WHAT'S AHEAD?...
The U.S. Economy

WHAT'S AHEAD?...
The U.S. Economy

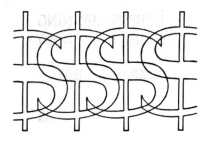

by Edward Boorstein

International Publishers   New York

Library of Congress Cataloging in Publication Data

Boorstein, Edward, 1915-
    What's ahead?—the U.S. economy.

    Bibliography: p. 213
    Includes index.
    1. Economic forecasting—United States   2. United
States—Economic conditions—1981-   .   I. Title.
HC106.8.B65   1984   338.5'443'0973   84-15867
ISBN 0-7178-0613-8
ISBN 0-7178-0614-6 (pbk.)

To my wife Reggie

ACKNOWLEDGMENTS

Professor Martin Hart-Landsberg read an early draft of these pages and provided a great many valuable criticisms. Betty Smith sensitively and creatively edited the manuscript, making a number of important recommendations both on style and substance. Louis Diskin and Daniel Rubin gave several useful suggestions. All helped make this a better book and I am grateful.

CONTENTS

WHAT'S AHEAD?...
The U.S. Economy

PART I

BACKGROUND TO CRISIS

1

The Capitalist System

Over the last fifteen years nothing in the U.S. economy has worked right. We have suffered from worsening "stagflation," a combination of severe recessions, high unemployment, and inflation. Periodically, the value of the dollar has plummeted in the international markets. Shortages of oil and natural gas have struck us several times, disrupting the whole economy.

A wave of plant closings has been sweeping over our industry, causing countless workers to lose their jobs, devastating communities, and bringing decline to entire regions. Several major industries—steel, auto, and others—are sick, with hundreds of thousands of workers thrown permanently out of their jobs.

Our cities are in decay. Large stretches of some of them look like bombed-out Berlin just after World War II. Our infrastructure—roads, bridges, water supply systems, etc.—is crumbling. The social security system has passed through several financial crunches. The health care system is in crisis.

All this has hit our people hard. The quality of life for the great majority has worsened. The working class, besides being ravaged by unemployment, has seen its real wages go down. The Afro-American, Hispanic and other oppressed minorities have suffered the most.[1] The snail-like progress that they previously were making toward closing the big economic gap between themselves and the white majority has not only halted but reversed. Many of our youth, especially minority youth, are cut off from the economy with no chance of a job.

Many specific causes help to produce these phenomena. We must try to understand these causes concretely, the way a good mechanic understands the workings of a car. But these phenomena are not separate and independent; they are interrelated. Together, they constitute a *comprehensive crisis* afflicting the whole U.S. economy. Basically, this crisis expresses a process of decay in U.S. capitalism.

If we wish to understand the crisis well, not just partially and superficially, we must begin with a preliminary discussion of fundamentals. What is capitalism? Under what phase of capitalism's development are we now living and how does this affect the workings of the economy? How have the enormous U.S. military expenditures helped produce the process of decay?

LENIN GIVES A clear, simple definition of capitalism:

> Capitalism is the name given to that social system under which the land, factories, implements, etc. belong to a small number of landed proprietors and capitalists, while the mass of the people possesses no property, or very little property, and is compelled to hire itself out as workers. The landowners and factory owners hire workers and make them produce wares of this or that kind which they sell on the market.[2]

This very nature of capitalism gives rise to contradictions. The most fundamental, the one which most broadly explains the workings of capitalism, is the contradiction between the social nature of production and the private form of ownership.

Production under capitalism is social. The goods we use (food, clothing, autos, etc.) are not the product of individuals, but social products, the result of the collaboration of countless workers. People work together in large enterprises, using materials and equipment produced by others, and producing goods for use by others. The economy is marked by an extensive and complex division of labor.

But the means of production are privately owned. The process of production is privately controlled, and the products of production are privately appropriated—they belong to the capitalists.

Why are social production and private ownership contradictory? Because each has its own logic and requirements which are incompatible with those of the other; because a process of production that is social cannot be properly managed and controlled under a system of ownership that is private.

For example: An economy with a developed division of labor

requires a central plan to mesh its different parts and ensure that various types of goods are produced according to social need and in the right proportions to one another. Privately-owned companies, however, don't operate according to a central plan, but anarchically, according to what will give them the greatest profits.

This contradiction, the combination of social production with private ownership, hasn't always existed. In the Middle Ages ownership was private but production was small-scale and individual, not social. What the medieval artisan owned was not a large enterprise employing many people, but the tools he worked with himself. Capitalism turned the medieval workshops into giant factories and produced an extensive division of labor. It created the contradiction by socializing production.

As capitalism develops, it socializes production more and more. Science and technology open up activities which can be carried on only through the collaboration of large numbers of people. Enterprises grow ever bigger. The division of labor becomes ever more extensive. Yet ownership remains private, so that the contradiction not only continues, but becomes increasingly acute.

THE GOAL OF THE capitalist is profits. As a chairman of U.S. Steel, Edgar Speer, once put it, the business of the steel industry is not to make steel, but to make money.

The pursuit of profits is not so much a matter of the individual capitalist as of the system. It is part of the basic dynamics of capitalism: the use of capital to make profits and the conversion of profits into capital to make still more profits. Corporations must make profits or die. Those that make profits grow ever larger and make still more profits. Those that fail to make profits go out of business. The stockholders of a corporation will forgive its managers almost anything except the failure to make profits. The making and accumulation of profits is a holy law for capitalism. Or, as Marx put it, "Accumulate, accumulate. That is Moses and the prophets!"[3]

The basic capitalist standard is: *How will profits be affected?* The profits standard governs corporate action on wages, hours of work and productivity, as well as health, safety and pollution. Directly or indirectly, it governs corporate action on everything.

As Lenin wrote:

It is understandable that the employers always try to reduce wages; the less they give the workers, the greater their profit. The workers try to get the highest possible wage in order to provide their families with sufficient and wholesome food, to live in good homes, and to dress as other people do. . . . A constant struggle is, therefore, going on between employers and workers over wages.[4]

For the same reason that they fight to keep wages down, the capitalists also fight to keep the working day long. It took a long, stubborn struggle by the working class to reduce the working day to what it is today. But the pressure of the capitalists never ends. It can be seen in the system of forced overtime that has grown up in the United States since the 1950s after the labor movement was weakened by McCarthyism. The corporations calculate costs and their effects on profits very carefully. They can often make more money if, instead of hiring new workers, they force already employed workers to work overtime. Thus they save on training costs, social security taxes, workers' compensation, hospital insurance, pensions, and vacation pay.

The capitalists also maintain an incessant drive to increase productivity, to squeeze the maximum output out of each hour of work. They tighten discipline and carry out crackdowns to speed up workers. They introduce new, more automated equipment and robots. Often they take advantage of the new machinery to lay off workers by the thousands.

In their concentration on profits, the capitalists respect nothing, not even the health and lives of the workers. Health and safety standards cost money, so the corporations resist them. They resist the measures necessary to give workers adequate protection against mine accidents, explosions, and Black Lung in the coal industry; cancer-causing coke oven fumes in the steel industry; Brown Lung in the textile industry. They gamble with the health and lives of the workers in the chemical industry with its innumerable dangerous substances and processes.

Just as the capitalists don't respect workers, they also don't respect the environment. Left free to do so, they pollute and destroy. They release poisonous chemicals into our air and water and establish dangerous toxic waste dumps. When the government, under pressure from the people, proposes or institutes controls, the companies resist. The chemical companies of New Jersey fight proposals to reduce emissions of known carcinogens from their plants. The American Iron and Steel Institute lobbies for an extension of the deadline for reducing the discharge of toxic substances into waterways by the iron and steel companies. General Motors presses for easing the Clean Air Act governing auto emissions.

The corporations apply the profits standard to countless other things besides their immediate operations. Every proposed law or government action of significance, the material that appears on television and radio or in newspapers, what takes place in our schools and universities—the companies examine all through the prism of profits and act accordingly. The effect of the capitalist profits standard pervades all corners of our society.

With the private appropriation of profits, the capitalist system inherently involves the exploitation of the working class by the capitalist class. Workers' labor creates all wealth. It creates the profits which the capitalists accumulate, the capital which results from the accumulation. Like serfs before them, wage workers under capitalism work only part of the time for themselves, the rest for someone else—in their case the capitalists.[5]

A CAPITALIST economy is an anarchic economy. It consists of a multitude of separate, private enterprises, each producing what it thinks will give the greatest profits. There is planning within the enterprise—for maximum profits—but the economy as a whole is not run according to plan, and anarchy prevails.

Capitalist economists deny that capitalism is anarchic. For example Paul Samuelson, a Nobel prize winner, writes in his best-selling textbook *Economics* that the system is not one of "anarchy. . . . A competitive system is an elaborate mechanism for unconscious coordination through a system of prices and markets. . . ."[6]

Milton Friedman (another Nobel prize winner) and his wife Rose offer an example to explain how the market does its work:

> Suppose that for whatever reason, there is an increased demand for lead pencils—perhaps because a baby boom increases school enrollment. Retail stores will find that they are selling more pencils. They will order more pencils from their wholesalers. The wholesalers will order more pencils from the manufacturers. The manufacturers will order more wood, more brass, more graphite—all the varied products used to make a pencil. In order to induce their suppliers to produce more of these items, they will have to offer higher prices for them. The higher prices will induce the suppliers to increase their work force to be able to meet the higher demand. To get more workers they will have to offer higher wages or better working conditions.[7]

Capitalist economic theory from its beginning is full of explanations, ranging from this kind of example to "elegant" mathematical formulations, of how capitalism "coordinates." The market (some call it the price mechanism or the competitive system) "regulates." It "allocates resources" according to what is required. It determines what will be produced, how much, and for whom. If too little of something is produced, the price will rise, this will attract "resources," and bring about an increase in production. If too much is produced, the price will fall, this will cause "resources" to flow elsewhere and again bring about the necessary adjustment.

Differences about the market exist among capitalist economists. The Friedmans hold that our economic problems are due to "interference" with the market, and that "the government is the major source of interference. . . ."[8] Paul Samuelson, after explaining how "unconscious coordination" takes place through "prices and markets," cautions his readers not to go to an "extreme and become enamored of the beauty of the pricing mechanism, regarding it as perfection itself, the essence of providential harmony and beyond the touch of human hands."[9] Such differences can be of great practical significance; they reflect differences among various groups of capitalists concerning the proper role of government in the face of economic problems. Nevertheless, for both Friedman and Samuelson, as well as almost all other capitalist economists, the market is the great coordinator which prevents capitalism from being anarchic.

Whether a capitalist economy is anarchic, however, can only be settled by looking at reality, by seeing how capitalism actually works, not by becoming enmeshed in the abstract logic of capitalist economists. What does a look at reality tell us?

It tells us, to begin with, that capitalism is beset by the business cycle; that it suffers from periodic crises of overproduction followed by declines in output and large-scale layoffs of workers. If the market is such a great coordinator, why doesn't it coordinate away the crises and the unemployment?

The examples given by capitalist economists require scrutiny. The Friedman example is pretty. Demand rises, companies have to employ more workers and pay higher wages, and everyone lives happily. But let's vary the example. Let's suppose that the item isn't pencils, but autos and that demand isn't rising, but falling because we are in the downswing of the business cycle. What does the great coordinator—the market—do then? It throws more than a million auto, steel, and other workers out of their jobs.

THE BUSINESS CYCLE is a disease of capitalism. Many specific factors such as fluctuations in investment, production and profits, help shape business cycles, but fundamentally they flow from the nature of capitalism; from the contradiction between social production with its division of labor and private ownership.

If either half of this contradiction is missing, there is no business cycle. There was no business cycle before capitalism because production wasn't social. There is no business cycle under socialism; ownership is no longer private.

Before capitalism, there could be no business cycle because there was no developed division of labor. Producers operated independently of one another, turning out goods for separate local markets. What happened to a blacksmith or flax weaver in one locality had no effect on blacksmiths and flax weavers in other localities. The different parts of the economy were not interdependent. A stimulus or disturbance in one part couldn't spread by a chain reaction to others and eventually cause the whole economy to move up or down. Natural calamities occurred, such as droughts or floods, but they were not the same as the periodic crises of the business cycle with their overproduction, layoffs, etc.

Under industrial capitalism with its division of labor, each enterprise, each part of the economy, is one element in the broad process of social production. Each enterprise depends on the prosperity of its customers who, in turn, depend on the prosperity of theirs. A supplier to steel companies depends on their prosperity; they in turn depend on the prosperity of metalworking companies; the different parts of the economy are interdependent. A disturbance in one part can start a chain reaction which spreads to all of it.

Capitalism systematically produces disturbances in such a way as to generate the business cycle. As Marx pointed out, for an economy with a developed division of labor to work smoothly, its different parts have to mesh with one another; proper proportions among them must be maintained. For example, the total value of consumer goods must be in proper proportion to the purchasing power of the people who are to buy them; if more goods are produced than people can pay for, part of them will be left unsold. Investment in productive capacity must be in proper proportion to the value of consumption; if it is too high, excess capacity will appear. Capitalism, with its limitless drive for profits and its anarchy, generates a systematic upsetting of the proper proportions.

Marx explained how. There is a limit to how fast consumption can grow; the income that people receive imposes a limit. But the capitalists don't gear production to consumption. Driven by the need to make profits or die in the competitive struggle, they anarchically expand production without limit. Production increases faster than consumption can grow. After a while, an overproduction of goods develops as part of what is produced cannot be sold. This causes the rate of profit to decline. Since profits are the goal of the capitalists, they must take corrective action to stem the decline. They cut production and lay off workers. "Crises," said Marx, "are forcible solutions of the . . . contradictions. . . ."[10]

The movement of auto inventories provides an illustration of the dynamics of the business cycle. When auto sales are rising, the manufacturers and the dealers attached to each of them push up inventories much faster than sales, which means that production is rising much faster than sales. The manufacturers and dealers push up inventories as part of the competitive pursuit of profits. The greater the variety and number of cars a dealer has, the greater the sales and profits; failure to have a certain model available for quick delivery can mean a sale lost to competitors. Neither the manufacturers nor the dealers can worry at this point where the process by which inventories are rising faster than sales will ultimately lead; they have to get their profits while the getting is good. But inventories cannot go on increasing faster than sales indefinitely. An inventory sufficient to cover sixty days of sales may be better than a forty- or fifty-day supply; but an eighty- or ninety-day inventory begins to be excessive. Eventually a correction must come. Such a correction is made urgent by the fact that dealers finance their inventories with borrowed money, which is expensive. If a dealer is stuck too long with unsold cars, the financing costs can put him out of business. So when signs appear that sales are flagging, dealers not only stop increasing their inventories, but start reducing them, forcing production to decline sharply. Now there is a new disproportion between production and sales, only this time production is not above, but below sales. This is also a state that cannot be maintained indefinitely; the reduction in inventories lays the basis for the next upturn in production.

The movement of investment in plant and equipment is another example of how the cycle works. In "good times," the individual enterprises press to expand their productive capacity. They gear their actions to calculations of their individual profits. They operate separately, without controlling the overall effects of their actions. The result is to expand capacity more rapidly than consumption and output are expanding. The high plant and equipment expenditures produce a chain reaction on the whole economy; they help push overall economic activity to a high level. But after a while the inevitable result appears: growing excess capacity. With the growth of excess capacity, capacity whose output can't be sold, the rate of profit tends to drop. So the enterprises slash their capital expenditures, and this, again by a chain reaction, helps push the whole economy down. A period of low capital expenditures prepares the economy for the next upturn.

The business cycle is inevitable under capitalism. This is confirmed not only by the way it flows from the very nature of capitalism, but by history. Business cycles have been noted in the United States since the early 19th century. There have been over forty cycles, eight after World War II.

Capitalist economists don't like to face the business cycle and its inevitability under capitalism. Till after World War I, the main capitalist economists practically ignored the business cycle—economic crises were aberrations, flukes, they said. Alfred Marshall, whom both Samuelson and Friedman call a "great economist," published an 850-page *Principles of Economics* in 1890. He devoted two paragraphs to the business cycle:

> The chief cause of the evil is a want of confidence. The greater part of it could be removed almost in an instant if confidence could return, touch all industries with her magic wand, and make them continue their production and their demand for the wares of others.[11]

The Great Depression of the 1930s forced at least some capitalist economists to deal with the problem of the cycle, imposing a dose of realism on their theories. But they still can't face the truth squarely. Samuelson, in the 1967 edition of his *Economics*, admits that some past slumps were "disastrous" and writes:

> Such, in brief, *was* the so-called "business cycle" that used to characterize the industrialized nations of the world for the last century and a half. . . . Nevertheless, now that the tools of income analysis are understood and their use is politically mandatory, the probability of

recession in any one year is less in the mixed economy than it used to be. Expansion periods tend to be longer and fuller than in the past: the periods of recession . . . tend to be less frequent and shorter. Perhaps only half the customary number of recessions will take place; and many of them may last scarcely a year. (Italics added-E.B.)[12]

Reality—in the form of the deep, prolonged recessions that hit us in the 1970s—made hash of these half-baked comments.

Some capitalist economists went further than Samuelson. During the long economic upswing tied to the Vietnam War, they began to propound the view that the cycle had been eliminated. But the cycle cannot be eliminated under capitalism; this can only be accomplished when capitalism is done away with.

THE ACCURSED PHENOMENON of unemployment also flows from capitalism. People need jobs to live. But the power over jobs, aside from those in the government, is privately held by capitalists through their ownership of the means of production.

Capitalists, to begin with, need a certain number of unemployed, as Engels concluded from his observations of the workings of British capitalism in the 1840s. "It is clear," he wrote, "that English manufacture must have at all times save the brief periods of highest prosperity, an unemployed reserve army of workers, in order to be able to produce the masses of goods required by the market in the liveliest months."[13]

On top of the general capitalist need for unemployment come the effects of economic downturns, the introduction of new machinery and equipment, and plant closings. As a result, capitalist economies are never, except occasionally in wartime, without unemployment. From time to time, the unemployment shoots up to what are high levels even by capitalist standards.

In 1933, during the Great Depression, the unemployment rate averaged 24.9 percent according to the official figures. In 1939, the year World War II began, it was still 17.2 percent.[14]

The capitalist economists ("salesmen of capitalism," as Lenin called them) have been quick to claim that the problem of unemployment is under control. Here again is Samuelson's *Economics*: "By proper use of monetary and fiscal policies, nations today can successfully fight off the plague of mass unemployment and the plague of inflation."[15]

More hash.

2

Monopoly Capital—
Finance Capital—Imperialism

That our economy is capitalist determines its most fundamental features. We are living, however, not just under capitalism, but a particular stage of capitalism, the monopoly and imperialist stage.

The monopoly nature of our economy is now a commonplace. Production and most other economic activities are concentrated in a small number of huge corporations. Pick the industry—steel, autos, insurance, the mass media—a handful of gigantic corporations dominate it.

The entry of capitalism into the monopoly stage meant a sharpening of the contradiction between social production and private ownership. The privately-owned monopolies have powers over prices and many other things which the enterprises of the pre-monopoly stage of capitalism didn't have.

With truly free competition, the market fixes the price. A small farmer selling his milk along with thousands of other small farmers doesn't have the power to determine the price. He can't make the price go up by withholding his infinitesimal share of the output. He can only take or leave the price fixed by the market.

But General Motors and U.S. Steel have the power to determine their prices. They can fix prices high. They know that keeping prices high reduces their sales, but this doesn't stop them. For a long distance up the price scale, they can make more profits by selling *less* at a higher price than more at a lower one.

To have this power over prices, a corporation need not be the only one producing the product. When even twelve companies, to say nothing of three or four, control the output of a product, each has this control to a certain degree. In addition, when there are only a small number of sellers, it is easy for them to act in collusion to keep prices high. In a situation of great market power and easy collusion, it is primarily monopoly considerations, not competitive forces, that determine prices. This is the reason for using the term monopoly, not just in those cases in which an industry is controlled by one corporation, but also when it is controlled by a few.

Monopolies have great power to determine what goods are produced. Capitalist economists talk about "consumer sovereignty," maintaining that what is produced is determined by "the votes of the consumers." But in the world of monopolies this is fiction. Monopolies can manipulate demand through advertising. They can create demand for harmful products like junk food and dangerous products like cigarettes. They can fail to produce goods which people need and want, like sensible television programs.

Capitalist economists tend to stress the market power of the monopolies; that is, their power over prices and products. But market power is only a small part of the power of the monopolies.

The monopolies have the power to shut down large plants employing thousands of people, in the same way that a medieval artisan could dispose of the tools with which he himself worked. A few oil companies can underinvest in exploration and drilling and leave the whole country with insufficient oil-producing capacity in the future.

It is the monopolies who determine the structure of our economy. They determine what industries we will have or not have and where these industries will be located; what sort of transportation system, one dependent on the automobile and truck with their heavy use of oil, or one which makes adequate use of mass transportation, etc. The monopolies hold the fate of different localities in their hands; they can doom communities, cities, and even entire regions by moving out.

The monopolies are not concerned with the structure of the economy. When they make their decisions about erecting, shutting down or moving plants, they are not concerned with the broader economic and social effects of their actions. They are concerned with profits. From the point of view of profits, their actions are rational but from the point of view of the economy, they are anarchic. It is the sum of the anarchic actions of the monopolies that determines the structure of the economy.

The development of monopoly kicked out the last possible prop supporting the theory that capitalism is not anarchic. This theory was always a paper theory. Capitalism has never, even in its competitive stage, worked the way this theory says it does. The competitive market did adjust disproportions in the economy, but it did so, as Marx wrote, by the creation of crises and unemployment.

But even to work just on paper, the theory has to assume free competition. Only by assuming free competition can one argue that prices will be fixed in a fair and orderly way, that resources will be allocated to where they are most needed, etc. The basis of the market theory is that prices will work against disproportions; that when demand falls, the price will decline and this will cushion the fall in demand. But what happens when in real life monopolies maintain or even increase their prices when the demand goes down? The basis of the market theory has disappeared.

Monopoly does many things to an economy. It tends to make economic downturns more severe since, in the face of crisis, the monopolies maintain their prices rigid and let production drop. Monopoly power over prices is a key element in the creation and continuation of inflation. The ills of some industries are partly due to the monopolies; for example, the long refusal of the auto industry to make small cars is part of the reason for its present troubles.

Though even the paper basis for the market theory is now gone, the theory lives on. Students of economics learn it as a kind of theology. Conservative businessmen and economists use it as a justification for doing nothing about even our most serious problems. Let the market decide, they intone. If some of our basic industries, like steel, are declining, never mind—let the market decide what industries we will have. If many of our cities are in decay, why do anything? Where is it written that cities shouldn't die?

But letting the market decide is just a highfalutin way of saying to hell with the needs of the people and the economy, let anarchy decide. And with the continued growth of monopoly, the anarchy is getting worse.

OUR ECONOMY is characterized not only by the concentration of production in monopolies, but also by the combination of monopolies into conglomerates; i.e., companies engaged in a variety of unrelated activities. One conglomerate may produce oil, gas, and coal, own hotels, and engage in the retail mail order business. Another may produce asphalt roofing materials and chemicals, as well as own a radio station and other enterprises.

What is the basic logic underlying conglomerates? They are a means of managing money (capital) so as to achieve the maximum profits from it. They release capital from being stuck to particular products which can limit its profit-making ability. If, as Speer argued, the business of the steel industry is not to make steel, but money, why should capitalists engaged in steel production limit themselves to this one activity? Why shouldn't they move their profits into other activities if they can make more money by doing so? By combining a variety of activities, the capitalists gain maneuverability; they can shift their capital from activity to activity, according to what will give them the maximum profits.

Fortune, the magazine of big business, explained:

> Formerly, men in, say, the cement business knew exactly what to do with their profits: pay out part of them to stockholders and reinvest most of the balance in cement plants. But anyone who sets out to clarify his ultimate objective comes, fairly rapidly, to the proposition that his main objective is maximizing the return on his capital and, thereby, raising the value of his stock. And when he gets to *that*, he proceeds inexorably to the thought that alternate investments may yield higher payoffs than cement. When he gets used to the idea that alternate investments are not only legal and moral, but profitable, he is pretty far along the road to becoming a conglomerator.[1]

Other reasons for conglomerates, besides the maneuverability of capital, also exist. The process of forming conglomerates lends itself to financial manipulation, in which there is big money. Owning companies that produce different products can reduce risks. Sheer size adds to monopoly power. A subsidiary of a conglomerate is backed by the resources of the whole company, which it can use against competitors or to ride out a strike.

Litton Industries, the conglomerate that makes everything from microwave ovens and cash registers to guided missiles and computerized security systems, is an example. According to the *New York Times* (4-24-83), William P. Winpisinger, president of the International Association of Machinists, said in 1983: "Litton has the dubious distinction of having displaced J.P. Stevens as America's No. 1 labor law violator."

Various unions which have been involved in organizing campaigns against Litton divisions say that it has a company-wide policy of illegally harassing and intimidating union sympathizers and, if all else fails, shutting down unionized plants. An official of the United Electrical, Radio, and Machine Workers explains how Litton gets its power:

> Formerly, when most workers at a plant faced a single-facility employer, there was equal bargaining power. . . . But when a conglomerate takes over, and one plant goes on strike while the rest, which produce completely different products, are working and pumping in profits, they can afford to let people hang out there.[2]

Conglomerates are a form of finance capital. Those who construct and run them are not industrial managers, but financiers primarily concerned with the buying and selling of companies and shifting capital around.

Finance capital results from the intertwining of the capital of banks and other financial monopolies (such as insurance companies) with the capital of industrial monopolies. The intertwining takes place in many different ways. The banks and other financial institutions penetrate into industry. They own or control shares in industrial companies, participate in the organization and merger of industrial companies, etc. The industrial companies also penetrate into banking and finance: General Motors and Ford own giant finance subsidiaries that lend money; National Steel owns banks; and ITT owns Hartford Insurance.

Interpenetration also occurs through interlocking directorates. Directors of banks become directors of industrial companies and vice versa. Far-reaching webs of interlocking directorates arise, providing personal interconnections between financial and industrial monopolies.

Here is an example from a congressional report of the workings of finance capital:

> In January 1964, Chase [Manhattan Bank] convinced Gulf and Western to open a line of credit with Chase. In the next six years, Gulf and Western's mergers became increasingly ambitious, transforming it into one of the major U.S. industrial corporations. . . . Chase provided short-term loans to Gulf and Western to purchase the stock of takeover target companies. . . . "One phase of the relationship included a flow of information from Chase about companies in which G&W had

an interest, including suggestions for acquisition." In return, Gulf and Western had new subsidiaries transfer their checking accounts to Chase, deposit payroll and withholding taxes with Chase, and transfer pension plans to Chase Manhattan's trust department.[3]

Here is another example:

Levitt & Sons plans, develops, builds, and sells entire residential cities in the United States and abroad. . . . Sales of $72 million in 1966 made Levitt the largest private builder in the world. In March of that year the [investment banking] firm of Lazard Freres described to ITT acquisition managers the captive market the conglomerate would acquire for myriad other products upon purchase of Levitt & Sons. . . . ITT purchased Levitt & Sons for $93,446,000 in February 1968. . . . In public testimony and with impressive authority, Felix Rohatyn, a Lazard Freres partner and director, who is also an ITT director and ITT executive committee member, described a system of interlocking directorships which keeps the acquisition process well greased. At least one of the brokerage firm's partners was on the boards of directors of 27 of the companies involved in the 68 mergers the firm arranged from 1964 through September 1969.[4]

Finance capital carries the logic of profits to its conclusion. It is unhampered by ties to any particular industry or place. It flows back and forth among industry, banking, finance, real estate, communications, and transportation, and among different countries—moving to wherever the highest profits are to be found. As Lenin put it in 1915:

Finance capital . . . is particularly mobile and flexible, particularly interknit at home and internationally, and particularly impersonal and divorced from production proper; it lends itself to concentration with particular ease, and has been concentrated to an unusual degree already, so that literally a few hundred multimillionaires and millionaires control the destiny of the world.[5]

To concentrate control over finance capital and take advantage of its mobility is, from the point of view of profits, the culmination of rationality. But this very concentration and mobility increases the power of the capitalists to do damage to the economy. A small number of banks and other companies can, for speculative or other reasons, transfer gigantic sums of money in or out of the country and bring about undesirable fluctuations in the value of the dollar. A handful of people can decide that because some industry isn't yielding a high enough rate of profit, they will let it decline by transferring capital to some other activity or moving operations overseas. Therefore, the growth of finance capital constitutes a further increase in capitalist anarchy.

IMPERIALISM IS the monopoly stage of capitalism. Some people think of imperialism as a policy: A president who follows a policy that leads the United States into war in Vietnam or aggressive actions in the Caribbean is imperialist; another who follows a more restrained course is not. While policy differences can be of great or even crucial importance, imperialism is not a policy. It is a system.

The monopolies spread beyond the boundaries of their home countries into all areas of the world that offer promise of profit and allow them to operate. The monopoly drive to spread is as limitless as the drive to accumulate profits of which it is an expression.

The key way in which the monopolies spread is through the export of capital. As Lenin wrote: "Typical of the old capitalism when free competition held undivided sway, was the export of *goods.* Typical of the latest stage of capitalism, when monopolies rule, is the export of *capital.*"[6]

The difference between the export of goods and the export of capital is basic. Countries can exchange goods and remain equal. But the export of capital means power. When a group of banks makes a loan to a foreign country it gains the power (which it often uses openly) to tell that country what economic and other policies to follow. When corporations make "direct" investments (that is, investments in enterprises) in foreign countries, they gain ownership of mines, utilities, plantations, factories, retail stores, etc. which are nuclei of economic and political power in that country. The export of capital is the basis upon which the United States and a few leading capitalist countries exploit and dominate the rest of the capitalist world.

A glance at the statistics of U.S. direct investment helps understand the scope of U.S. imperialism. In 1940, U.S. direct investment abroad stood at $7 billion. By the end of 1980, it had reached $213 billion. Investment in manufacturing rose even more spectacularly than investment in general—from $1.9 billion to $89 billion.[7]

U.S. corporations have established an enormous economy abroad. The output of U.S. foreign subsidiaries is several times larger than total U.S. exports. The total sales of foreign subsidiaries engaged in manufacturing was almost three times as large as total U.S. exports of manufactured goods in 1976.[8] Sidney Rolfe, an expert on the multinational corporation, wrote in 1970: "International investment has by-passed exports as the major channel of international economic relations."[9]

For the corporations, the enormous foreign investment means enormous profits. But what does it mean for the economy and people of the United States? Where will the continuing growth of such investment eventually lead?

Foreign investment means the transfer abroad of thousands of factories which could be located in the United States. Often the factory abroad is directly tied to a shutdown here. But even when not so tied, it frequently means the loss of one that could have been built here. The transfer of factories means the export of jobs; existing jobs and new jobs that might have been created.

Besides costing jobs, foreign investment does other damage. It reduces U.S. exports; many goods that would otherwise be shipped from the United States are shipped from the foreign subsidiaries. It increases U.S. dependence on imports; we import from the foreign subsidiaries many goods that would otherwise be produced here. It helps give the United States an unfavorable trade balance which weakens the dollar.

The mouthpieces of the multinationals tell us not to worry. If we leave things to the international market every country, including the United States, will automatically get the economy it needs. But the experience of the underdeveloped countries gives the lie to this argument. The market has left these countries with deformed, lopsided economies, incapable of providing their people with all the jobs they need; with economies in which the foreign corporations and a small local minority do very well, while the great majority live in misery. Imperialism—the imperialist international market in investment and trade—is also deforming the U.S. economy, de-industrializing it, making it lopsided.

3

The Government Role: Economic Regulation; Military Expenditures

A key feature of the U.S. economy since the early 1930s has been the government's attempts to regulate its workings. To fully understand the economy, we must understand how the government's intervention affects it. Government economic intervention is part of what Lenin called state monopoly capitalism, the system into which capitalism has evolved.

Originally, U.S. capitalists furiously opposed government regulation of the economy. They didn't want the government interfering with them. But as the economy grew larger and more complex and subject to big disruptions, government regulation became increasingly necessary. In 1907, for example, a disruption occurred, a financial panic in which the banking system broke down. In 1913 the government set up the Federal Reserve System in the hope that by regulating banking it could prevent future breakdowns. World War I brought large-scale, though temporary, government regulation. Only with such regulation could the economy be harnessed for the war effort.

The decisive movement toward large-scale government economic intervention came during the Great Depression of the 1930s. As the depression developed, President Hoover kept repeating Alfred Marshall's refrain: The crisis was one of "confidence." But with a fall of 37 percent in industrial production between 1929 and 1933; with five thousand banks closed in three years and panic-stricken people lining up to withdraw their money from those still open; with millions of farmers bankrupt; with unemployment hovering during its peak months at one-third of the labor force;

with many of the unemployed building shantytowns and calling them Hoovervilles; with breadlines and millions starving, mass pressure from the people forced the government to do something.

The government intervened under the New Deal of Franklin D. Roosevelt. It tried to regulate the production and sale of industrial goods through a National Recovery Administration (NRA); provided loans and other financial help to banks, railroads, and agricultural and industrial enterprises; tried to raise farm prices and income through programs for destroying crops and reducing the amount of acreage sown; took action to protect farmers and homeowners against mortgage foreclosure; provided some financial relief for the unemployed; and established public works programs to create employment and increase mass purchasing power.

The basic purpose of the New Deal was to save capitalism. Wherever possible, it favored the monopolies. Representatives of the major corporations dominated the administration of the NRA and promoted regulation (so-called "codes of fair competition") that helped extend monopoly. The money lent to banks went mainly to the bigger ones.

Besides accelerating the movement toward government economic regulation, the depression also produced a theory for it, formulated by the British economist John Maynard Keynes in his book, *The General Theory of Employment, Interest, and Money,* published in 1936. The Keynesian theory, as propounded by Keynes himself and later by followers, became the main answer of state monopoly capitalism to the problem of the business cycle and unemployment.

Although Keynes's book is loaded with high-sounding jargon and impressive-looking mathematical formulas, its scientific character is limited. It is not intended as an objective probe of the causes of depression and unemployment and what is necessary to get rid of them, regardless of what this means for capitalism. It is intended to help save capitalism. Keynes's criticism of previous capitalist economic theory and his recommendations for changes in government policy went only so far as was necessary, in his view, to save capitalism.

The danger to capitalism created by the terrible unemployment of the depression forced Keynes to admit that capitalism does not automatically regulate itself. The spontaneous forces of the market will not automatically produce full employment. Government intervention is necessary. Keynes was far from the first to promote the necessity of government intervention. The Roosevelt administration (as well as the governments of several other countries) had already been acting for several years when Keynes's book appeared. The book provided an intellectual rationale for the intervention.

Keynes doesn't find that the capitalist system is the basic cause of unemployment, doesn't analyze the characteristics of capitalism that lead to unemployment. He simply relates unemployment to a shortage of effective demand as though this could happen under any economic system.

Keynes's argument is as follows: Effective demand is made up of consumption and investment. When the community's aggregate income increases, its aggregate consumption also increases, but not by as much. Part of the increase in income is saved. This means that consumption alone is not enough to absorb total output. To maintain demand, new investment equal to the additional savings is required. This generally does not occur. "The effective demand associated with full employment is a special case . . ." rarely realized.[1]

But if capitalism does not regulate itself and if full employment rarely occurs when the economy is left alone, then government intervention is required. Keynes talks of "the vital importance of establishing certain central controls in matters which are now left in the main to individual initiative. . . ."[2] But even while recommending an expansion in the role of the state, he is careful to fix strict limits. "It is not the ownership of the instruments of production which it is important for the State to assume. If the State is able to determine the aggregate amount of resources devoted to augmenting the instruments and the basic reward to those who own them, it will have accomplished all that is necessary."[3]

What Keynes specifically recommends are measures to take up the slack in effective demand: public works; lower taxes and interest rates to stimulate private investment and consumption; and deficit financing—the government pumping more money into the economy than it takes out.

The following quotation gives the essence of Keynes's thinking at the same time that it tells us something about the irrationality of capitalism:

Pyramid-building, earthquakes, even wars may serve to increase wealth. . . . If the Treasury were to fill old bottles with banknotes, bury

them at suitable depths in disused coal mines which are then filled up
to the surface with town rubbish, and leave it to private enterprise on
well tried principles of *laissez faire* to dig the notes up again . . . there
need be no more unemployment. . . . It would, indeed, be more
sensible to build houses and the like; but if there are political and
practical difficulties in the way of this, the above would be better than
nothing.[4]

Keynes understood clearly why he was recommending large-
scale government intervention in the economy. He wrote:

While . . . the enlargement of the functions of government . . . would
seem to a nineteenth-century publicist or to a contemporary American financier to be a terrific encroachment on individualism, I defend
it, on the contrary, both as the only practicable means of avoiding the
destruction of the existing forms in their entirety and as the condition
of the successful functioning of individual initiative.[5]

Keynes's theory was as superior to the capitalist theory that
preceded it as Roosevelt's economic policy was superior to that of
Hoover. Both the New Deal and Keynesianism were based on
recognition of a crucial truth: Capitalism can no longer survive and
manage without large-scale government intervention in the economy.

The New Deal and Keynesianism succeeded in easing the severity of the depression. They contributed to an environment in which
the American people were able to wrest important reforms and
concessions from the government and the monopolies. But they did
not even come close to getting rid of the depression. World War II
did that.

Keynes's followers and government economists further developed the principles of state economic intervention. The government could try not only to put the unemployed to work, but also to
fight inflation and promote growth. In periods of economic upswing, it could restrict credit (through the Federal Reserve) and
raise taxes to prevent the economy from "overheating" and generating inflation. In periods of recession, it could ease credit and
lower taxes to promote a turnaround. If the rate of growth was
deemed unsatisfactory, it could provide special tax incentives to
monopolies to get them to expand investment.

For twenty years after World War II, U.S. capitalism enjoyed
favorable conditions and the government applied Keynesianism
with a certain degree of success. The success was limited. Unem-

ployment and the business cycle were not eliminated. Inflation was not eradicated. But these ills were—for a capitalist country—kept within bounds.

Keynesianism has been useless, however, against the comprehensive crisis that has been making itself felt with increasing force since the late 1960s. It has provided no answer even to the problems to which it was mainly addressed, depression and unemployment. And it did not even envisage such problems as declining industries, decaying cities, and rotting infrastructure. As eminent a capitalist economist as John Kenneth Galbraith has declared Keynesianism "obsolete."[6]

The inherent limitation of Keynesianism has rendered it bankrupt. This limitation is simple. Keynesianism springs from capitalism, defends capitalism, and refuses to lay hands on the prerogatives of the monopolies. It is, therefore, itself entangled in the contradictions of capitalism.

Keynesianism is a one-dimensional theory grappling with a multi-dimensional economy. It proposes to regulate the whole economy through one or two so-called indirect controls, such as the budget and credit mechanism run by the government, plus public works. Keynesianism's reason for stressing indirect controls, for insisting that control of "aggregate" investment is "all that is necessary," is that it wants to preserve the unrestricted rights of the monopolies.

Under Keynesianism, the government operates its indirect controls and the monopolies, operating anarchically, have the power of decision over the hiring and firing of workers, the level of production, the fixing of prices, the amount, type and location of investment, etc. But a modern economy, with its innumerable interlocking parts, cannot be managed by simply manipulating indirect controls. A central plan which meshes all the main parts is required.

Keynes's own thinking was exceptionally one-dimensional. Because he was writing at a time when inflation happened not to be a problem, he ignored it. He recommended deficit financing as a remedy for unemployment without regard to whether such financing would produce or aggravate inflation. But what does one do if the economy is suffering simultaneously from both unemployment and inflation? This is a contradiction for which Keynesianism has no answer.

Keynes's confident assertion, "It is not the ownership of the means of production which it is important for the State to assume," is wrong. Without public ownership of the means of production, the government cannot have true control of the economy. The private monopolies control it. Keynes's assertion highlights the fundamental reason for the shipwreck of Keynesianism. It ran afoul of the contradiction between social production and private ownership.

THE U.S. ECONOMY does not, of course, exist in isolation. The world situation and the U.S. reaction to it help shape our economy. What are the central features of that situation? A titanic competition is going on between two systems, capitalism and socialism. A world revolutionary process is under way with revolutions erupting now here, now there. The U.S. reaction has been to build a gigantic military machine. The effects of the enormous U.S. military budget pervade all aspects of our economic life.

From 1946 through 1980, even before the big Reagan arms buildup, U.S. military expenditures added up to $5.2 trillion (in 1980 dollars). This sum is 3.5 times as big as total U.S. military expenditures during World War II, twice as big as the gross national product of 1980, four times more than that of 1960.[7]

Marx once remarked that war (and this can be taken to include all military expenditures) is equivalent to casting part of a nation's capital into the water. The amount cast into the water by the United States since World War II has been more than the total value of its fixed, non-residential business capital in 1980—its factories, mines, railroads, office buildings, stores, etc.[8] It was enough, if used for housing, to have built a $90,000 house for every family in the country. It was enough, in sum, to have rebuilt our country from top to bottom.

But the direct loss of resources is only part of the story. The steady hemorrhage, continued year after year for decades, also has indirect and cumulative consequences. Military expenditures are a key cause of budget deficits and inflation. The pumping of dollars abroad to maintain troops on foreign bases contributes to the international instability of the dollar. The Pentagon's hogging of a large share of the country's scientific effort helps account for a slowing down of productivity growth. The heavy cost to the economy of maintaining the military machine acts as a drag on export competitiveness.

These problems, in turn, help cause or aggravate others. Several times during the last fifteen years the government has acted to deliberately provoke recessions and hold down recovery, as a means of combatting inflation and a weak dollar.

No part of the economy is immune to the effects of the voracious military budget. It chews up resources that could otherwise be used to deal with our long list of problems by providing jobs to the unemployed, rebuilding our decaying cities and crumbling infrastructure and guaranteeing strong social security and health care systems.

There is, of course, something else for us to think about in connection with the military budget: It could get us all blown up.

PART II

DECLINING MANEUVERABILITY

———————————————————

4

Inflation vs. Unemployment

Since the early 1970s, the U.S. economy has been suffering from stagflation: a combination of severe recessions, high unemployment, and inflation. In periods of economic upswing, the unemployment has gone down a little while the inflation has flared up. During recessions, the inflation has abated while unemployment has shot up. We have not had ordinary business cycles, but cycles in which downswings have been getting worse and the unemployment rate has been rising from one cycle to the next.

The worst recession of the postwar period struck during 1974-1975. Then followed something still worse—two back-to-back recessions from 1980 through 1982.

The decline in the rate of growth was steep. Between 1948 and 1973, the gross national product grew at an annual rate of 3.8 percent. Between 1974 and 1982, it grew at a rate of only 1.9 percent.[1]

A good part of the reason for the deep recessions, low growth, and high unemployment was the upsurge of inflation that got under way during the Vietnam War. Keynes had not provided a prescription for dealing with unemployment when it is combined with inflation.

An economy suffering simultaneously from inflation and high unemployment is like a person suffering from two diseases of such a nature that the medicine for each aggravates the other. The government's remedy for inflation is to slow down the economy, to provoke recession and greater unemployment. Its remedy for high unemployment is deficit financing, which fuels inflation.

To say that the government deliberately provokes recessions is not to imply that if the government did not do so, there would be none. As noted in Chapter 1, the business cycle with its economic downturns is inevitable under capitalism. Nevertheless, it can make a big difference in the frequency, severity, and duration of recessions whether the government tries to fight against them or deliberately provokes them.

During the administrations of Nixon, Ford, Carter and Reagan, the government tried to fight inflation with the standard remedy of provoking a recession. All it accomplished was to push the economy ever deeper into a trap of simultaneous high inflation, low growth, and high unemployment.

SEVERAL DIFFERENT factors help cause inflation. One is war and military expenditures. The chart on page 29 shows the movement of wholesale prices from 1800 to 1970. The association between war and inflation is unmistakable. The major inflations in the United States have occurred during wars and their aftermath—the War of 1812, the Civil War, World War I, World War II, the Korean War. The upsurge of inflation from which we are suffering today began during the Vietnam War.

HOW DO WARS and military expenditures produce inflation? Inflations, which are systematic, sustained increases in the general price level (not isolated, sporadic increases in a few individual prices), result from pumping too much money into the economy in relation to the supply of goods available. Wars and military expenditures cause the pumping of excess money into the economy.

Arms programs and wars cause deficits in the federal budget; these are financed by what amounts to printed money, money created by the banking system. The technical details of how this happens are less important than the fact that it happens. Both the Federal Reserve System and the commercial banks buy government securities (Treasury bills, bonds, etc.) with money that they create. If the reserves of the commercial banks are insufficient to support the necessary purchases of government securities, the Federal Reserve takes the technical action required to increase these reserves. Before the establishment of the Federal Reserve System, the mechanics were different, but the essence of what happened was the same. The equivalent of printed money was used to cover the deficits.

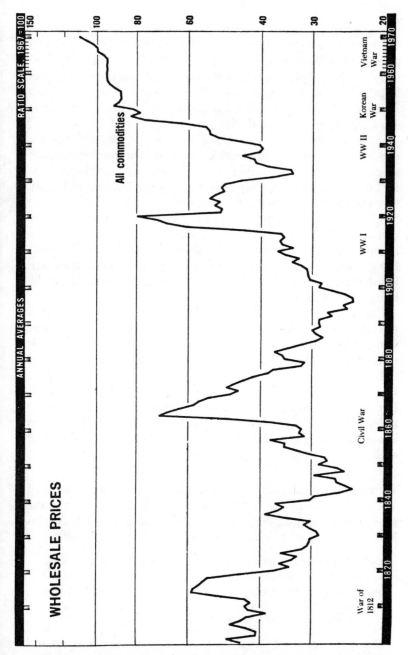

WHOLESALE PRICES

ANNUAL AVERAGES

RATIO SCALE, 1967=100

All commodities

War of 1812

Civil War

WW I

WW II

Korean War

Vietnam War

150
100
80
60
40
30
20

1820 1840 1860 1880 1900 1920 1940 1960 1970

Source: *Historical Chart Book,* 1971, Board of Governors, Federal Reserve System, p. 101. War captions added.

Each of the major upsurges in inflation shown in Chart I was associated with an enormous deficit. In 1811, the federal budget showed a big surplus; in 1812, with war, expenditures were twice as large as receipts. During the Civil War (1862) they were nine times as large; during World War I (1918), three and a half times; and in 1943, during World War II, three times.[2]

If the government were able and willing to pay for military expenditures with money withdrawn from the market through taxes or savings, there would be no increase in the money supply to fuel inflation. This helps explain why the post-World War II military expenditures in the Soviet Union have not led to inflation. In the Soviet Union, since the means of production are publicly owned, the government directly controls the main sources of revenue. It operates a planned economy which gives it incomparably greater control of budget receipts and expenditures than capitalist governments have. It does not engage in deficit financing; the budget is balanced.

One must not conclude from the Soviet experience that it is possible for the United States to have a big arms buildup or war without budget deficit and inflation. The question is not what is possible in the abstract or in a socialist economy, but what happens in fact under capitalism with its anarchy, and its class struggle over how the social product is to be distributed. Capitalist governments find it politically difficult, one could almost say impossible, to raise taxes enough to cover big arms buildups and wars. In fact, there has never been a big U.S. arms buildup or war without budget deficit and inflation.

ANOTHER FACTOR helping to cause inflation is monopoly control of strategic sectors of the U.S. economy. The price behavior of the steel industry during the 1950s, writes one economist, illustrates how companies with "market power" can contribute to inflation.

> By 1953, the wartime inflation had spent itself, and during 1953-55 the wholesale price index remained stable. Thereafter, it began to rise. Steel prices played a major role in these increases. Between 1953 and 1959, finished steel prices rose by 36 percent, in contrast to an 8.5 percent increase for all wholesale prices.

Steel prices rose not only during periods of business upswing and rising output, but also during periods of recession and falling output. "Steel prices were increased in 1954 despite the fact that capacity utilization fell from 95 percent in 1953 to 71 percent in 1954." Prices were increased again in 1958 although capacity utilization had dropped to 61 percent from 85 percent the year before.[3]

The increase, or even just maintenance, of prices in the face of falling demand is a clear manifestation of monopoly. As John Kenneth Galbraith once wrote:

> Only where monopoly power is present could it be possible for industries to show the price . . . behavior which we are considering. Under anything approaching pure competition . . . it would be impossible for the prices of the products of an industry to remain constant while production found its own level. Where numerous producers compete freely . . . the inevitable sequence of reduced demand is lower prices. . . . Should one producer attempt to maintain his prices, his production would [drop] to zero.[4]

Many economists have noted that in concentrated industries prices are "inflexible"—they almost never go down. In 1934, Gardiner Means (then an economic consultant to the Secretary of Agriculture) noticed that despite the tremendous decline in demand brought about by the Depression, many prices didn't fall. Analyzing the problem, he drew a distinction between what he called "market" prices and "administered" prices. Market prices are determined by competition, and when demand falls, they also fall. Administered prices are determined by the administrative action of the monopolies and are inflexible. Means pointed out that the economy was moving more and more toward administered prices:

> Gradually as our great corporations have been built up, more and more of the coordination of individual economic action has been brought about administratively. . . . As we go from the atomistic to the concentrated industries we find more administered prices and the administered prices becoming more rigid. In spite of many exceptions, the more concentrated the industry in relation to its market, the more inflexible do prices become. . . .[5]

Other economists have called attention to the practice by General Motors, du Pont and other companies of what is known as "target return pricing." Under this method, the company first sets a profits target, say 20 percent of its investment, and then fixes its prices at whatever level is required to produce profits at the target level.[6]

One study examined how price "markups" over costs moved

during the first five recessions after World War II. It found widespread increases in markups during recessions, and offered the following explanation:

> Consider a firm operating in a concentrated market. . . . Then introduce a recession. . . . If the firm loses revenue through a sales reduction during the recession, it will try to recoup the lost revenue from those diminished sales by increasing the price markup for its remaining sales so that it can get closer to the target profit rate it started with.[7]

As John Blair (formerly chief economist of the U.S. Senate Antitrust Committee) put it, prices in the concentrated industries "no longer remain 'rigid.' They have become flexible—*upward*."[8]

MANY OTHER FACTORS can contribute to inflation. Bad crops can drive up food prices. Rising oil prices can push up the general price level. A decline in the international value of the dollar can cause the dollar price of imports and related goods to rise.

The various factors that help cause inflation interact with one another and with the overall state of the economy, so that there is often no simple correlation between these factors and the movement of prices. Thus, although a budget deficit *tends* to produce inflation, this doesn't mean it will always do so regardless of its size and duration or the state of the economy. For example, inflation can be counteracted by an economic decline. The effects of bad crops will vary depending on whether they occur in an economy in which prices are stable or one in which a strong inflation is already underway. Of the different factors, the two most important are military expenditures and monopoly power over prices.

DURING THE YEARS 1960-65, the rate of inflation in the United States was comparatively low. Then, as the Vietnam War escalated, so did the inflation. The following table gives the annual increase in the consumer price index for the years just before and after 1965.[9]

Year	% Increase Before Escalation	Year	% Increase After Escalation
1960	1.6	1965	1.7
1961	1.0	1966	2.9
1962	1.1	1967	2.9
1963	1.2	1968	4.2
1964	1.3	1969	5.4
		1970	5.9

There can be no doubt that the surge of inflation from 1965 on was brought about by the Vietnam War, both through its effects on the economy in general and by causing big budget deficits. The increased activity of the manufacturers producing for the military resulted directly in increased prices. These manufacturers competed with the civilian sector of the economy for raw materials and other resources, helping to bid up prices. Rising military orders caused bottlenecks to develop, creating conditions favorable for monopoly price gouging.

There was also the effect of rising budget deficits. During the fiscal years 1960 through 1964, the deficit averaged $4 billion. However, because President Johnson was afraid to ask for a tax increase to finance the hated war, the deficit soon began to soar. In the fiscal year 1968, it reached $25 billion. The Vietnam War was the cause of this rise. Between 1965 and 1968, "national defense" outlays rose from $50 to $81 billion.[10]

After World War II, military expenditures dropped by ninety percent in three years. By 1947, the budget was in balance. After the Korean War, military expenditures dropped by twenty percent in two years and soon the budget was in surplus. But after the Vietnam War, military expenditures did not go down; they rose. And the budget ran one large deficit after another: $45 billion in 1975, $66 billion in 1976, $60 billion in 1980, even before Reagan became president.[11]

THE GOVERNMENT does not, of course, relate its enormous deficits to military expenditures. It tries to lay the blame on social expenditures, claiming that it spends more on "human resources" than on the military; but this claim is based on tricky budget accounting.

Till 1969 the government kept the finances of such systems as Social Security, Medicare, and Railroad Retirement separate from the general budget. These systems operate through trust funds that are financed by separate taxes. The government acts only as a caretaker for these funds. It cannot spend the money in them except for the specific purposes for which it is earmarked.

In 1969 President Johnson added the trust funds to the general budget to make the cost of the Vietnam War look smaller. The added trust funds made the total budget look bigger; therefore, the cost of the Vietnam War became a smaller percentage of it.

This device is still used to mislead. There is a category in the government's budget publications called "Outlays for Income Security." This category now contains outlays not only for the food stamps that the government pays for but also the more than ten times larger outlays for Social Security for which the government does *not* pay. Including Social Security and other trust funds in the general budget under "Income Security" enables the government to inflate this category into the biggest item of expenditures in the budget. The misleading charts distributed for publication in newspapers make it appear that for every two dollars the government spends on National Defense, it spends more than three dollars providing income to the people.

Social Security outlays, regardless of how much they have been growing, have had nothing to do with creating the federal budget deficits. These trust funds have financed themselves. The deficits have been in the general budget.

What is required to control the deficits in the general budget? What are the main outlays? Even after the end of the Vietnam War, fifty to sixty percent of total outlays have been war-related: current military expenditures, veterans' benefits, and interest on the national debt, the bulk of which arose through past military buildups and wars.

With these items costing so much, no amount of cutting of the rest of the budget could have eliminated the enormous deficits. To have eliminated the deficit in 1975, for example, it would have been necessary to slash the non-military part of the budget by 42 percent; for 1976, by 52 percent. Slashes of such proportions lie outside the boundary of budgetary reality.

After all, the government must continue to operate the Departments of Agriculture, Commerce, Justice, etc. Many federal programs involve what the government calls, in its statistics, "relatively uncontrollable outlays." Even programs that involve "relatively *controllable* outlays" can be cut only within limits.

Reagan worked hard to create the impression that the government's food stamp and public assistance programs are a big cause of its financial problems. But the maximum cuts in these programs that even the most hardhearted budget cutter could have carried out would hardly have dented the deficits of the 1970s not to speak of the deficits created by Reagan.

Controlling military expenditures is the key to controlling the federal budget. Experience since the escalation of the Vietnam War has shown that when military expenditures rise, the budget goes out of control; only by slashing military expenditures can the deficits be eliminated.

WHAT ROLE HAVE wage increases played in the inflation since the escalation of the Vietnam War? This question cannot be answered (at least not fairly and accurately) in the abstract, but only by considering the development of the inflation and the movement of wages concretely and historically. The questions to be kept in mind are: What started the big wave of inflation in the first place? Was it wage increases? What caused workers to demand bigger wage increases? Did this happen out on the blue or was it the workers' response to inflation? Even with the increases in workers' nominal wages, have their *real* wages (wages adjusted to take price increases into account) been rising or declining?

Most capitalist economists prefer to discuss the relation between wages and inflation in the abstract. This enables them to put the blame for inflation on workers' wages and to justify policies that lay the burden of controlling inflation on the backs of the working class.

John Kenneth Galbraith is an example. He writes in his book, *The New Industrial State:*

> At any reasonably high level of demand, prices and wages in the industrial system are inherently unstable. This is certainly so when the demand is strong enough to begin enrolling the hard core of the more or less unemployable unemployed. Then wages and prices press each other up in a continuing spiral. It is convenient in describing this spiral, to break into it at the point where wages act on prices. But it is a continuous process and no causal significance should be attached to wage increases merely because they are the starting point.
>
> When unemployment is small, the bargaining position of unions is, in general, strong. Members can face a strike with the assurance that they cannot be replaced. . . .
>
> Employers, on their side, will deem it wise under such circumstances to grant increases in wages. The strong demand insures that the added costs of the higher wages can be passed along to the consumer or other buyer.[12]

Galbraith spins out his theory from an armchair. He doesn't examine either the history of inflation or the concrete facts of any recent inflation. He devotes a whole chapter to "The Control of the Wage-Price Spiral" and not a single line to the historical connection between wars, military expenditures, and inflation.

Galbraith's theory may appear to have a certain plausibility, but only so long as one doesn't ask it to explain, not some vague, hypothetical inflation, but what actually happens in the real world. Why did a big wave of inflation get under way in 1941, after the United States began to arm for World War II, even though unemployment stood at the high level of ten percent? Why did another wave of inflation get under way in 1950, the first year of the Korean War? Unemployment at 5.3 percent was far from low. Why was inflation receding in 1955, after the Korean War had ended, even though unemployment stood at the lower level of 4.4 percent? Galbraith's theory can't explain why the highest inflation in a hundred years occurred during the 1970s and early 1980s, when unemployment was not low, but at the highest levels since the Great Depression.

What has been happening, in fact, since the current wave of inflation got under way in the mid-1960s is completely different from Galbraith's loaded, hypothetical example. The Vietnam War, not wage increases, set off the inflation. The demand for bigger wage increases didn't come out of the blue—it was an attempt by workers to defend themselves against the inflation created by the war. As the inflation grew, *nominal* wage increases got bigger. But *real* wage increases, wage increases adjusted for inflation, got smaller.

The increase in *real* average hourly earnings during the years 1965-70 was smaller, according to the government's statistics, than that during 1960-65. In 1973, real earnings actually began to fall. By 1980, they were 7.5 percent below their peak in 1972 and lower than they had been at any time since 1967.[13]

Despite nominal wage increases, workers are not the cause of inflation, but its victims. When they fight for wage increases, they are simply defending themselves. Given the inflation, where would they be if they didn't fight?

Blaming inflation on the workers is simply an excuse for trying to cut wages and control the inflation by forcing sacrifices on the working class. Making the working class sacrifice is not only unjust and cruel, but it won't solve the problem of inflation. This problem can only be solved by attacking its true causes.

 THE SO-CALLED *monetarists* claim that they have *the* way of attacking the true cause of inflation. Milton Friedman is the leading monetarist. Here is the way he and his wife present the monetarist view:

> Just as an excessive increase in the quantity of money is the one and
> only important cause of inflation, so a reduction in the rate of
> monetary growth is the one and only cure for inflation. The problem is
> not one of not knowing what to do. That is easy enough. Government
> must increase the quantity of money less rapidly. The problem is to
> have the political will to take the measures necessary. Once the
> inflationary disease is in an advanced state, the cure takes a long time
> and has painful side effects . . . lower economic growth, temporarily
> high unemployment, without, for a time, much reduction of infla-
> tion.[14]

The Friedmans' analyses of what causes inflation and what
should be done about it go together. An excessive increase in the
quantity of money is the "one and only important cause" of inflation
and therefore what must be done is simple—cut this increase. This
argument is a formalism, a mechanistic oversimplification which
leaves out ninety percent of the problem. The problem is not just
that an excessive increase in the quantity of money causes inflation,
but what causes the excessive increase in the quantity of money and
how it can best be halted.

One must not look at formal, hypothetical examples, but at the
actual facts. The main factors causing an excessive increase in the
quantity of money have been military expenditures and monopoly
pricing. When the government turns to the banking system for the
money to cover a budget deficit caused by military expenditures,
what can the Federal Reserve do: Manage the system in such a way
that the government *doesn't* get the money? The Federal Reserve
may be independent in theory, but in fact it is a subordinate arm of
the government and has to go along. It is government borrowing,
not the Federal Reserve, that is increasing the money supply.

When the monopolies raise their prices during economic downswings as well as upswings, this swells the amount of money that
businessmen and consumers borrow from banks and also increases
the money supply. How much can the Federal Reserve do about it
without squeezing credit so much as to produce a depression?

Excessive increase in the money supply, military expenditures,
and monopoly pricing are all causes of inflation. Military expenditures and monopoly pricing provide the content which explains the
excessive increase in the money supply.

Friedman and the other monetarists pay no attention to this

content. They act as though it doesn't matter how the increase in the money supply is cut, just so it is cut. What does this mean in practice? The Federal Reserve can't do anything to stop the government from borrowing or the monopolies from raising their prices. Cutting the increase in the money supply means imposing restrictions elsewhere such as cutting the supply of credit for the housing industry, for the purchase of autos, for the economy generally, and creating recession and unemployment.

What distinguishes the monetarists, however, is not only their absolute disregard of anything except the money supply, but the extremes to which they want to carry their remedy, regardless of what happens to the economy and unemployment. When Friedman says that the problem is one of "political will" he means that the policy of cutting the money supply must be carried through to the end come hell or high water.

It is no accident that Friedman has never been given public office. The leading circles of U.S. state monopoly capitalism have thus far not accepted his view about rigidly pushing the monetary remedy to its extreme. They recognize the political dangers of such a course. They see that the problem is more than one of political will. The fightback of the people must be taken into account.

No government of a democratic country has ever attempted to apply the Friedman method. Only Pinochet's Chile has done so; there the Friedman method was backed by fascist bayonets. Even so, it has failed.

However, the standard state monopoly capitalist remedy for inflation contains a strong dose of Friedmanism. Those who apply the standard remedy knowingly create and use recession and unemployment. They just want to manage them flexibly, to hold them within politically tolerable limits. Since the beginning of the 1970s, faced with a high and stubborn inflation, they have expanded their idea of how much recession and unemployment are politically tolerable.

AN INFLATION RATE OF five percent seemed high in 1969. The Nixon administration applied the remedy of tightening credit and provoking recession. The tight credit policy and recession didn't solve the problem. The inflation had gathered too much momentum and it was still being fed by the war and budget deficits. The best the government could do was reduce the growth rate of the consumer price index from 5.9 percent in 1970 to 4.2 percent in 1971. The unemployment rate, which had been 3.5 percent in 1969, leaped up to 6 percent. The government eased its policy; Nixon didn't want to face the 1972 presidential election with recession and high unemployment.

Still Nixon couldn't just ignore the inflation. He needed a method that offered hope of containing it while leaving the government free to pump up the money supply and stimulate the economy for the election. So he turned to wage and price controls, despite his long record of opposition to them.

For a year, the controls resulted in a small reduction in the rate of price increases. However, at the same time that the government was applying the controls, it was producing a sharp increase in the budget deficit. It was increasing the inflationary pressure with enormous deficits while trying to contain this pressure with wage and price controls.

With the deficits and an expansion of economic activity, a boom in world commodity markets, and a devaluation of the dollar that caused import prices to rise, the inflation accelerated again. Despite controls, consumer prices rose sharply in 1973.

As usual under capitalist governments, the wage and price controls were administered against the working class. Here is what a publication of conservative central bankers, the Annual Report of the Bank for International Settlements, said:

> The price regulations imposed under the Economic Stabilization Act were not very effective . . . even though the wage aspects of the policy were not subject to serious challenge. . . . First year pay increases under the new contracts in 1973 averaged less than 6 percent, the lowest figure in several years. . . . By contrast, consumer prices in December 1973 were nearly 9 percent and food prices alone 20 percent higher than twelve months before.[15]

The government dismantled the controls in early 1974; the monopolies didn't want even lax controls on their prices. Given the inflationary pressure that had been building up, the elimination of controls had an effect like the release of a pressure valve. The big increase in oil prices came on top of everything else; the OPEC countries had hiked oil prices and the U.S. oil monopolies had added on their own price gouging. The consumer price index went up 11 percent in 1974.

As the government did away with the controls, it went back to a restrictive monetary policy. What followed was the longest and deepest recession of the postwar period till then, combined with double-digit inflation. Industrial production fell over a period of sixteen months by a total of 14 percent. The gross national product fell by 6 percent from the last quarter of 1973 to the second quarter of 1975. Unemployment, even by the official figures, rose to a peak of 9 percent in May 1975.

But even the powerful recession of 1974-75 didn't bring the inflation under control. The rate of increase in the consumer price index was reduced to 5.8 percent in 1976; not as bad as double-digit, but still out of control. As the recovery from the recession got under way, the inflation flared up once more. A process of ratcheting up both inflation and unemployment was under way.

The rate of inflation rose steadily from 1977 to 1979, and then during the first quarter of 1980, it exploded to an annual rate of 18 percent. Again the government applied the standard remedy, the same one (tightening credit and provoking recession) that Nixon had applied ten years earlier. But now the economic mess was far worse. The rate of inflation was three times higher, and the official rate of unemployment 6.3 percent instead of 3.5 percent.

As always, the government and the capitalist press understood clearly what the tightening of credit meant. A few months earlier, at a prior stage of the tightening of the monetary screws, the *New York Times* carried a story headlined: "Tight Money: Here Goes Housing" (12-21-79). Commenting on the effects of a one percent increase in the Federal Reserve discount rate on loans to banks, it said:

> The percent increase may not sound like much, but the AFL-CIO estimates that the increase in the discount rate from 11 to 12 percent results in 170,000 lost jobs and a $6 billion increase in the cost of new construction. Moreover, each percentage point rise in mortgage rates pushes up a home buyer's carrying costs about 7.5 percent. The overall effect is to reduce the availability of mortgage money and to depress the total housing market. The effect of a downturn in housing is certain to strain the entire economy.

Now the credit tightening was far tougher; again the *New York Times* carried a story (3-30-80):

> The word on [the] availability [of mortgages] is tight. Citibank was holding to its week-old rise to a 16½ percent interest rate on home

loans. But a higher rate at Citibank could be only a few days away. . . . The Bank of America has increased its down-payment requirement on real estate loans from 20 percent to 25 percent and will increase the rate it charges on mortages on one-family homes. . . . The squeeze is also being applied to second mortgages.

Citibank says it will no longer issue any new Master Cards or Visa Cards—even to depositors. The Bank of America . . . raised the minimum monthly payment on its Visa and Master Cards to 6 percent from 4 percent or from $10 to $25, whichever was higher. . . .

The Bank of America is restricting personal loans to current customers. For those Californians prone to borrow for swimming pools, spas, or hot tubs, the Bank of America now says, "forget it". . . .

Chase Manhattan will accept applications [for auto loans] from depositors of six-months standing or who have a good payment record of six months. The same with Citibank. No others need apply.

The government, with its tight credit policy, was deliberately destroying jobs of construction workers, lumber workers, auto workers, workers generally—millions of jobs in all.

The government temporarily loosened credit policy before the elections of 1980 and the economy began a slow, weak recovery. The recovery didn't last long. The Reagan administration quickly re-tightened credit and the economy resumed its recession.

5

Reaganomics

The only valid point made by Ronald Reagan when he took office was that the economy was in a mess. His policy guaranteed a worsening of the mess.

President Reagan brought with him a philosophy that the government was too big and doing too much. It should not concern itself with such problems as poverty, hunger, medical care for the needy, decent social security for old age, the environment, safe and healthy working conditions, etc.

Reagan also brought with him a strategy of showing labor who is boss; in fact, of showing all groups who disagreed with him who is boss. As governor of California he had pressed college authorities to deal harshly with students demonstrating against the Vietnam War. Labor must be handled the same way.

Of a piece with Reagan's anti-labor outlook was his racism—a crass lack of concern for the economic and social problems of Afro-American, Hispanic, and other minority peoples. If they were suffering (which he questioned), that was part of the natural order of things.

The counterparts to Reagan's anti-labor and racist philosophy at home were his militarism and warlike foreign policy. His military goal was ambitious and dangerous: to reestablish the nuclear superiority of the United States over the Soviet Union. He set the tone of his foreign policy by calling for a "crusade" against the Soviet Union ("the focus of evil"), and strong action to halt the process of revolution in Central America and the Caribbean, the Middle East, and elsewhere.

The economic policy Reagan put into effect contained four main parts: (1) an enormous hike in the military budget; (2) lower taxes on the big corporations and the rich; (3) slashed government help to working people and the poor; and (4) an extremely tight monetary policy by the Federal Reserve.

What the Reagan policy came down to was simply to give more to the corporations and the military and make the people, especially labor and the minorities, sacrifice. This policy was already taking shape before Reagan. The Carter administration had begun a big increase in military expenditures and had called for "wage restraint" and a reduction in the U.S. standard of living. But Reagan took this philosophy much further than Carter, with an even bigger military buildup, more blatant favoritism toward the monopolies, and a tougher line on labor.

The difference in degree is important. It is one thing to increase military expenditures 5 percent per year, and another to increase them 8.5 percent and to combine this increase with a big tax reduction benefitting the corporations and the rich.

But Reaganomics means more than just a difference of degree. The Reagan philosophy of "cutting down the role of government" marks a break not only with the Carter administration, but with all other administrations of the last fifty years. It is a throwback to the days before U.S. monopoly capitalism became state monopoly capitalism. The last president who subscribed to this philosophy was Herbert Hoover.

REAGAN BEGAN to implement his economic policy with assurance and optimism. He would carry out a big increase in military expenditures, a big decrease in taxes, and still balance the budget in 1984. In 1985 and 1986, the budget would show a growing surplus.

During the 1980 presidential campaign, one of Reagan's opponents, John Anderson, had asked: "How can you increase expenditures, lower taxes, and balance the budget all at the same time? It's easy; you do it with mirrors."

Reagan had an equally easy and sure method—supply-side economics. The tax cuts and the business confidence he was creating would immediately cause the recession-ridden, stagnant economy to start growing like mad. The rate of growth would be four to five percent per year. This rapid growth would cause an increase in receipts big enough to change what would otherwise be enormous deficits into surpluses.

Reagan also claimed that, even as the economy was bursting into growth, the rate of inflation would come down. He explained how this would happen. "The final aspect of our plan requires a national monetary policy which does not allow money growth to increase consistently faster than the growth of goods and services. In order to curb inflation, we need to slow the growth in our money supply."[1]

Reagan's program was based on illusion and contradiction. To expect the economy to grow at a rate of four to five percent per year over a five-year period is to live in a dream world. The only times since 1965 that the economy has grown at a rate of four percent or more has been after recessions in which it had first declined. Even then the high growth rates have lasted only two or three years, and were followed by further declines.

True, the economy grew at sustained high rates during the early 1960s, a precedent often cited by the Reaganites. But many things were different then. In particular, the rate of inflation was so low as to be almost without significance.

Now the rate of inflation was anything but insignificant and the method Reagan was relying on to lower it—tight credit—contradicted the goal of achieving a high growth rate. If the Federal Reserve kept credit as tight as Reagan requested, the economy could not grow as he had projected. If these growth goals were not realized, the great gap he was creating between budget expenditures and receipts would not be closed. All possibility of attaining the promised balanced budget by 1984 would vanish, giving way to a prospect of deficits unprecedented in size.

Where would this tangle of contradictions lead? There were only a few possibilities. The Federal Reserve could tighten credit all the more to compensate for the large budget deficits; the result would be deeper recession, more prolonged stagnation, higher unemployment. Or the Federal Reserve would not be able to tighten credit enough to compensate; the result would be stronger inflation. Given the deficits, the Reagan administration could not eliminate the inflation short of provoking a major, prolonged depression. Although one of the components of the high inflation-high unemployment trap might temporarily ease, the combination would worsen.

That the Reagan administration put into effect a program of the type it did shows its adventurism. Many recognized this adventurism. The *New York Times* stated: "President Reagan's economic program represents a daring gamble that a sweeping application of an untested economic theory can improve the American economy radically and quickly."[2]

The economist, Lester Thurow, entitled an article on the Reagan program, "How To Wreck the Economy."[3]

THE MILITARY BUILDUP called for by Reagan was much bigger than the buildup during the Vietnam War. Between 1965 and 1970, military outlays went up from $50 billion to $80 billion (by 60 percent). The Reagan program called for them to rise from $159 billion in 1981 to $336 billion in 1986 or by 110 percent.

Military expenditures in 1981 had already been increased by Carter to well above the level of preceding years. If this high level were maintained through 1986, total military expenditures for the six-year period 1981-86 would total $950 billion. Reagan called for annual increases over the 1981 level that would raise total expenditures for the period to $1,450 billion, that is, $500 billion more.

The increased burden on the budget from military expenditures didn't stop Reagan from proposing huge tax cuts for the corporations and the rich. From a famous interview with Reagan's Budget Director, David Stockman, published in the *Atlantic*, we get a description of how Reagan's tax proposal was worked out:

> The tax lobbyists of Washington, when they saw the outlines of the Reagan tax bill, mobilized the business community, the influential economic sectors from oil to real estate. In a matter of days, they created the political environment in which they flourish best—a bidding war between the two parties. . . . Stockman participated in the trading—special tax concessions for oil-lease holders and real-estate tax shelters, and generous loopholes that virtually eliminated the corporate income tax. . . . "Do you realize the greed that came to the forefront?" Stockman asked with wonder. "The hogs were really feeding."[4]

The Reagan administration had the gall to claim that its tax cuts provided tax relief for everyone. But what its program really did was slash the taxes of the corporations and the rich and place more of the tax burden on those with lower incomes.

The cuts in individual income taxes favored the wealthy. Those with incomes below $15,000 received an average cut of $95; those with incomes above $50,000 got $2,900, and those with incomes above $200,000 got more than $25,000.

The picture becomes even worse if one takes into account Social Security taxes and the effects of inflation in pushing incomes into higher tax brackets. Here is what an AFL-CIO report says:

> Estimates of the Congressional Joint Committee on Taxation which take into account inflation and increased Social Security taxes show that the tax cut is an illusion for low and moderate income workers.... By 1984, taxpayers with incomes under $15,000 will be paying more in taxes than they are paying now. . . .[5]

The corporations received an even bigger bonanza than rich individuals. The Reagan tax cut meant a drop in the effective rate on corporate profits from 28 to 14 percent. This drop came on top of large previous declines in this rate. In 1960, it was 43 percent.[6]

The Reagan tax cuts mean a big shift in the federal tax structure. The percentage of federal tax receipts derived from corporate income taxes will go down by a third between 1980 and 1986. The percent derived from Estate and Gift taxes (which fall mainly on the rich) will be virtually nil. But the percentages derived from taxes on individuals, from Social Security taxes, and from consumer excise taxes will all go up.

The AFL-CIO justly noted that "the most dangerous feature of the tax cut is that it imposes a huge, continuing drain on the federal treasury."[7] Reagan's budget estimates indicated that the revenue loss would amount to over $700 billion during 1981-86.[8]

Reagan proposed a cruel slash in federal social spending. His budget called for cuts in such programs as Food Stamps, Medicaid, Aid to Families with Dependent Children, and rent subsidies. It proposed eliminating the floor under Social Security benefits. It called for a reduction in federal aid to states with high unemployment which had enabled them to extend the payment of unemployment benefits from 26 to 39 weeks.

Reagan also proposed to slash government support for a variety of economic activities. His budget called for the elimination or reduction of subsidies for the development of synthetic fuels, solar energy, and water resources; for the promotion of railroad travel and the construction of new mass transit systems.

For all the cruelty and severity of the Reagan budget cuts, they could not even remotely solve the budget problem. The total expenditure reduction added up to less than $350 billion. This could not make up for the gap of more than $1 trillion created by increased military expenditures and tax cuts.

Despite its hardheartedness and lack of realism, the Reagan budget swept through Congress in early 1981.

ECONOMIC REALITY in the form cf recession struck the Reagan program in the summer of 1981. Many predicted this recession. Here, for example, is Edward Cowan in the *New York Times* (12-14-80):

> The seemingly relentless upward march of interest rates—the prime rate at 20 percent . . .—is pulling the economy down into a second dip that analysts are likely to regard as a continuation of the steep business recession that began in the first half of 1980.

Even before the recession, unemployment stood at the high level of 7.2 percent, which prior to the 1970s would have been considered intolerable by almost everyone even at the trough of a recession. Now, starting from this high level, unemployment began to climb. By April 1982, the official rate stood at 9.3 percent, a new postwar record; by December, it had reached 10.8 percent. Between July 1981 and December 1982, official unemployment increased by over four million people, from 7.8 million to 12 million. The real increase was much bigger, since these official figures omit the large increase in the number of workers who become too discouraged to look for work.

This recession was, as Cowan dubbed it beforehand, "President Reagan's recession." It was precipitated by the tight monetary policy Reagan had demanded from the Federal Reserve. Its severity and duration were also tied to Reagan policy. Right through the downswing and despite the mounting unemployment, the Federal Reserve persisted in maintaining tight credit and high interest rates. Reagan, as befit his ideology, pressed the policy of fighting inflation with recession and unemployment further than any previous president. Even conservatives like Nixon and Ford didn't tighten the monetary screws as hard.

Besides the immediate damage it did to both the people and the economy, the recession killed the earlier rosy Reagan predictions that the budget would switch from deficit to surplus by 1984. In his 1982 Budget Message, Reagan projected not only a deficit of $92 billion in 1983, but one of $83 billion in 1984 and $72 billion in 1985.

Even these revised projections were criticized as unrealistic. The *New York Times* (2-7-82) said:

> In its 1983 budget released today, the Reagan administration appears, at least to some analysts, to be ignoring the restraint on economic growth imposed by the Federal Reserve Board's tight monetary policy, which the president endorses in his Budget Message to Congress.

The Congressional Budget Office also issued budget projections. Its projections showed rising, not falling, deficits—deficits that would reach the astronomic levels of $188 billion in 1984 and $208 billion in 1985.[9]

As the prospect for the future deficits became clear, even many in Wall Street became disenchanted with the Reagan program. Big budget deficits mean inflationary pressure and inflationary pressure means that the Federal Reserve will keep interest rates high. Stockbrokers don't like high interest rates; they tend to make stock prices go down because they cause investment money to flow away from stocks to whatever is offering higher yields. The prospect of huge deficits boded ill for the stock market.

Many economists and others became concerned about the effects of the enormous deficits on the economy. They worried: Won't these deficits fuel inflation far into the future? If the Federal Reserve tries to counter the deficits with tight credit and high interest rates, what will be the effect on the housing, auto, and other industries? And on the economy as a whole? Don't the deficits guarantee that we will have a stagnant economy far into the future?

REAGAN NOT ONLY brought about a great increase in unemployment, but he also resisted the creation of government programs to ease it. Although he claimed that "I bleed for the man or woman able and willing to work who can find no job opening,"[10] the only jobs bill he went along with was a token measure that he felt would undercut demands for a meaningful jobs program.

Unemployment was part of an environment that Reagan was working to create for wringing concessions from labor, concessions desired for several reasons: to control inflation at labor's expense; to free resources for the massive military buildup; and to give the monopolies higher profits.

Another way Reagan worked to create the environment he

wanted was his action in the air traffic controllers' (PATCO) strike. When his administration broke the air traffic controllers' union, it had more in mind than this particular strike. It was acting to create for itself an image of authority and toughness, to set the general tone for dealing with labor.

The government's uncompromising, union-busting stance began to have wide effects immediately. A few weeks after the PATCO strike began, *U.S. News & World Report* (2-21-81) ran a story headlined, "A Hard Line Against State, Local Unions Too." It said in part, "The tough reaction by Reagan set a precedent that mayors and governors won't ignore. The bitter confrontation between the White House and striking air-traffic controllers is setting a harsh new tone for government dealings with public employee unions."

The campaign by private industry for labor givebacks, already under way for some time, acquired additional impetus. In the months following the air-traffic controllers' strike, one company after another—Firestone, Goodyear, Uniroyal, International Harvester, Ford, General Motors, National Steel, and others—demanded that the workers give up hard-won gains in wages and benefits. The monopolies used several weapons to support their demands, including often the threat to shut down plants. The environment created by Reagan was a great help to them.

THE REAGAN administration quickly proved itself to be exceptionally bullheaded in insisting that its program be carried out regardless of whether developments showed it to be working, or leading to a deepening of troubles. Nothing worked the way Reagan had said it would. But he blithely disregarded not just the recession and unemployment (which is not surprising for Reagan) but also the spectre of soaring budget deficits which he had long claimed to abhor.

The prospective deficits showed (for those who needed proof) that lower taxes on the rich is not the magic solution Reagan said it was; you can't lower taxes, hike military expenditures and balance the budget. As the size of the looming deficits became clear, many observers, including some friendly to the Administration, suggested that the program be modified. The military buildup could be reduced. The later stages of the tax cut could be postponed. The administration reacted with a rapid, "No, we must stay the course."

What Reagan did propose was further cuts in Food Stamps,

Welfare, Medicaid, employment training, and aid to mass transit.
Here is the adminstration's justification for these cuts: "With programs such as Medicaid and Food Stamps rising far faster than
inflation, income supplementation programs have become a major
source of persistent deficits, excessive taxes, and poor economic
performance."[11]

This was too much even for the *New York Times*, which com-
mented (2-14-82):

> It takes a lot of nerve for an administration that is calling for a $758
> billion budget and a $92 billion deficit to blame its troubles on $11
> billion in Food Stamps and $18 billion in Medicaid. That makes the
> unskilled and unemployed not merely victims but villains.

Reagan shifts the blame for everything bad that happens during
his administration to government social spending, to his pre-
decessors, to everything and everybody but himself. But no amount
of cutting social programs can solve the problem of the deficits.
The gigantic deficits are Reagan deficits, produced by his military
and tax programs and his stubborn refusal to allow the necessary
changes in them to be made. He represents economic thinking that
is exceptionally unconcerned with reality.

REAGAN BROUGHT great benefits to the monopolies and the military
with his tax cuts and arms buildup, but to the people and the
economy he brought calamity.

His administration not only pushed unemployment to record
postwar levels, but created a situation in which, unless something is
done, it will remain outrageously high for years. The projections
churned out by government agencies vary from one another but
they all agree on one thing: Unemployment will stay high for a long
time.

Reagan was quick to claim a reduction in the inflation rate as an
accomplishment of his program. The consumer price index in 1982
was 6.1 percent higher than the year before. In 1981, the increase
had been 10.4 percent and in 1980, 13.5 percent. But what does this
slowdown in inflation mean? Inflation was exchanged for unemployment. Besides, Reagan was favored on the inflation problem
by good harvests, a decline in oil prices, and a rise in the international value of the dollar to an overly high level that can't last
indefinitely.

Even with the sacrifices forced upon the people, Reagan did not eliminate the inflation, and the enormous deficits created by his policy loom over the economy.

What will be the effect of these deficits? The possibilities are few. They will tend to reinvigorate the inflation. The Federal Reserve will face a choice between giving the inflation free rein or again deliberately slowing down the economy. We will get either higher inflation or more recession, stagnation, and unemployment, or some combination of the two—probably the combination.

For an economy which is already suffering from high unemployment and an inflation that is far from cured, this is an ominous prospect.

6

Stagflation—No Easy Solution

There is no easy, neat solution to the mess that the economy is in from years of fighting inflation by provoking recession and unemployment. We are dealing with an anarchic, capitalist economy which resists control. Nevertheless, things can be done that would improve the economy and help the people.

The problem of inflation should not be viewed in isolation from the problem of inflation-recession-unemployment (stagflation) of which it is a part. What is required is not just to reduce the inflation, but to treat the whole problem.

We must end the government's practice of fighting inflation by provoking recession and unemployment. Instead of eliminating the deficits which are feeding the inflation, the government tries to compensate for them by slowing down the entire economy. This method doesn't get rid of the inflation but just temporarily contains it, while the government continues its military expenditures and deficits. These, of course, reinvigorate the inflationary pressure.

Besides a switch to better methods of fighting inflation, a massive government jobs program is urgently needed. Such a program could employ workers to rebuild our dilapidated roads and bridges, sewer and water systems, and railroads and subways, to upgrade our parks and other public facilities, to construct housing, schools, and hospitals. It makes no sense to have so many things which need doing left undone, while millions of people are forced to suffer unemployment.

But a jobs program should be properly financed so that it doesn't aggravate inflation. In fact, a true program for getting the economy out of stagflation must, even while taking action to relieve unemployment, also attack the problem of inflation.

Can this be done? Is it possible to fight unemployment and inflation simultaneously? Most capitalist economists say no, but they are wrong. It isn't easy, but ways can be found to do it.

The key lies in a very important fact, established by many researchers: Dollar for dollar, military expenditures create far fewer jobs than do civilian expenditures. This means that if the arms budget were slashed, part of the money could be saved to help bring down the budget deficit (and inflationary pressure), and the rest used to create more jobs than did the old level of military spending.

A report by the Council on Economic Priorities (CEP) on *The Costs and Consequences of Reagan's Military Buildup* states, "While military spending creates jobs, almost any alternative use of the same money would create more jobs." It summarizes the studies that back this statement. Here are three examples:

> Roger Bezdek, then an economist with the U.S. Department of Commerce, published a study in 1975 that traced the effects over five years of three levels of military spending. . . . Bezdek found that employment and net output would be 2.1 percent higher if the military budget were cut than if it continued at the same level. If military spending were increased by 30 percent, employment and output would be 1.3 percent lower than if the budget remained stable. Marion Anderson, of the Employment Research Associates in Lansing, MI, has also studied the employment effects of military spending. . . . She estimated that every billion dollars spent in the military sector resulted in a net loss of 9,000 jobs compared with spending the billion dollars in the private sector, and a net loss of 35,000 jobs compared with spending the money in the state and local government sector. Anderson estimated that over a million jobs were foregone in the whole economy during 1977 and again in 1978 as a result of military spending.
> Most recently, in *Misguided Expenditures,* economist Gail Shields of the Council on Economic Priorities compared the job creating potential of the MX missile with a range of alternative industries. . . . All five alternatives [mass transit, public utility, railroads, housing, solar energy-energy conservation] would create more jobs than the mobile missile project.[1]

The report presents an explanation for the low job yield of military spending and some interpretations of its significance:

> The major reason why military spending creates fewer jobs than most civilian alternatives is that arms production requires a greater concentration of highly skilled, well-paid engineers and technicians than does civilian industry. . . .
>
> On average nine out of every ten jobs in U.S. industry are production jobs, but in such areas as guided missiles and electronic communication, only three jobs out of ten go to production workers, and in aircraft just five out of ten. The Air Force is now engaged in research to develop a highly automated "factory of the future" for aerospace production which will further reduce labor input and increase the capital intensity of military production.
>
> The increasingly low job yield of military spending means that such spending can do little to reverse the problems of structural unemployment and income maldistribution. . . . In 1968, at a time of high aerospace employment, Herbert Northrup concluded that formidable "institutional" factors limit black employment opportunities and the chances for promotion in aerospace. . . . The two main factors behind Northrup's conclusions were the high skill and educational requirements for aerospace jobs, which penalize those who have not had access to the needed education or prior work experience, and the location of aerospace facilities away from urban areas with concentrations of minorities.[2]

Thus slashing military expenditures could help to eliminate the budget deficits and at the same time provide funds to create more jobs.

It is also necessary to increase taxes on the corporations and the rich to balance the budget. Actually, the United States needs a tax reform even apart from the desirability of balancing the budget. The tax system is riddled with loopholes by which the corporations and the rich escape taxes. A tax reform would end some blatant inequities as well as help solve the problems of budget deficit and inflation.

As a supplement to fighting inflation by balancing the budget, emergency price controls could be instituted. The idea that price controls could do the whole job of eliminating inflation is mistaken. While price controls were the main method during World War II, they were relied upon then because there wasn't much choice;

reducing military expenditures was not an option. The price controls helped, but they didn't prevent a strong inflation from getting underway. Price controls by themselves do not work well. A flooding of the economy with money created because of budget deficits will overwhelm them sooner or later. But price controls can be useful as a supplement to measures which eliminate the flooding.

A program based on the considerations above that could get us out of the stagflation trap would include the following:

1. The complete scrapping of the Carter-Reagan program for increasing military expenditures and an immediate return to the 1979 level, to be followed by annual ten percent reductions in each of the next five years.

2. A massive, federally-financed jobs creation program, with comprehensive affirmative action guarantees.

3. An increase in taxes on big corporations and individuals with incomes above $50,000 a year which, when combined with the reduction in military expenditures, would provide sufficient funds to finance the jobs program, restore all the Reagan cuts in social and economic programs, and bring the budget into balance within one year.

4. Emergency price controls for two years.

5. Federal Reserve action, as the budget is brought into balance, to reduce interest rates to their traditional levels.

The basic logic of this type of program is simple: to curb budget deficits and inflation by slashing military spending and raising taxes on the corporations and the rich, and to release the economy from the Federal Reserve's chokehold. The emergency price controls would hold the price line while the other measures are taking effect.

The federal jobs program is necessary because a large part of the unemployment is now "structural"—it will not go away even if the economy grows more rapidly. Most of the unemployment among Afro-American, Hispanic and many white youth, and much of that among workers in steel, auto and other troubled industries must be dealt with by targeted job and job-training programs.

The program outlined here will not work perfectly and is not a cure-all for state monopoly capitalism, but it would be a great improvement.

PART III

DECLINING INTERNATIONAL STRENGTH

7

An Unstable Dollar

Since the 1950s, the international value of the U.S. dollar has fluctuated widely and there have been several severe dollar crises. These fluctuations and crises are not just technical phenomena, of interest only to international bankers. They affect the whole economy and all of us.

A falling dollar helps feed inflation in the United States; when the dollar buys less of a foreign currency, it takes more dollars to pay for imported articles and their prices here rise. A rising dollar, on the other hand, makes imported goods cheaper in the U.S., but makes it harder for U.S. goods to compete in the world's export markets.

Fluctuations in the dollar upset the monetary mechanism of the whole capitalist world. The dollar is the capitalist world's key currency, held as a reserve by many countries. An excessive decline in its value could cause the whole mechanism to break down.

What happens to the dollar affects the level of economic activity in the United States. The government's main method of fighting a declining dollar is to slow down the economy by jacking up interest rates. It reasons as follows: A decline in the dollar is caused by the United States spending more abroad than it earns there, which floods the world with dollars and lowers their value. Slowing down the economy reduces the U.S. demand for imports; high interest rates attract money from abroad which also helps the dollar.

Although the dollar has had ups and downs and was considered "strong" during 1983, fundamentally it has been weakening over the years. Such weakening reflects a decline in the international strength of the U.S. economy, including a decline in its ability to support a large military establishment abroad. Just as the decline in the ability of Britain to maintain its empire was reflected in a fall in the value of the pound, so the decline in U.S. economic strength is reflected in a weakening of the dollar.

U.S. IMPERIALISM came out of World War II riding high. The U.S. economy was unscathed; the economies of the other major industrial countries were severely damaged, in need of reconstruction. The United States enjoyed export markets in which there was virtually no competition. It sold far more than it bought, ringing up enormous trade and payments surpluses. The other main capitalist countries needed large imports, which only the United States could supply, to feed their people and reconstruct their economies. But they were unable to earn enough dollars to pay for these imports. The capitalist world outside the United States suffered from a "dollar shortage."

The dollar was not only scarce, but backed strongly by gold. In 1949, the United States gold reserve was $25 billion, 70 percent of the world's monetary gold stock. Because of its scarcity, and its gold backing, the dollar was the world's most valuable currency.

The U.S. economy seemed capable of accomplishing almost anything. The United States mounted the Marshall Plan to transfer dollars to Western Europe. It took on the Korean War. It inflicted an enormously costly arms race upon the Soviet Union, which had lost so much in the war against fascism. It set up a worldwide network of military bases which cost billions of dollars in upkeep. Its corporations were able to transfer billions of dollars abroad and acquire strategic positions in the economies of foreign countries.

The economic and military strength of the United States was reflected, of course, in its international position. It was able to form a military coalition directed against the Soviet Union, to channel economic reconstruction of other capitalist countries into directions that were to its liking, to exert a dominant influence on the international economic institutions that grew up after the war. For example, the international monetary system for the capitalist world, set up at Bretton Woods in 1944, was largely a creation of the United States.

Under this system, the dollar was to be maintained at a fixed relation to gold, and the other main currencies at a fixed relation to the dollar. Currencies could fluctuate within a narrow range around their fixed relations or parities. Under certain circumstances and in agreement with the International Monetary Fund (set up at Bretton Woods), the parities themselves could be changed; but the basic system was one of fixed rates—currencies didn't "float" in relation to one another.

The method by which countries were to keep their currencies at parity was simple. To keep the dollar at parity in relation to gold—$35 an ounce—the United States was obligated to exchange dollars presented by foreign central banks for gold at that price; and vice versa, to exchange gold presented for dollars. The foreign central banks would, therefore, know that they could get an ounce of gold for $35, and $35 for an ounce of gold, and this would maintain the dollar at parity. Similarly, other countries could keep their currencies at a fixed price in relation to the dollar by standing ready to buy and sell them for dollars at that price.

The Bretton Woods system provided U.S. imperialism with a great advantage: It helped make the dollar the world's main reserve currency. Other countries used dollars not only to buy goods and services, but also to hold in their reserves. This meant that, by the amount of dollars going into foreign reserves, the United States would enjoy the privilege of spending more than it was earning. If, for example, in a given year, other countries added $1 billion to their reserves, the United States could spend abroad $1 billion more than it had earned.

Theoretically, this privilege was limited to the amount of dollars that other countries wanted for their reserves. If, through balance of payments deficits (an excess of spending over earnings), the United States pumped out more dollars than other countries wanted, they could present the excess dollars to the United States for exchange into gold. The loss of gold was supposed to get the United States to mend its ways and eliminate the deficits.

But this limitation was only theoretical. As the system came to operate in practice, the United States would often use its political power to get out of the obligation to pay gold for dollars. To use an expression common in the literature, it was able to run large balance of payments deficits "without pain." It didn't always have to pay out gold for excess dollars. And it didn't—despite the excess—have to suffer a decline in the value of the dollar either. Other countries had to maintain its value by accepting unwanted dollars; by being forced, in effect, to lend resources to the United States that would probably never be repaid.

This ability of the United States to run balance of payments deficits without pain helped U.S. imperialism finance many things—foreign investments, foreign military bases, foreign wars.

AS LENIN POINTED OUT, capitalist countries develop unevenly. The overwhelming economic superiority of the United States could not last. Western Europe and Japan were bound to recover from their low postwar level. In addition, the U.S. monopolies were making massive transfers of technology to the other major capitalist countries through investments and licensing arrangements. The economic growth of West Germany and Japan was furthered by the restrictions placed on their rearming. They didn't have to suffer the drag on growth that the huge cost of armaments and wars would be placing on the United States economy.

Still close to its peak strength, the U.S. economy seemed to take the Korean War in stride. This war did not give rise to a major dollar crisis as did the Vietnam War later. But even aside from the inflation it inflicted on the American people, the war did great damage. The expenditures of U.S. dollars for military purposes in Korea and Japan shot up. The U.S. trade surplus declined sharply; the surge to a war economy brought about a big increase in imports, while the military drained off resources that might otherwise have gone into exports. The balance of payments shifted from surplus to deficit. The United States was now pumping out more dollars than it was taking in, and other countries found that they had more dollars than they wanted. The dollar shortage had given way to an excess of dollars.

Countries holding more dollars than they wanted began to present the excess to the United States for exchange into gold. U.S. gold reserves began to shrink. Between 1950 and 1955, they declined by $2.5 billion, or 10 percent.[1]

While the United States was engaged in the Korean War, the other main capitalist countries were rebuilding, and by the second half of the 1950s, it was clear that a change had taken place in their relative economic positions. The other main capitalist countries had not only rebuilt but had modernized their economies. The countries of Western Europe, especially West Germany, were becoming ever fiercer competitors of the United States in the world market. Japan had entered a period of rapid growth from which it would emerge an even more formidable competitor. Not only did these countries vie with the United States in its export markets, but they began to invade the United States internal market with Volkswagens, television sets, radios, cameras, and many other goods.

In 1958, the U.S. balance of payments took a sharp turn for the worse. The outflow of gold, which had stopped after the end of the Korean War, resumed at an accelerated pace. During 1958-60, $4.7 billion flowed out, 20 percent of the total gold stock in 1957.[2]

In 1960, a dollar crisis flared up, the first of many. The price of gold in the London free market jumped from its official price of $35 an ounce to $41. Because of the flood of dollars pumped out by the United States, the market value of the dollar had fallen below the value at which the United States was artificially maintaining it.

What did the U.S. government do? It used its political power to get other countries to bear as much as possible of the burden of the problem. It pressured them to refrain from converting as many of their dollars into gold as they would have liked. And it pressured its allies to pay bigger shares of the cost of U.S. military bases on their soil; to buy more military equipment from the United States; to open their markets wider to U.S. exports. Two things it did not do: stop, or even reduce, the flow of corporate foreign investment or shut down military bases abroad.

Other crises followed. The United States met them by getting the other main capitalist countries to enter a series of stop-gap agreements for shoring up the dollar. The United States was afraid and unwilling to use solely its own declining gold reserve for this purpose, so it persuaded other countries to provide gold from their reserves as well.

This artificial support of the dollar was futile. Maintaining the high price of the dollar by massive government intervention simply papered over the problem. Meanwhile, the growing flood of dollars the United States was pumping out was upsetting the workings of the capitalist world's international monetary mechanism.

Pumping out excess money internationally has the same effect as doing it domestically—it produces inflation. When foreign exporters receive dollars for shipments to the United States, they convert them into their local currency which is what they work with in their own country. The ultimate source of the local currency is the central bank, equivalent to our Federal Reserve. To buy the dollars coming from the exporters, the central bank prints and issues the local currency. A large increase in the dollar reserve of foreign central banks means therefore, a large expansion in the supply of local currency. By pumping dollars abroad through its payments deficits, the United States was exporting inflation to the rest of the capitalist world on a grand scale.

Other countries objected to the United States' flooding the world with dollars. France, through de Gaulle and others, spoke out against the monetary imperialism of the United States. Pointing out that for a country to accumulate dollars is equivalent to its lending, or even giving, money to the United States, de Gaulle asked why France should help finance U.S. policies—policies in which it had no voice and with which it often disagreed. Why should it help finance the takeover of French businesses by U.S. corporations or the escalation of the war in Vietnam?

The Vietnam War exacerbated the dollar problem. It caused a sharp increase in the already large U.S. military expenditures abroad. It set off a wave of inflation which reduced the competitiveness of U.S. exports by raising their price. By blowing up the general demand for goods, it increased the demand for imports. Previously, the one strong positive element in the balance of payments had been the trade surplus. Now this surplus began to shrink. In 1971, it disappeared altogether. The U.S. trade balance moved into deficit for the first time since 1893.[3] The switch from trade surplus to trade deficit, coming on top of the increased outflow of dollars for military expenditures abroad, caused the deficit in the overall balance of payments to skyrocket.

In May, 1971, a panicky flight from the dollar occurred. Holders of dollars rushed to change them into gold, or West German marks, Japanese yen, and other currencies. As dollars poured into central banks abroad, swelling their reserves, many banks refused to accept dollars.

Because of the strength of its currency, which everyone felt was "undervalued" (that is, would increase in value), West Germany received an especially large proportion of the unwanted dollars. Previously, West Germany, as a defeated country, had been more accommodating to U.S. policies than its economic power justified. Now it, too, rebelled. It released the mark from its fixed relation to the dollar, allowing it to "float." The exchange rate would be determined by the supply and demand for the two currencies.

This measure was designed to protect West Germany from a further excessive inflow of dollars. If too many dollars were being presented for exchange into marks, the dollar would fall and the mark would rise until the dollar was no longer overvalued with the mark undervalued. This would end the pressure to exchange dollars into marks.

In the following months, several other leading capitalist countries, including Japan, refused to support the dollar, and began to let their currencies float. In August, 1971, the United States announced that it would no longer convert dollars into gold.

After crisis meetings, the leading capitalist countries made a last-gasp attempt to restore a modified form of fixed rates. But they gave this up in early 1973. The Bretton Woods system of fixed rates which had been crumbling for many years had broken down completely.

UNDER THE NEW SYSTEM, the dollar and other currencies "float"; that is, fluctuate in value in relation to one another, although governments may still intervene with purchases of gold and currencies to control the fluctuations. Floating means that the United States can no longer systematically run balance of payments deficits without pain. Running deficits and flooding the market with dollars will now tend to cause the dollar to fall in value.

The floating rate system is not a step forward from the fixed rate system. The fixed rate system provided far more order to international economic relationships. Everyone (exporters, importers, and others) knew what the rate would be and could plan accordingly. The fixed rate system was given up reluctantly because it could no longer be maintained.

The U.S. trade deficits not only continued after the breakdown of the old system, but soared to new record levels. The 1971 deficit which helped cause the breakdown of the old system was $2.3 billion. The deficit during the years 1977-80 averaged $29 billion.[4]

The increase in the deficit reflected a long-term trend toward a worsening of the U.S. export-import position. The U.S., once an exporter of oil, was now importing large amounts and at prices that OPEC had begun to hike sharply in 1973. Even more important over the long run, the United States was becoming an ever larger importer of manufactured goods; for example, imports of autos and parts, which were less than $1 billion in 1965, climbed to $25 billion in 1980.[5]

In 1976, a new dollar crisis began, the first to show what could happen under the new floating rate system. The dollar had been comparatively strong in 1975 when the United States was in a recession and the trade balance was in surplus. A year later, as the United States pulled out of the recession, the surplus turned to deficit and the dollar began to fall.

As the deficit widened in 1977 and 1978, the fall of the dollar became steeper. Between September, 1977 and September, 1978, the dollar fell 34 percent against the Swiss franc, 29 percent against the Japanese yen, 15 percent against the West German mark, and 11 percent against both the French franc and the British pound.[6]

Such a decline helps fuel inflation in the United States. One in every five dollars worth of goods now sold here is imported. A decline in the dollar not only raises the prices of these goods, but indirectly, the price of many domestically produced goods. The *New York Times* reported on November 13, 1978 that the chairman of the Council of Economic Advisors "has produced new data for the president [Carter] showing that a 20-percent trade-weighted depreciation of the dollar over the last 18 months has been responsible for as much as one-third of the accelerating inflation."

Because the dollar is the key currency of the capitalist world's monetary system, such a decline also causes many international economic problems. It arbitrarily reduces the value of the dollar reserves of other countries. It creates harmful uncertainty; for example, according to the 1978 Annual Report of the International Monetary Fund, producers in many countries were reluctant to invest because exchange-rate "volatility" had made them "uncertain about the profitability of future export sales."[7]

A decline in the dollar, if it went fast and far enough, could lead to a general disaster. A panicky flight from the dollar could occur, with institutions and people in different countries refusing to accept dollars because they were dropping too rapidly. The value of foreign exchange reserves held in dollars would plummet. Many countries would find it necessary to slash their imports which would cause others, in turn, to do the same. The monetary and trading system of the capitalist world could be thrown into chaos.

As the decline of the dollar went on, the United States came under increasing pressure from the other leading capitalist countries to take action to stop the process. On July 26, 1978 the *New York Times* carried a revealing story from Paris, headlined, "OECD Backs Slash in Growth to Help Dollar." (The Organization for Economic Cooperation and Development is made up of 24 major capitalist countries.) "President Carter," the story began, "should accept a sharp reduction in economic growth next year and a possible rise in unemployment as necessary to reduce inflation and strengthen the weakened dollar, the [OECD] said in a report... released today." The report cited "the key role of the dollar in the international monetary system" as a major reason for giving "top priority" to an attack on the dollar problem.

The U.S. government had been taking action in driblets. It had raised the Federal Reserve's discount rate (the rate the Fed charges private banks who borrow from it) by small steps, in order to raise interest rates and reduce the flow of credit. Now it began to raise the rate more rapidly. Still the dollar dropped. By October, 1978, according to the *New York Times* (11-10-78), "There was a sense of panic, a sense of fear of the unknown."

In November the government took drastic action. It jacked up the discount rate by a full percentage point to what was then a record 9.5 percent. As recently as August, 1977, it had been 5.75 percent.

The Department of Commerce predicted that because of the tighter monetary policy, housing starts would decline 17.5 percent in 1979. Within a few weeks, a decline appeared in the statistics. This decline in housing construction helped produce a slowdown in overall economic growth in 1979.

The government's action stemmed the decline of the dollar, but at the cost of a restriction on housing construction and economic growth, and without attacking the basic causes of the dollar's weakness. How deep-seated many of these causes are is confirmed by a study of the U.S. competitive position in world markets, submitted to Congress by President Carter with the observation that it was the most comprehensive analysis of the problem ever undertaken by the government. Here, in the study's own words, are some of its main points.[8]

> Over the past two decades there has been an erosion in the U.S. competitive position in foreign and domestic markets[9]. . . . The product areas in which the decline in the U.S. export position in world

markets has been most pronounced include: automotive equipment, dyes, textile and metalworking machinery, domestic electrical equipment, steel, rubber manufactures, copper, furniture, footwear, and miscellaneous manufactures. . . .[10]

The countries which have tended to displace U.S. exporters' sales . . . have been Japan and certain of the more advanced developing countries[11]. . . . Much of the increase in consumer imports since 1971 has come from Japan and the more developed Asian exporters like Taiwan, [South] Korea, and Hong Kong.[12]

The United States still has a competitive advantage in technology-intensive products [aircraft, computers, electrical machinery, etc.[13]. . . .] But the evidence suggests that the advantage is beginning to erode.[14]

Competition will continue and increase in the 1980s because the United States continues to lag behind other countries in net real investment growth and because of the relative decline in our research and development effort.[15]

On top of the declining U.S. competitiveness comes the shift to a more aggressive military policy begun under Carter and accelerated under Reagan. This shift means an increase in military expenditures not only within the United States but also abroad.

After the crisis of 1979, the dollar strengthened. As usual under capitalism, once the problem ceased to be acute, it was forgotten. But the problem must be understood in historical perspective.

Since the mid-1950s, the dollar problem has followed a pattern of becoming acute, then easing, then becoming acute again. The easing occurs for several reasons. Interest rates in the U.S. have been jacked up periodically to high levels. At times, business downturns may be worse here than in other countries, causing imports to decline more. Both phenomena tend to strengthen the dollar. But temporary oscillations should not be allowed to obscure the basic fact that the international competitive position of the U.S. economy is getting worse and the underlying tendency is for the dollar to weaken.

This tendency has far-reaching implications. The ambitious, arrogant U.S. foreign policy is paid for in dollars. For many years, the dollar—and therefore the financing of foreign bases and wars—depended on three main supports: a surplus of exports over imports; the willingness of other countries to accumulate enormous amounts of dollars; and sales from the U.S. gold reserve.

These supports are now either gone or far weaker than they once were. The former trade surplus is now (in most years) a huge deficit—$69 billion in 1983. The willingness of other countries to accumulate dollars is much reduced. A good part of the U.S. gold supply has been lost to other countries.

Therefore, the U.S. economy simply cannot do what it once did. It was able to take on the Korean War and many other burdens at the same time. It was far less able to handle the Vietnam War. It is still less able to deal with foreign adventures today.

The precedent of Britain stands before us; the loss of competitive strength, the long-run balance of payments deficits, the weakening of the pound, etc. Britain was eventually forced to dismantle its once far-flung system of foreign bases.

The emergence of the dollar problem marks a watershed for the U.S. domestic economy. Before the Bretton Woods system broke down, U.S. policymakers were free to try to promote economic growth and a higher level of employment without concern for the effects on the balance of payments and the dollar. Now they must take these factors into account.

These new constraints explain the action of U.S. officials in 1978-79, when following the advice of OECD, they slowed down U.S. economic growth. Repeated balance of payments deficits and a weak dollar will induce the government to slow down the economy again and again, unless it is forced to change its way of dealing with the problem.

Slowing down the economy and increasing unemployment is only part of the story. The government has also been working with the monopolies for the past decade to lower real wages, to solve the dollar problem by forcing U.S. workers to provide their labor power more cheaply.

In sum, state monopoly capitalism is trying to place the burden of the problem on the backs of the working class and the people in general. The system doesn't want to give up its aggressive foreign and military policy. It wants to hold down the lid on the revolutionary caldrons that have been boiling over now in Africa, now in the Middle East, now in Central America. It wants to reverse revolutions that have been successful and even dreams of doing away with socialism, including in the Soviet Union. To back these dangerously unrealistic desires, it has undertaken a huge military buildup that it knows requires an enormous amount of resources. So it has been working to reduce the flow of resources to the people by increasing unemployment and reducing the standard of living.

The dollar problem thus reflects one of the key contradictions at work in the United States today—between the foreign and military policy and the needs of the economy and the people. The choices are sharp. Until the costly foreign/military policies are changed, an ever-weakening, stop-go, low-growth, high-unemployment, low-wage economy will be inflicted on the American people.

As with inflation, the first thing necessary for coping with the dollar problem is to end the government's way of dealing with it. Raising interest rates and slowing down the economy is a costly, superficial measure which temporarily contains the problem at the workers' expense without doing anything to solve it. Truly attacking the dollar problem means to slash the military budget, shut down bases abroad and bring the armed services personnel home. Above all, it means staying out of war.

8

The Oil Crisis

In 1973 and 1979, the United States suffered oil shocks—periods of oil shortage, long lines at the gas pumps, and enormous price hikes. Presidents Nixon, Ford and Carter, the media, and economists talked of an "energy crisis."

But in 1982, a world oil glut developed, international oil prices began to slip, and talk about an energy crisis faded. Some writers went so far as to proclaim that the energy problem had been solved. The market had worked its wonders and solved it—high prices had brought about so much energy conservation and so great a reduction in demand that we no longer need worry about the adequacy of future supplies.

But just because a glut developed in the midst of a severe worldwide recession doesn't prove that there is no oil problem. No one can tell exactly when or in what form this problem will manifest itself, but it continues to exist and will be making itself felt. The oil shocks of the 1970s have already done great damage. Over the longer run, the oil problem has the potential of shaking the U.S. economy to its foundations.

How much can we expect from capitalism in dealing with the oil problem? Capitalism—state monopoly capitalism—with its greed and lack of foresight or planning, is itself the basic cause of the problem. The monopolies and the government, working together, based the economies of the capitalist countries, especially the United States, on an irrational, wasteful use of energy and a weak, unstable energy foundation.

FROM THE BEGINNING, the history of the energy complex of the capitalist world is a tale of incredible greed and lack of foresight.

The different forms of energy—coal, gas, oil, etc.—are available in different amounts. U.S. coal reserves are many times larger than its reserves of gas and oil. Aside from being available in far lesser quantity, oil is a "premium" fuel compared to coal. Oil has uses for which coal will not serve: as a fuel for motor vehicles and aircraft; as a raw material for producing certain chemicals and synthetics.

Elementary prudence would have counselled that account be taken of the reserves available and whether a fuel is premium or not. No form of energy should be wasted, but especially not one of which reserves are small. As much as possible, oil should be reserved for uses to which it alone is suited and not wasted doing things that coal can also do.

However, rational planning is not the method of capitalism. If autos provide more profits than mass transit, then promote the auto; never mind that mass transit, among other advantages, requires less energy and can be run on electric power generated from coal or water, thereby saving oil. If oil provides more profit than coal, then promote it over coal in all possible uses without worrying about how long it will last.

The monopolies, with the help of the government, made the United States dependent on the automobile and truck. The auto, oil, and tire monopolies created a powerful organization to lobby for highways and the government lavished money on them. General Motors created companies to buy up and do away with struggling mass transit systems.

The highway lobby contributed to political campaigns, invited congressmen and other politicians (at big fees) to address meetings, placed people in key government posts, etc. It persuaded most state legislatures to dedicate the proceeds of gasoline taxes exclusively to highway construction. Bradford Snell, in a well-documented study prepared for a Senate committee, wrote:

> By promoting these highway "trust funds" [the highway lobby] has discouraged governors and mayors from attempting to build anything other than highways for urban transportation. Subways and rail transit proposals have had to compete with hospitals, schools, and other governmental responsibilities for funding. By contrast, highways have been automatically financed from a self-perpetuating fund which was legally unavailable for any other purpose. Largely as a result, highways, not subways, have been built.[1]

The lobby also promoted interstate highways. In 1956, the federal government passed a law providing for the construction of a 42,500-mile, $70-billion Interstate Highway System—the most gigantic building program in U.S. history.

For examples of how state monopoly capitalism made the United States dependent on the automobile, we have only to look at the experience of New York and Los Angeles. The New York metropolitan area once had an excellent mass transit system—a cheap, clean, reliable subway and efficient commuter rail links to the suburbs. Then the authorities began to build for the auto in a frenzy and to starve the mass transit system. One highway after another was rammed through the city and into the surrounding area. One highway bridge after another was put up. Subway construction halted. Expansion of the commuter rail network ended. The city's electric trolley car system was converted to buses, partly on the ground that trolley cars got in the way of auto traffic.

The highways drew customers away from the subway and commuter lines which responded by increasing fares and cutting services. But this only caused a further loss of customers, which in turn was met by further fare increases and cuts in service.

Now the energy-efficient subway, the main transportation for New York's workers, poor, and many others, is expensive and in a dangerous state of dilapidation. The commuter lines are also costly and offer but a fraction of their previous services. The highways in and around the city are filled with cars and trucks in a tremendous oil-consuming congestion.

Mayor Tom Bradley of Los Angeles described what happened to that city. Bradley spoke to the same Senate committee which published Bradford Snell's book.

> Thirty-five years ago, Los Angeles was served by the world's largest interurban electric railway system. The Pacific Electric System branched out from Los Angeles for more than 75 miles, reaching north to San Fernando, east to San Bernardino, and south to Santa Ana. The "big red cars" . . . ran literally all over the Los Angeles area. . . .
>
> In 1938, General Motors and Standard Oil of California organized Pacific City Lines (PCL) . . . to "motorize" West Coast electric railways. . . . [In 1940] PCL began to acquire and "scrap" portions of the $100 million Pacific Electric System, including rail lines from Los Angeles to Burbank, Glendale, Pasadena, and San Bernardino.
>
> Subsequently, in December 1944 . . . American City Lines was financed by GM and Standard Oil to "motorize downtown Los

Angeles." . . . American City Lines purchased the local system, "scrapped" its electric cars, tore down its power transmission lines, uprooted the tracks, and placed diesel buses fueled by Standard Oil on Los Angeles city streets. By this time, Los Angeles's 3,000 quiet, pollution-free, electric train system was totally destroyed.[2]

Bradford Snell sums up:

By 1949, General Motors had been involved in the replacement of more than 100 electric train systems with GM buses in 45 cities, including New York, Philadelphia, Baltimore, St. Louis, Oakland, Salt Lake City and Los Angeles.[3]

The decay of the U.S. railroad system paralleled that of the urban and suburban mass transit systems. The railroads were, of course, bound to lose some traffic to the airplane, auto, bus and truck. But with a rational transportation system (one planned so that the different components mesh with one another), the loss would not have been nearly as great as it was and need not have led to decay.

While the government was showering billions on the interstate highway system, it was giving zilch to the railroads. A vicious circle set in here, too. As they lost business to the highways, the railroads also cut service, allowed trains and stations to decay, and let the roadbed deteriorate. This limited train speeds, caused accidents and, as a consequence, the railroads suffered a further loss of passenger business.

Not only did the railroads decline in favor of the energy-inefficient auto, bus and truck, but they were converted from coal-burning steam locomotives to oil-burning diesels. Before World War II, the railroads ran almost completely on coal. It would have been possible to get away from the inefficient steam locomotive without turning so completely to oil by electrifying a good part of the railroad system. As this would have required the investment of large sums of money in the declining railroad industry, only a minute proportion of the U.S. railroad system was electrified.

The monopolies also pushed oil and gas over coal in electric power stations and industry as well as in commercial and residential use. The consumption of coal fell by a third in the fifteen years following World War II.

CAPITALISM PUT ITS stamp not only on how oil was used, but how it was obtained. The oil industry became a prime example of imperialism. Seven immense companies obtained a monopoly of the key oil concessions of the whole capitalist world: in the Middle East, Venezuela, Africa, Indonesia, and elsewhere. Five of these companies (Exxon, Gulf, Mobil, Socal, and Texaco) are American. One (Shell) is British-Dutch and one (British Petroleum) is British.

These companies didn't get their concessions by their own efforts alone. Their governments not only helped, but often played the key role. Robert B. Stobaugh, the Harvard energy expert, writes that after World War I, "the U.S. government and the big American oil companies, especially Standard Oil of New Jersey . . . [now known as Exxon] pursued a common goal—to place as many foreign sources of oil as possible in American hands."[4] The government got the Dutch to open up the Netherlands East Indies, formerly reserved exclusively for Shell, to U.S. companies. It struggled with Britain and France for control of the oil of the Middle East, obtaining an "open door" into their zones of influence for U.S. companies. By its fierce diplomatic pressure, the government made possible the entry of Exxon and Mobil into Iraq, Gulf into Kuwait, and Socal into Bahrein. During World War II, the government gave lend-lease aid to Ibn Saud, ruler of Saudi Arabia, to further the interests of Aramco, the consortium of U.S. companies which operated there.

The power of the oil companies in the countries in which they held concessions was enormous. They monopolized the technology of finding, extracting, and refining oil, owned the tankers used for transporting it, and controlled the final markets. Behind them stood their governments, ready to defend their interests, if need be by conspiring to overthrow governments or even using armed force.

In 1951, the Iranian government, under Prime Minister Mohammed Mosaddegh, nationalized the properties of British Petroleum (then Anglo-Iranian) in Iran. The seven supergiants instituted a boycott of Iranian oil, increasing production in Kuwait, Saudi Arabia, and Iraq to make up for the loss. When a Panamanian ship took on Iranian oil, Royal Air Force planes forced it into the harbor of Aden in Yemen, then a British colony, where the authorities impounded its cargo.[5] The decisive blow came from the United States—the CIA organized a coup which overthrew the Mosaddegh government and installed the Shah as the ruler of Iran.

The monopolies used their power to rob the host countries by keeping the price of foreign oil lower than that of U.S. oil. From

1949 through 1953, the price of Middle East crude oil was $1.80 a barrel while the price of U.S. crude was $2.50.[6] In 1959 and again in 1960, the monopolies cut the price of foreign oil. Stobaugh describes how they did this: "As was the habit in those days, Exxon did not negotiate with the oil-producing nations; it simply announced the price cuts."[7] Throughout the 1960s, when a growing inflation got underway in the capitalist world, the price of foreign oil declined, reaching a low of $1.00 to $1.20 a barrel in the Persian Gulf at the end of 1969.[8] The oil-exporting countries watched helplessly as the price of their product shrank, while the prices of the goods they imported leaped upward.

The monopolies found that they could realize far bigger profits from the dirt-cheap foreign oil than by fully developing domestic sources. So the irrational, wasteful system of oil use in the United States became increasingly dependent on oil extorted at miserable prices from poor, underdeveloped countries through the use of imperialist power.

For a long time this arrangement "worked." But beneath the surface, various processes were operating to undermine it. The oil-exporting countries were chafing at being robbed. In 1960, shortly after the second price cut forced on them by the monopolies, they formed OPEC (Organization of Petroleum Exporting Countries) to defend their interests by united action. At first, the oil monopolies and their governments acted as though OPEC didn't exist. But it was bound to grow in strength.

Within the United States, the cheapest and most accessible sources of oil and gas were being used up. Knowledge of how to run the oil industry was steadily growing among the oil-exporting countries. With the growing strength of the socialist countries and the increasing political power of the underdeveloped countries, the general balance of forces in the world was moving against the imperialists.

The energy complex of the United States and the rest of the capitalist world was a fool's paradise which contained the makings of deep trouble.

IN THE EARLY 1970s, the fool's paradise began to collapse. Both production and proved reserves of oil in the United States, which had previously been increasing, began to decline. U.S. oil imports began to climb. These phenomena were important not only in themselves, but because of their effect on the balance of forces between the oil-exporting countries and the imperialists. By increasing U.S. dependence on foreign oil, they strengthened the position of the oil-exporting countries.

Also by the 1970s, the change in the general balance of forces in the world had ripened to the point where the oil-exporting countries felt able to take drastic action to defend their interests. The weakened position of imperialism reduced the chances of U.S. military intervention or other forms of strong counteraction.

Libya, under Muammar el-Qaddafi, was the first oil-exporting country to act. In 1970, it forced a price increase of thirty cents a barrel and an increase in its profits tax from 50 to 58 percent on Occidental Petroleum, a company almost wholly dependent on Libyan output. The next year OPEC forced through a price increase on the major companies—30 cents a barrel immediately, up to 50 cents by 1975. During the negotiations, OPEC used the threat of an embargo to get its terms accepted. U.S. domination of the world oil market was rapidly ending.[9]

The climax came in 1973. The Arab OPEC countries, acting to support Egypt in the Israeli-Egyptian war, imposed an embargo on the export of oil to the United States and the other main capitalist countries backing Israel. Prices shot up simply because of the embargo, but soon OPEC was reinforcing the embargo with deliberate, concerted action. In a series of increases, it lifted the price of crude oil from $2.50 a barrel to over $11.

Important though the embargo and the OPEC actions were, they do not by themselves explain the shortages, the gas lines and the large price increases that followed in the United States. On top of the OPEC actions came the deliberate withholding of supplies and price gouging by U.S. oil companies.

For the monopolies, the embargo and the OPEC price increases created an opportunity for making a killing as well as striking a blow against price controls on domestically produced oil. With supplies tight, the monopolies could withhold oil without any risk that they would lose sales and be stuck with unsold supplies. By deliberately aggravating or even creating shortages, they forced retail prices much higher than did the OPEC increases. They blamed the shortages and price increases on OPEC while arguing that price controls limited U.S. production and created vulnerability to embargoes.

These monopoly actions paid off. Between October, 1973 and
October, 1975, the retail price of gasoline rose 48 percent.[10] OPEC
price increases accounted for a third of this jump; monopoly price
gouging accounted for the remainder.[11]

In 1978, when the revolution in Iran disrupted its oil exports,
OPEC put through another series of large price increases. Like the
earlier ones, these did not occur in a vacuum. The inflation had
been raising the prices of goods imported by the OPEC countries
even faster than before 1973, while the value of the dollar in which
they got paid for their oil had dropped sharply.

Again there were shortages, gas lines, and big jumps in the retail
price of gasoline and heating oil in the United States. Again, the
monopolies accounted for a bigger part of the increase than OPEC.

The soaring prices were, of course, bound to bring soaring
profits. Here, from a report by Chase Manhattan Bank, are figures
for the net income of the twenty-six leading oil companies, including the big seven, from 1970 through 1980:[12]

Year	Billion dollars	Year	Billion dollars
1970	6.6	1976	13.1
1971	7.3	1977	14.4
1972	6.9	1978	15.0
1973	11.7	1979	31.5
1974	16.4	1980	35.2
1975	11.5		

The "shortages" of 1973 and 1979 brought skyrocketing profits.
By 1980, oil company net income was over five times more than in
1972.

THE ERUPTION of the oil crisis had a number of effects on the people
and economy of the U.S. The hike in prices was equivalent to a pay
cut for many workers who must drive long distances to work.
Increased heating oil costs forced many families to make a choice in
cold weather between heating and eating.

There were also indirect effects. The oil price increases further
boosted the general inflation. They also acted as a kind of tax,
reducing the people's purchasing power and helping slow down the
economy. The expenditure of tens of billions of additional dollars
on imported oil increased the U.S. balance of payments deficits and

helped weaken the dollar. The oil crisis thereby contributed to the stagflation which has plagued our economy since the early 1970s.

The auto industry suffered a hard blow. It hasn't been the same since the gasoline shortage and price hikes which accompanied the Iranian revolution in 1979. Not only did total auto sales plummet with the onset of the shortage, but the proportion of sales accounted for by large U.S.-made cars declined in favor of smaller, fuel-efficient imports.

WHAT IS THE BASIC long-run oil supply situation? This question must be viewed from a number of angles: the reserves in the U.S. and other countries; the limitations that can be placed on supply by the oil-exporting countries; and the possible interruption of supply by wars, revolutions, etc.

The problem of reserves is full of uncertainties. Experts differ even in their estimates of reserves in the same known field. Estimates depend in part on assumptions about the development of improved recovery techniques and the future price of oil. Assuming a higher future price makes the estimate go up because it increases the amount that it will pay to spend to get the oil out. For a full picture of the future oil situation, it is necessary to go beyond the known fields and form an idea of the number and size of oil discoveries yet to be made—which is, of course, still more uncertain. To cap it all, most of the data underlying the estimates, as well as the estimates themselves, come from the monopolies who cannot be trusted—they can tilt the data and estimates to whatever suits their purpose.

Despite the uncertainties, certain judgments are warranted. First, U.S. oil production, already below its peak, will probably decline further. The Office of Technology Assessment of Congress and various experts, such as Stobaugh, project a decline between 1980 and the year 2000 of 30 to 60 percent.[13] The evidence suggesting decline is strong. For example, despite a sharp increase since 1973 in the number of wells drilled, proved reserves declined and in 1980 were 20 percent lower than in 1974.[14]

Big new discoveries could cause the projections of decline to be wrong. But how likely are they? The United States has already been intensively explored. As Stobaugh points out, "over two million wells have been drilled in the United States—four times as many as in all the rest of the [non-socialist] world combined."[15]

A second judgment is that for the world as a whole, limits on physical availability will place increasingly severe constraints on oil production in the coming decades. The period of most rapid growth in the availability of oil is now behind us. Between 1950 and 1975, world proved reserves shot up from 76 billion barrels to 712 billion. In three of the five following years, they declined, standing in 1980 at 10 percent below the 1975 peak.[16]

Future world oil production will be limited not just by physical availability, but also by the restraints placed on output by a number of the leading oil exporting countries. Saudi Arabia and several other OPEC exporters often limit their output to levels below capacity. They do this for several reasons—to help maintain prices, to avoid receiving more dollars than they need, to space their oil earnings so that some will be left for future generations.

The Office of Technology Assessment has projected with "high confidence" that oil production in the non-socialist world will be between 40 to 62 million barrels a day in the year 2000, compared to 52 million in 1979.[17] The lower limit would mean a 23 percent decline from 1979; even the upper limit would mean only a 19 percent increase. Between 1960 and 1979, production rose by 290 percent.

What conclusions can one draw from the OTA and other such projections? The best guess is that world oil production in 2000 will be about the same as in 1980. This means that a big change lies ahead since before 1980 production was climbing rapidly. Production may rise by 2000, but the increase will probably not be large, and it would be imprudent to count on it. Production may also decline, perhaps sharply.

The OTA projections assume that there are no "major" disruptions to production "such as the revolution in Iran" or a war, but a large part of the oil imported by the United States and most of the oil imported by the other main capitalist countries comes from the unstable Middle East where the possibility of war and revolution is ever present.

In sum: U.S. production will probably decline during the next fifteen years; world production will at best not rise by much and may also decline; sharp interruptions in supply could occur.

WHAT ABOUT THE demand for oil? To some extent, oil demand will vary with the gross national product; growth of GNP tends to increase oil demand. To some extent demand will depend on how oil is used, on how much the amount of oil required to maintain a given level of GNP can be lowered by rationalizing oil use.

The arithmetic of economic growth is sobering. A GNP which grows at the modest rate of 3.0 percent annually will increase by 34 percent in ten years, 80 percent in twenty years, and 140 percent in thirty years. For many years in the past, oil use in the United States moved in lockstep with GNP and in some other countries even faster than GNP. Such a relationship is no longer sustainable.

Actually, the lockstep relationship has been loosened in the United States during the last several years. The spread of smaller, more fuel-efficient cars, some switch away from oil in electric power generation and other uses, and the adoption of measures to use less energy have lowered the ratio of oil use to GNP.

In 1975, the government passed a law requiring that the average fuel economy for new manufactured or imported passenger cars reach 27.5 miles per gallon in 1985. It had been 14 miles per gallon in 1974. Since less than ten percent of the total auto fleet is replaced annually, it will take years for the whole fleet to approach this level. Even so, given the high proportion of petroleum use accounted for by the automobile, the potential savings are large.

However, there are limits to how far such measures can hold down oil demand. Working in the opposite direction will be growth in the number of autos, trucks, buses, and planes; in industrial requirements, in the size of the population and GNP. Besides, with the easing of the oil market in 1982, the auto companies began again to work on selling big cars and soon General Motors and Ford were saying that they would not be able to meet the fuel-efficiency requirements for 1983 and several years thereafter because their big models were selling too well.[18]

In many countries, the potential savings in oil use are less than in the United States. They have always had smaller, more fuel-efficient cars. They are not richly endowed with coal to substitute for oil in electric power generation.

The underdeveloped countries will be requiring far more oil as they industrialize and develop. They contain four-fifths of the world's population, but at present consume only a minute proportion of its oil.

Combining the outlook for the supply and demand for oil, what do we get? It is possible that as a result of conservation measures of the type thus far undertaken, the demand for oil can be held down in the United States for a time. But the decline in U.S. production that is in prospect could easily more than counter-balance these savings. And the demand cannot be held down indefinitely—with time, the growth of the GNP will start it up again. The United States will, therefore, continue to depend heavily and after a while, increasingly, on imported oil.

Similarly with world supply and demand. World demand may be held down for a while, but then it will grow again. World supply will be able to match this growth only if the more optimistic forecasts are realized. Even if production does run high for a while, it will probably be leveling off and turning down in the not too distant future.

The world faces an oil crunch. One can argue about when this crunch will make itself felt—whether by 1990, 2000, or 2010. But a crunch is coming.

THE OIL SHOCKS of the 1970s marked a turning point for the U.S. economy. The era of an abundant, cheap, reliable supply of oil on which that economy was built was over.

What happened after the gasoline shortage of 1979 is but a token of what could happen if we get other such episodes or if, even without sharp interruptions, oil supply gradually tightens. The auto industry is a central industry—a major consumer of steel, rubber, glass, plastics, and many other products. A number of other industries (chemicals, plastics, and recreation, for example) also depend greatly on oil. Trouble in oil strikes at the heart of the U.S. economy.

There is another side to the fact that a growing GNP will increase the demand for oil. To the extent that the supply of oil doesn't expand enough to meet this increased demand, the growth of GNP will not take place.

Although changes in the way oil is used can decrease the amount required to sustain growth, the changes so far undertaken are far from enough to meet the problem of oil tightness that is looming ahead. Eventually, deep structural changes in the economy, in the transportation system and in the way cities and suburbs are built, will be required.

Not only will it be necessary to build a new structure, but to undo parts of the old one. The monopolies—auto, banking, real estate, etc.—would not be true to their nature if they didn't merrily pursue the big profits they get from the present structure and use their power to resist the necessary changes. Capitalism would not be capitalism if it could make an adjustment as profound as the one required without suffering big shocks in the process.

IF HOT AIR COULD solve the oil problem, the government would have solved it long ago. Nixon announced a "Project Independence" to make the United States "self-sufficient" in energy by 1980.[19] Carter called the energy problem "the moral equivalent of war."[20] And here is an example of Reagan administration rhetoric:

> When fully implemented, the Economic Recovery Program will release the strength of the private sector and ensure a vigorous economic climate in which the Nation's problems, including energy problems, will be solved primarily by the American people themselves—consumers, workers, managers, inventors, and investors.[21]

Aside from the law requiring increased fuel efficiency in autos and a few measures to encourage electric power utilities to switch from oil to gas, the government has done either very little or the wrong thing.

Carter spoke of building a "more efficient mass transportation system,"[22] but the talk was phony. It called for spending $10 billion over ten years, an average of only $1 billion a year. Just extending the New York subway system would eat up the bulk of the money. Under Reagan the program died completely.

In 1980, the government set up a company to aid private industry to develop the production of synthetic fuels. Two years later, the *New York Times* (10-18-82) reported that "the company still has not committed its first dime for a project."

When Reagan took office, the United States had a standby plan for rationing gasoline in case of shortage. Reagan abolished it in favor of "reliance on market forces . . . even during an emergency."[23] This is a recipe for disaster. During a shortage, important users of gasoline, such as farmers, will not be able to get enough, while the rich, to whom high prices mean little, will go on driving as usual.

The monopolies, concerned only with profits, and quick profits at that, are also doing nothing about the long-run oil supply problem. The government created the environment they clamored for by lifting price controls on oil. Decontrol was supposed to provide an incentive to the monopolies to increase their exploration and drilling and to work on synfuels, and thereby expand the supply of oil. But what actually happened?

When prices skyrocketed after the oil shocks, the monopolies increased their exploration and drilling and began to show interest in the development of synfuels. But with the oil glut and price drop in 1982, the drilling boom became a bust and the monopolies lost interest in synfuels. The number of oil rigs in operation in the United States plummeted and several oil equipment firms went bankrupt. Dozens of sponsors of synfuels projects withdrew from them; one project after another was scrapped.

The monopolies also lost interest in saving oil by rationalizing consumption. According to Daniel Yergin:

> Industrial-fuel users in the United States are beginning to switch away from natural gas to what is in some regions, surprisingly enough, a cheaper fuel—oil. Coal conversion projects are stalling or stopping altogether in the United States, Western Europe, and Japan.[24]

Capitalism is being true to its history and its nature. It is gambling in the way it deals with oil.

WHAT SHOULD BE done about the oil problem? The first thing is to nationalize the oil and energy industry. To begin with, without nationalization, we are blind. We have to depend on the lying monopolies for the most basic information and can't trust what we are told about the size of reserves, the cost of exploration and extraction, the cost of producing synthetic fuels, etc.

Without nationalization, we cannot have a full-scale effort to increase the supply of oil, both natural and synthetic. Except when oil prices and profits are super-high, the oil conglomerates will not carry out a large amount of drilling and big synthetics projects because they have too many other opportunities to invest their capital for enormous profits.

Finally, in the tightening oil situation that is in prospect, it is just asking to be gouged if we allow the industry to remain privately owned. The monopolies will create shortages, jack up prices, and rip us off again and again as the opportunities arise.

Along with nationalization, the government could mount a strong, sustained effort to increase the supply of oil. It could set up a crash program of exploration and drilling for natural oil. It could determine how far synthetic production can be developed without excessive damage to the environment, and develop it. Both programs would not depend on the short-run movement of oil prices, but would rather be carried out as a matter of national policy, as a form of insurance for the future.

The effort to increase the supply of oil should be part of a broader energy supply program. The production of coal should be increased to replace oil wherever possible. How to use coal with a minimum of pollution and what effects the continued large-scale burning of fuels will have on the earth's temperature and climate should be systematically investigated. A crash program to investigate and, where promising, develop the unconventional ways of producing energy—using the sun, wind, oceans, and biomass—should be undertaken.

While working to increase the supply of oil and other forms of energy, the government should also be taking measures to rationalize the use of oil and energy. The federal fuel-efficiency standards for autos should be made higher and standards should be set for trucks, buses and airplanes. The switch away from oil in electric power generation and as an industrial fuel should again be pressed.

But the most important measure that the government can take for the long-run rationalization of oil use is to promote the development of mass transportation. It should use some of the billions now going down the military drain—say $20 billion a year—for the development of mass transit systems around the country. Instead of helping to close down railroad routes, it should promote their extension and take measures to increase the electrification of the railroads.

What is the essential difference between the program just outlined and what the government has been doing? The government has been guided by the interests of the oil and auto monopolies and U.S. militarism, and these interests stand in the way of making a meaningful attack on the oil problem. The program just outlined is based on what is best for the economy and the people.

PART IV

INDUSTRY IN CRISIS

9

Plant Closings

Stories of plant closings have become a standard feature of the news in the United States. Here are a few examples:

The Firestone Tire and Rubber Company said yesterday that it would close its truck tire plant here early next year. The move will cost 1,345 jobs and will leave this city, which is known as the center of the tire industry with only one operating factory. After the Firestone closing, the General Tire Company's 65-year old factory will be the last tire-making factory still operating in Akron. No passenger tires have been made here since Goodyear and Firestone closed plants in early 1978.

New York Times, 10/23/78

The United States Steel Corporation announced yesterday that it was closing 15 plants and mills in eight states. About 13,000 production and white collar workers will lose their jobs.

New York Times, 11/28/79

The Ford Motor Company announced sweeping cutbacks in its workforce today, saying it would close three plants, including its big Mahwah, N.J. passenger car assembly plant. Company officials said that 6,100 salaried employees would be dismissed effective May 1, and that 9,000 hourly workers, most of them involved in manufacturing, would be dismissed beginning April 25 and continuing through the remainder of the year. In addition to the Mahwah plant, Ford will permanently close two smaller manufacturing plants in Dearborn, Michigan, and Windsor, Ontario.

New York Times, 4/16/80

The Singer Company is closing its mammoth [sewing machine] plant here [Elizabeth, N.J.]. Moving on to a marketing strategy of more cost-effective foreign production and diversification in aerospace products, it is finished with this aging city now.

New York Times, 2/23/82

Idle Mills, A Dearth of Hope Are
Features of Ohio's Steel Towns

The first iron furnace came to Ohio's Mahoning Valley in 1803. By 1875, 21 blast furnaces were producing 250,000 tons of steel annually. By 1925—the whole valley wreathed in smoke and flame—production was four million tons a year. . . .

Now, a visitor can drive south from Warren, down through Niles and McDonald, Girard and Youngstown, on to Campbell and beyond to Struthers, and see silent, empty steel mills stretching mile after mile
. . . .

Wall Street Journal, 1/20/83

Plant closings have been hitting all industries and all regions. In their book, *Capital and Communities: The Causes and Consequences of Private Disinvestment,* Barry Bluestone and Bennett Harrison estimated that closings destroyed "at least" 15 million jobs between 1969 and 1976, an average of 2.5 million jobs per year.[1] Plant closings constitute a major problem. Why has this problem become so big in recent years? Several factors are responsible: automation, foreign investment, the growth of conglomerates, the decline in the U.S. competitive position, and economic stagnation.

AUTOMATION PRODUCED a shift of plants from cities to suburbs after World War II. The typical old industrial plant was a multi-storied building located in a city, with easy access to rail transport. Automation makes it desirable to carry out operations in single-story plants which require more land than the old multi-story ones. Land is easier to get and cheaper in the suburbs. Also, with the development of truck transport, many companies consider it better to be on a good highway than near a railroad.

A plant relocation in 1965 by the Jello Division of the General Foods Corporation is an illustration. This Division had five main plants, located in Hoboken, N.J., Leroy, N.Y., Chicago, Ill., and Dorchester and Orange in Massachusetts. A quasi-official account of the relocation described two of them as "multistoried, 'vertical' plants, inefficient when compared to modern, horizontal plant layouts," and located in "crowded, urban areas where expansion would mean acquiring high-cost land." Two others, "even though located in small towns, were hemmed in by railroad tracks, streets and—at Leroy—a cemetery."[2] General Foods decided to shut down four of the five old plants and transfer their operations to a new plant outside the city limits of Dover, Delaware.

TECHNICAL IMPROVEMENT, as Marx pointed out, is one way for a capitalist to increase profits, and paying workers less is another. The endless search of the corporations for freedom from unions, lower wages, and higher profits brought about a great shift of industry to the South after World War II.

In 1950, 62 percent of all jobs in the apparel industry were in the Northeast, only 17 percent in the South. By 1974, the share of the Northeast had dropped to 36 percent, while that of the South had jumped to 44 percent.[3] What was the South's attraction? Weak union organization and low wages.

Companies in many other industries have also transferred plants South. Examples abound: GTE Sylvania transferred its color TV assembly operations from Batavia, N.Y. to Smithfield, N.C.[4] White Motor Co. transferred truck production from Cleveland to Roanoke, Va.[5] And in "1978, when the United Rubber Workers would not make wage concessions the company wanted, Goodyear closed Akron's Plant 2, their last passenger car tire factory in the city.... Now, Goodyear makes their U.S. car tires in the South...."[6]

The southern states have made no bones about what they offer the corporations. North Carolina issued a document boasting that its local right-to-work law

PRESERVES the right to manage;
CURBS union monopoly power;
LESSENS union abuses and violence;
REDUCES featherbedding;
INDUCES unions to fulfill contracts;
FREES employees from labor boss domination.[7]

South Carolina has advertised in the *Wall Street Journal that*

WE DON'T HAVE LABOR PAINS.
South Carolina has the lowest work stoppage rate in the country....
Our "right to work law" insures the right to work regardless of

membership or non-membership in any organization. So consider locating in South Carolina. You'll be able to do business painlessly here.[8]

And an advertisement for Texas in *Business Week* announced that "Texas workers in general don't feel that anybody owes them a living."[9]

But despite these attractions, the South itself suffers from plant closings. Bluestone and Harrison have even found that between 1969 and 1976, the rate of closings of large manufacturing plants was *"actually higher in the south than in any other part of the country!"*[10] The South has offered the corporations lower wages and "a good business climate." But some foreign countries offer still lower wages and an even better "climate."

THE VAST EXPANSION of U.S. foreign investment after World War II has meant the shutdown of countless U.S. factories. The sewing machine plants of the Singer Company are an example which Professor Seymour Melman of Columbia University wrote about some years ago:

> The Singer Company operates a factory in [Elizabeth] New Jersey, that has a special claim for distinction. It is the last place in the United States where household sewing machines are manufactured. About 10,000 people worked there in 1947. By 1964, about 3,000 workers were left to man a factory composed of primarily antiquated manufacturing equipment. . . .
>
> All the sewing machines needed in the United States used to be manufactured by American factories. . . . [But] since the Second World War, the Singer Company has expanded in the following ways: new sewing machine factories have been erected abroad; production of new products has been undertaken abroad, either directly or by other firms to Singer's order; sewing machines and other products produced abroad have been sold there and also imported into the United States for sale through Singer's far-flung retailing organization.[11]

Now the Elizabeth plant is also closed. A *New York Times* story (2-23-82) gave a brief history of the plant and workers' comments on the closing:

> The gargantuan red brick plant was built here in 1873, during America's industrial revolution. The city of Elizabeth grew up around it,

with neighborhoods representing the waves of immigrants who came to the plant from Ellis Island, a few miles away: German, Italian, Irish, Jewish, Polish, Lithuanian, and others. . . . S. L. Jones summed up the prevailing mood of the rank and file workers, many of whom said they believed the company capitalized on cheap immigrant labor until the union negotiated the first contract in the 1940s, then began moving its operations overseas to capitalize on other oppressed workers.

The workers were right. Originally, the U.S. capitalists used immigrants to provide themselves with a reserve army of labor. But now, given modern transport and communications, they use the labor force of the whole capitalist world. The apparel, garment, shoe, electronics and many other industries have closed plants in the United States while erecting them in foreign countries.

The process by which the U.S. lost its sewing machine industry is underway in many other industries. In 1977, the North American Congress on Latin America (NACLA) published a compilation of runaway electronics plants it was able to identify from government and company reports. It found 680 runaways—193 in Mexico, 140 in Puerto Rico, 45 in Hong Kong, 45 in Taiwan, 32 in India, 30 in Singapore, as well as others in the rest of Asia and the Caribbean area, and in some of the poorer countries of Western Europe.[12] Even when they appear in the United States under U.S. brand names, practically all radios, most black-and-white TV sets, and a large part of many other consumer electronics products are produced abroad.

CONGLOMERATION ALSO makes for plant closings. These closings are a manifestation of the mobility of capital. Geographic mobility is one form of mobility. Another is the ability of capital to switch from one type of activity to another. The growth of conglomerates reflects an increase in this second form of mobility.

Conglomerates, with their diversified activities, have a wider range of investment opportunities than ordinary corporations. As we have seen, the basic logic of conglomerates is to maximize profits by maneuvering money from those activities which give lower rates of profit to those which give higher ones. If producing steel gives a ten percent rate of profit while running cargo ships gives twenty percent, the trick is to get the money out of the first activity and into the second.

Conglomerates ruthlessly exploit every possible way of extracting cash from less profitable activities, including the diversion of funds that would ordinarily go to the upkeep of plant and equipment. They deliberately allow plant and equipment to run down. Sometimes, they consciously plan the eventual closing of the plants they are milking. Sometimes, allowing a plant to run down ends in a closing even though the conglomerate may not have planned to go that far.

From a Congressional committee report, we can follow the maneuvers that led to the closing of the Campbell Works of the Youngstown Sheet and Tube Company in 1977:

> Youngstown Sheet and Tube (YST) was the eighth largest integrated iron and steel company in the nation in 1969. The firm had 26,000 employees and over $1 billion in assets.
>
> Lykes Corporation was a holding company engaged primarily in the steamship business and had $376 million in assets. Although it was only one-third the size of YST, Lykes was able to borrow the money needed to acquire YST. The chief attraction of YST appears to have been the company's large cash flow of almost $100 million per year.
>
> In the steel industry, a firm's cash flow is its life-blood. In fact, at the time of the merger, YST management had this cash flow earmarked to fund one of two aggressive modernization strategies, vital to YST's continued viability because of increasing competition from more modern steel facilities in Europe and Japan.
>
> The company's new conglomerate parent apparently contemplated other uses for the cash flow, though. Lykes president F.A. Nemac was quoted in the business press at the time as saying, "I will not hesitate to use Youngstown's $100 million annual cash flow to move into other fields if our views on the future of steel should change.". . .
>
> Youngstown Sheet and Tube was forced to close its Campbell Works facility in September, 1977, laying off 4,200 workers and severely affecting the economy of Youngstown, Ohio. It appears that YST's cash flow was used by Lykes to pay its interest and carrying charges for loans taken to finance the merger, and to subsidize the conglomerate's shipping operations. . . .
>
> Ed Kelly, representing the Ohio Public Interest Campaign, told the Subcommittee the siphoning off of the steel mill's cash flow led to its demise.[13]

Not just conglomeration, but finance capital in general, is the system ultimately responsible for the Campbell closing. Lykes claimed it couldn't raise the money to modernize the Campbell

Works. One reason it couldn't was the action of the banks. Concerning this, Ed Kelly told the following:

> Lykes' bankers, which had really been vital to the takeover in the first place—they never could have taken over [YST] without them— began to reduce the credit availability to Lykes during the seventies, and at the same time began to greatly increase their loans to Japanese steel companies . . . . So you had a situation in which, while the steel industry was talking about imports hurting them, you had the very bankers of the steel industry lending money to the Japanese steel industries. . . .[14]

The finance capital system worked to steer the money necessary to Campbell away from it. The conglomerate, Lykes, milked Campbell so it could buy cargo ships, an insurance company, etc. The banks were willing to lend money to Lykes for the takeover at Youngstown, but not to support its steel operations. They could make more money by loans to Japanese steel makers. The 4,200 workers lost out because higher profits could be made elsewhere.

THE DECLINE IN the competitive position of the United States has also helped produce plant closings. A corporation is obviously more likely to close a plant that is not competitive against foreign plants than one that is. Thirty-five years ago, the U.S. plant that was less technologically advanced or efficient than a foreign plant was rare. But not now. While the rundown condition of many U.S. plants is due to their being milked by their owners, this is not the only reason for the decline of U.S. competitiveness. Another is the inevitable economic advance of the rest of the world.

The decline in U.S. competitiveness is an expression of Lenin's law of the uneven development of capitalism. As the experience of Britain has shown, countries can pull ahead during one period, then lose ground during others in a constant shifting that is part of capitalist anarchy.

The process of uneven development has by no means ended. Japan, West Germany and France have moved ahead of the United States in some fields. Even underdeveloped countries have begun to acquire industrial plants that either match those in the U.S. or are superior. Pockets of advanced technology joined to low wages in such countries make a formidable competitive combination.

Then there is the effect of low growth and deep recessions. A buoyant economy with a high level of demand causes companies to hang on to plants they would otherwise scrap. Low growth and deep recessions increase the excess capacity which companies see as a deadweight in their chase after profits. What are the implications for the future of U.S. industry?

THE POWER TO CLOSE plants is an enormous power over the lives of many people and their communities. It is a far more important power than that exercised by all but a handful of our elected public officials.

The companies claim that in closing plants they are acting according to what is "economic," but this is a perversion of language. To act economically would mean to take into account all the true costs of closings. But the companies don't take the true costs into account because they don't have to pay them. They get higher profits from closings, while the workers, their communities, and the people of the United States are stuck with the costs.

Plant closings should be met by the organized resistance of workers and their communities, using all possible forms of action, including street demonstrations and sit-ins. But the monopolies are expert in the way they time and manage their closings to keep workers in different plants and people in different communities from joining together in the common fight. The fight against plant closings requires drawing in not just those workers who are immediately threatened, but the workers of the whole company, the whole industry—all workers and their communities—many of whom will be threatened later.

Moreover, resisting threatened plant closings, while essential, is a defensive response to monopoly initiative, and wars are not won by defensive actions. Working people must go on the offensive with their own program to deal with plant closings.

Such a program would include federal legislation to (1) eliminate the untrammeled right of the companies to close plants; and (2) to force the companies to bear the full costs of those closings that are allowed.

Any law to restrict company power to close plants, though limited to a particular state or even city, is better than nothing. But the companies are skillful at playing off different states and communities against each other. They threaten those that consider passing laws to curb plant closings with boycott—with taking their investments and business elsewhere.

That's why we need federal legislation. Under such legislation, corporations would not be able to decide by themselves to close a plant. They would have to apply for permission to a public body set up to control plant closings. This body would determine whether a corporation wanting to close a plant is motivated by a genuine deficit in the plant or simply desires to get higher profits elsewhere; what the consequences would be for the workers and their communities; and whether or not a proposed closing is in society's interest.

The legislation would require corporations that are allowed to close a plant to do the following: give a long advance notice to the workers and communities affected; give appropriate severance pay to the workers (say a minimum of two years' pay); give an appropriate financial recompense to the community; pay for retraining the workers, and relocation expenses if they must move to obtain new jobs.

Besides helping workers and their communities when plants are closed, these requirements would have another useful effect. If corporations themselves had to pay the true costs of closings instead of being able to dump them on others, there would be many fewer closings.

Plant closings are one aspect of a broader problem—a spreading sickness in many of our industries that threatens them with shrinkage and even disappearance and is weakening the whole structure of the U.S. economy.

10

Sickness in Auto

Our auto industry is sick and this means sickness in the vitals of the U.S. economy. The auto industry is, by many standards, our most important industry.

According to a government report entitled *The U.S. Auto Industry 1980,* auto and truck production and services accounted for eight and one half percent of the U.S. G.N.P. and over one quarter of total retail sales. During past periods of peak output, the industry directly employed over 900,000 workers and supplier industries employed 1.4 million more. An additional 900,000 people earned their living in the auto dealer network.[1]

The auto industry is a major consumer of other industries' products. It utilized 21 percent of the nation's steel output; 60 percent of the synthetic rubber; 11 percent of the primary aluminum; 30 percent of the ferrous castings; 25 percent of the glass; 20 percent of the machine tools; and significant percentages of plastics and electronics.[2]

Anything significant that happens in the auto industry is bound to affect the whole economy.

THE CRISIS IN the auto industry broke out just after the oil embargo in 1973; the sale of domestically produced cars fell unusually sharply during the recession of 1974-75. But as the economy pulled out of the recession and the memory of the lines at the pumps faded, auto sales recovered, hitting highs in 1977 and 1978. Then in 1979, with the gasoline shortage that accompanied the Iranian revolution, the crisis erupted again and with far greater force. The sale of domestically produced cars fell for four years (1979-82), the first time in history that car sales fell over so long a period. Sales in 1982 were 45 percent below the 1978 level.

Part of the auto companies' response to the crisis was a wave of plant closings. The following table, taken from the government study cited above, gives "recent plant closings" (as of December 1, 1980)in the auto industry:[3]

Chrysler Plants	Job Loss
Lyons Trim, MI	700
Hamtramck Assembly, MI	5,600
Fostoria Iron Foundry, OH	650
Eight Mile/Outer Drive Stamping, Detroit, MI	2,400
Windsor Engine, ONT	2.400
Missouri Truck Assembly, St. Louis, MO	4,100
Warren R.V. Assembly, MI	2,000
Huber Av. Foundry, Detroit, MI	2,400
Cape Canaveral, FL	500
Mack Ave. Stamping, Detroit, MI	4,100
Employment Loss from Peak	24,850

Ford Plants	Job Loss
Los Angeles Assembly, CA	2,300
Mahwah Assembly, NJ	4,800
Dearborn Foundry, MI	1,100
Windsor Foundry, ONT	1,600
Flat Rock Foundry, MI (announced possible future closing)	—
Cleveland Engine, OH (indefinite)	2,300
Employment Loss from Peak	9,800

GM Plants	
Shutdowns	New Locations
Pontiac Assembly, MI	Orion Township, MI
St. Louis Assembly, MI	St. Charles, MO
St. Louis Corvette, MO	Bowling Green, KY
Detroit Cadillac Engine, MI	Livonia, MI
Flint Foundry, MI	(Consolidation)
Kansas City (possible)	Kansas City Area
Detroit Cadillac Assembly	Detroit (negotiation)
	Dayton, OH
	(mini-truck and engine)

Since this table was prepared, additional closings have occurred. Here is a partial list put together from newspaper accounts:

Ford Plants	Job Loss
Assembly plant, San Jose, CA[a]	2,386
(Plant employed up to 5,000 at times)	
Aluminum casting, Sheffield, AL[b]	1,000

GM Plants	Job Loss
Automotive trim plant, Euclid, OH[c]	1,250
Assembly plant, Fremont, CA [d]	2,500
Assembly plant, South Gate, CA[d]	2,550
Parts plant, Trenton, NJ[e]	3,615
Fort Street parts plant, Detroit, MI[e]	2,900
Coit Road parts plant, Cleveland, OH[e]	2,810
Plant No. 37, Detroit, MI[e]	256

[a]NY Times, 11/19/92; [b]NYT, 6/19/82; [c]Wall Street Journal, 2/8/82; [d]WSJ, 2/16/82; [e]NYT, 2/26/82.

Over 55,000 auto workers lost their jobs through these plant closings.

But unemployment among auto workers goes far beyond that caused by the shutdowns. In late 1979 during the gasoline shortage, the auto companies began massive layoffs even in plants that were not being permanently closed. Layoffs continued during the recession in the spring of 1980. By August of that year, 250,000 production workers—a third of the hourly work force—plus 50,000 salaried workers had been laid off. An additional 650,000 were unemployed in the parts and supplier industries.[4]

Auto unemployment has remained high ever since, even during periods of cyclical upswing. Workers in the auto industry are suffering from structural, long-term unemployment.

The unemployment strikes with special force at Black, Hispanic, and other minority workers, who previously found jobs in the auto industry in large numbers. As always the minorities suffer a disproportionate share of the layoffs because they generally have lower seniority than white workers.

The regional impact of the crisis in autos has been severe. The industrial belt extending from western New York, and Pennsylvania through Ohio, Michigan, Illinois, and Wisconsin accounts for over 90 percent of the production of motor vehicles, parts and accessories. In July 1980, when the rate of unemployment for the country as a whole was 7.6 percent, it was 14.8 percent in Michigan, 11.3 percent in Indiana, and 10.2 percent in Ohio. In Flint, Michigan, unemployment was 22.2 percent and in Detroit 14.6 percent.[5] The auto-producing belt was hit by a deep, long-lasting depression.

The crisis in autos also had a big impact on the economy as a whole. It dragged down output and increased unemployment in several other industries—steel, tires, glass, aluminum, machine tools.

WHAT ARE THE CAUSES of the crisis in the auto industry? How can we expect it to develop in the future? What is being done? What should be done?

Several causes worked together to produce the crisis: the operations of the monopolies which control the industry; the oil crisis; and the loss of the U.S. technological lead in automobile production.

The U.S. auto industry has long been marked by an exceptionally high degree of monopoly. For years prior to the upsurge in imports that began in the late 1950s, the domestic auto market was completely controlled by the three U.S. giants—General Motors, Ford, and Chrysler—that accounted for 95 percent of cars sold. General Motors alone has accounted for 40 to 50 percent (in some years even more) and continues to do so despite the imports. This corporation, one of the most profitable in the history of the world, put its stamp on the auto industry.

In the early 1920s, the industry was dominated by Henry Ford whose policy was to achieve a high volume of sales by providing basic transportation, a utilitarian black car that sold at a low price. The system of annual model changes with constant stylistic alterations did not yet exist.

General Motors changed all this. "The primary object of the corporation . . . was to make money, not just to make motor cars," wrote Alfred P. Sloan, Jr. president and chairman of the company from 1923 to 1956, and the intellectual father of most of its business and organizational policies. "The problem was to design a product line that would make money."[6] GM designed such a line; one based not on providing basic transportation, but cars that could be sold at higher prices and would therefore yield higher profits.

Whereas Ford put out only two cars, the Model T and the high-price, low-volume Lincoln, GM put out a range of cars designed to extract what the traffic would bear from several different income strata. "The core of the product policy," wrote Sloan, "lies in its concept of mass producing a full line of cars graded upward in quality and price."[7] GM had a Chevrolet for buyers with modest incomes, and then Pontiac, Olds, Buick, and Cadillac.

To further support high sales volume, high prices and high profits, GM introduced the system of annual model changes with its emphasis on style. Again Sloan's observation is revealing:

> Automobile design is not, of course, pure fashion, but it is not too much to say that the "laws" of the Paris dressmakers have come to be a factor in the automobile industry. . . .
>
> The changes in the new model should be so novel and attractive as to create demand for the new value and, so to speak, create a certain amount of dissatisfaction with past models as compared with the new one. . . . [8]

GM's strategy enabled it to wrest predominance in the industry from Ford. Henry Ford was a capitalist, like the owners and managers of GM. But he had started out as a mechanic and retained some of the criteria of a mechanic. With time, these criteria clashed with moneymaking. When a GM committee headed by Sloan declared in 1921 that the primary object of the company was to make money, not automobiles, they weren't simply stating a platitude, but something that had concrete meaning for the company's operations. They were stressing the need for pure devotion to capitalist principles and for always using these principles to guide specific decision-making. The stronger emphasis on capitalist principles not only won for GM; after a while, the whole U.S. auto industry was forced to convert to the GM-type strategy.

The auto monopolies geared themselves with ever increasing skill to profit-making. They used model changes and advertising with a success that went far beyond the dreams of the Paris dressmakers. They didn't just passively accept consumer demand. They manufactured it. They managed it. They pushed it in the direction of the highest profits.

No possibility for increasing profits was overlooked. The companies promoted "planned obsolescence"—the "dissatisfaction with past models" that Sloan wrote about. They promoted gadgetry, "extras" added to the basic model, which enabled them to greatly increase prices. They promoted "power" and big, heavy cars. Big cars meant big bucks while, as Henry Ford II once put it, "mini-cars mean mini-profits."

Part of GM's domination of the auto industry consisted of the power to act as price leader. John Blair, in his *Economic Concentration*, explains how GM's price leadership works:

> The effective leader in the automobile industry is not always the first to announce. In seeking to create the impression of an intensely competitive industry, General Motors sometimes considers it expedient for the initial announcement to be made by one of its rivals. . . . If the announced increases are more than what is called for by the formula, GM will theoretically announce smaller increases and Ford and Chrysler will be forced to adjust their prices downward; this incidentally has rarely, if ever, occurred. But if their advances are too small and GM goes higher, they can revise their quotations upward "to meet the competition."[9]

What is the pricing formula to which Blair refers? It is the practice of "target return pricing" followed by GM and other companies; the setting of prices at whatever level is required to yield a predetermined target rate of profit. Blair explains that GM's target rate of profit is 20 percent and he presents statistics to show how actual profits compared with the target for the years 1953 through 1968. "As compared to its target return of 20 percent, the weighted average of General Motors' actual rate of return on net worth was 20.2 percent."[10]

FOR MANY YEARS after World War II, all was bliss for the U.S. auto monopolies. In 1950, the United States accounted for three quarters of world motor vehicle production. Imports of passenger cars constituted three tenths of one percent of U.S. sales. As late as 1960, the United States still accounted for half of world motor vehicle production. But the decline in U.S. predominance had begun. Starting in 1956, U.S. car imports had begun to move upward, reaching 10 percent of sales in 1959.

The U.S. auto monopolies analyzed the threat from small car imports in order to decide what strategy to follow. They could have decided to try to prevent the imports from getting a foothold in the U.S. market by producing small cars themselves. With their great financial and technological strength, they were in a powerful position to fight the imports. The foreign exporters had to overcome strong disadvantages: distance from the U.S. market, consumer prejudice against foreign cars, and the need to build an extensive system for supplying spare parts for the cars they sold.

But the monopolies decided against this strategy. They calculated that if they produced small cars it would cut into their sales of big cars, that small cars would mean lower profits even if the foreign competition were kept out.

A Congressional committee, in a report on *The Auto Situation: 1980*, explains:

> U.S. manufacturers believed that the investment in equipment need-ed to produce a small car simply would not guarantee the return that a similar amount invested in equipment for a large car would return. The rationale was that they could not load a small car with the high return options such as power steering, brakes, windows; large V-8 engines; air conditioning; and automatic transmissions. It appears their strategy could be stated as follows:
>
> We know we will lose the small car market to imports, so what? Let them hold 15 percent of the U.S. market because these are low-profit models. We will produce a few small cars, but we won't spend much to develop them, and maybe we can still make a little money on small cars.[11]

John Z. De Lorean, in a book on his experiences as a high-ranking GM executive, tells of the problems of "Pushing Small Cars In A Big Car Company":

> When I was with GM, a $300 to $400 difference between the building costs of a Chevrolet Caprice and a Cadillac De Ville, a bigger car, was small compared to the $3,800 difference in sticker price. The dif-ference in profit to General Motors on the two cars is over $2,000.[12]

So GM held back on developing small cars despite an increasing consumer demand for them:

> Any auto analyst who studied the domestic car market during the 1960s knew well that the growth of the auto industry from 1965 on was in smaller, lighter-weight and more fuel-efficient cars. The dramatic rise in imported car penetration from that time forward proved the trend. . . . When the Arab Oil Embargo was enacted in October of 1973, the American interest in small cars jumped appreciably. . . . The domestic manufacturers, especially General Motors, which had ig-nored the sales charts when they clearly showed the trend to smaller cars, were now faced with a market demanding products they did not have. . . . The domestic automobile industry plunged into a severe

recession in part because the domestic manufacturers failed to heed the call from the marketplace as early as the mid-1960s. . . . Much of this trouble need never have been. There were several programs with which I was associated during the 1960s that proposed to management that General Motors move into smaller car markets and take size and weight out of its successful big cars to meet the future demands of the marketplace. Most of these proposals were turned down.[13]

De Lorean reflects on the broader significance of what he saw:

Never once when I was in General Motors management did I hear substantial social concern raised about the impact of our business on America, its consumers, or the economy. When we should have been planning switches to smaller, more fuel-efficient, lighter cars in the late 1960s in response to a growing demand in the marketplace, GM management refused because "we make more money on big cars." It mattered not that customers wanted the smaller cars or that a national balance-of-payments deficit was being built in large part because of the burgeoning sales of foreign cars in the American market.

Refusal to enter the small car market when the profits were better on bigger cars, despite the needs of the public and the national economy, was not an isolated case of corporate insensitivity. It was typical.[14]

Faced with little competition from domestic small cars, imports reached 18 percent of U.S. car sales in 1975 and 23 percent in 1979. In the latter year, imports pushed into the No. 2 spot in the U.S. sales ranking, surpassing Ford and trailing only GM. In 1980 Japan surpassed the United States in motor vehicle production for the first time and U.S. imports reached 27 percent of sales.

Even after the imports were running at such alarming levels, the companies remained less interested in fighting them than in promoting immediate profits. An example is what they did when the Japanese yen appreciated sharply in 1978, causing the dollar price of Japanese cars to jump. *Consumer Reports* tells us:

Freed from the restraints of Japanese competition, American manufacturers had two choices. They could keep their own price increases moderate, undersell the Japanese by more than $1,000, offer huge bargains to the car-buying public, and try to regain at least some of the business captured by the imports in previous years. Or they could capitalize on the absence of price competition to maximize profits now, without regard for long-range market share—and, of course, add to inflation here in the U.S.

The numbers show Detroit's choice. When the 1978 *Chevrolet*

Chevette was introduced in September 1977, it carried a base price of $3,354. During the year, GM raised the price of the *Chevette* twice. . . .

It was the same with the *Plymouth Horizon*. In November 1977, a four-door 1978 *Horizon* carried a base price of $3,706. A year later a *Horizon* was up about 11 percent; now, a 1980 *Horizon* is up an additional 24 percent.[15]

Although the monopolies did not attempt to hold back the imports by competing against them in price, they did pressure the government to restrict them. In 1981, the government negotiated an agreement with Japan to place "voluntary restrictions" on its auto exports to the United States for three years.

PART OF U.S. motor vehicle imports are "captive imports"—vehicles produced abroad but sold here under U.S. nameplates and on behalf of U.S. companies. In 1979, for example, 8.6 percent of the passenger car imports and 48 percent of the light truck imports from Japan were captive imports such as the Dodge Colt (Mitsubishi), the Buick Opel (Isuzu), and among the trucks, the Ford Courier (Toyo Kogyo), and the Chevrolet LUV (Isuzu).[16]

The captive imports cost U.S. workers jobs, but they are profitable for the companies. An example: According to the *New York Times* (12-11-80) in 1980, "Industry analysts estimate that Chrysler grosses about $100 million from the distribution of Mitsubishi cars."

Besides importing complete vehicles, the monopolies also import foreign-made parts for use in domestic production. Here is an explanation (from the *New York Times*, 3-3-80) of how they get parts from Mexico:

"Little Detroits" Boom in Mexico

Among the latest expansion efforts within the 14-year-old, narrow duty-free zone just inside the Mexican border are clusters of "Little Detroits," established by the General Motors Corporation and the Chrysler Corporation to take advantage of the sharply lower wage and production costs of assembly plants here.

These operations were set up under the Mexican in-bond, or Maquiladora industrialization program. . . . set up in 1966. It permits foreign and domestic corporations to post a bond for parts and materials imported for assembling in Mexico, avoiding the usual customs duties if the assembled parts are exported. And United States customs duties are imposed only on the value added to parts in Mexico. . . .

General Motors has four new plants in production in the free trade area, the oldest dating from 1978, and three under construction in Ciudad Juarez and Matamoros. . . .

Chrysler opened a 100,000-square-foot assembly plant last June in Juarez . . . [and has] a second plant in Piedras Negras. . . .

William L. Mitchell, marketing director of the . . . Industrial Park in Juarez, put a company's cost to maintain an assembly-line worker here, most of whom are women in their 20's, at $3,200 yearly, including wages, benefits and Government taxes for housing, social security, medical care and day-care programs. A company's cost would be 10 to 20 times that figure for wages, benefits and Government taxes for an American worker.

The network of suppliers abroad from whom the companies obtain parts is far-ranging: GM de Mexico, GM de Brazil, GM Strasbourg (France), and Isuzu; Ford-Mexico, Ford de Brazil, Toyo Kogyo, etc.; Chrysler de Mexico, Mitsubishi, Peugeot, etc. The range of parts imported is also wide, including engines, electronic control devices, aluminum cylinder heads, radiators, automatic transmissions, etc.[17]

The monopolies have been increasing the import of parts and intend to go on doing so. Here is an excerpt from a *New York Times* story (10-14-81) headed "GM Shift: Outside Suppliers":

The General Motors Corporation, historically the domestic automobile company most committed to producing its own components, is looking increasingly to outside suppliers as a means of lowering its labor costs, according to the company's chairman Roger B. Smith. . . . Mr. Smith [predicted] that the practice, known as "outsourcing," would become more common throughout the American automobile industry. He said that as a result of the General Motors effort, some of its plants might close.

Carter's Secretary of Transportation, Neil Goldschmidt, predicted that the import of parts would grow three percent per year during the 1980s. He expected the export of parts also to grow, but not as rapidly, so that the U.S. negative trade balance in parts (then already $2.5 billion a year) would "grow worse."[18]

How far can the movement overseas go? Very far—there is no clear limit. U.S. and West European auto companies have been talking about nothing less than a "world car"; the same car to be assembled in several different countries from standardized parts produced throughout the capitalist world.

The movement toward a world car is well under way. Already in 1980, the Ford Escort, for example, was being assembled in three countries, with the U.S. version containing parts from nine foreign countries—shock absorber struts from Spain, rear brake assemblies from Brazil, engine cylinder heads from Italy, etc.[19]

The monopoly strategists hope to gain several advantages from a world car: to transfer many operations to areas in which wages are lower; to place U.S. workers into ever increasing competition with foreign workers, which means downward pressure on wages in the United States; and to be able to play off the workers of one country against another during labor disputes.

The world car represents an international division of labor carried out by the monopolies according to their interests and standards. For them, it means higher profits; but for our people it means the transfer of a good part of the auto industry to other countries. The monopolies, with an eye on lower wages elsewhere, are bound to arrange things so that the U.S. economy loses more than it gains from a world car. For U.S. workers, the movement toward a world car means a loss of jobs and lower wages.

The superiority of U.S. technology over that of the underdeveloped countries will not protect the jobs and wages of U.S. workers. Where it suits their purpose, the monopolies are transferring technology to these countries. As the Secretary of Transportation put it in his report:

> Many . . . multinationals are building uniform components on a very large scale, distributing the production facilities through many countries. . . . In so doing, it becomes the multinational's goal to move newly developed technology into other countries rapidly, so that the previous competitive advantage of high technology countries now diminishes rapidly.[20]

BESIDES OBTAINING more cars and parts from abroad, the auto monopolies have been carrying out far-reaching plans for automation and robotization. At the beginning of the 1980s, they undertook a gigantic capital investment program to retool virtually the entire industry. Part of the aim was to create additional facilities for the production of small cars. Another part was to install the latest technology and slash labor costs.

Harley Shaiken, an expert on automation and the auto industry, wrote in 1980:

The tiny microprocessor—the heart of a computer on a sliver of silicon—is carrying automation to every corner of the industry, affecting design studios, engine plants, warehouses, foundries, tool rooms, and assembly lines. . . .

GM is considering using robots in every aspect of S car assembly . . . . The entire car will be made up of modular components so that robots can ultimately be used in the highly labor-intensive operations that are most difficult to automate. . . .

Chrysler has recently installed the most advanced autobody welding system in the United States—utilizing 128 robots—in its renovated plants in Newark, Delaware, and in Detroit. . . .

At Ford's new Batavia, Ohio, plant—a $500 million facility making automatic transmissions for Escorts and Lynxes—machine tools are linked to central computers and display screens in supervisors' offices for instant monitoring.[21]

Robotization was, of course, only beginning in 1980. GM is so serious about robots that in the midst of the recession of 1982, it joined with a Japanese partner to form a company to produce them— the GM Fanuc Robotics Corp. It expected GM Fanuc's robots to be rolling off an assembly line in the United States in 1984 and planned to use them in GM plants as well as sell them to others.

Robotization means a loss of jobs for auto workers. Shaiken noted that each 1980 robot welder could displace three or four workers. He expected that as robot technology became more sophisticated, this ratio would go even higher. The jobs created for maintaining and repairing the robots would be far fewer.

The effect of the auto industry's massive retooling program on labor requirements will be drastic. The Secretary of Transportation's 1980 report states that:

The assembly process will witness increased line speeds and productivity due to greater utilization of robots and other automated equipment. Labor requirements per unit will likely decrease by 20-30 percent as line speeds will be increased from 40-60 units per hour to 70-80 units per hour. If sales follow . . . middle demand projections . . . and if productivity were to improve by 5 percent per year in the industry, about 200,000 fewer workers would be employed in 1985 than would otherwise be the case.[22]

Just as the monopolies threaten workers with the import of parts from overseas and with plant closings to get them to accept lower wages and benefits, so they also use the threat of automation and robotization. GM's Roger B. Smith, at the same time that he was talking about looking increasingly to outside suppliers, also stated: "Every time the cost of labor goes up $1 an hour, 1,000 more robots become economical."[23]

THE CHRYSLER CORPORATION, in 1980, reported a deficit of $1.7 billion, the biggest in U.S. corporate history. It had already suffered previous deficits in 1978 and 1979 which had thrown it into a fight to survive.

In December 1979, Chrysler Chairman Lee Iacocca gave his opinion of how corporations in danger of going under should be dealt with: "There is the sound principle that the market place should be the final judge of success or failure, and if the government started routinely bailing out failing firms, there would be a breakdown of market discipline."[24]

But we live in the era of state monopoly capitalism and this statement was eyewash. For the monopolies, opposition "on principle" to government help through subsidies, tariffs or import curbs, loans or grants, or in any other way, applies only to others, not one's own company. Even as he was proclaiming the high principle of financial discipline, Iacocca was asking the government for financial help.

GM Chairman Thomas Murphy, Milton Friedman, and others argued that Chrysler should be left to fend for itself. But the government rejected this view. Chrysler was too big and important. Just its debt in commercial paper—short-term IOUs—amounted to $1.2 billion, according to *Newsweek*, and when the credit rating services downgraded this debt "tremors spread throughout the money markets."[25] Chrysler spent $800 million a month for materials and components.[26] It employed 110,000 people itself, its suppliers an additonal 180,000, and its dealers yet another 100,000.[27] Eventually, the government granted Chrysler a $1.5 billion loan guarantee.

The government bailout saved jobs as compared to what would have happened without it. But beyond this, it was geared not to saving jobs, but slashing them. The reorganization plan which the government insisted that Chrysler work out as a condition for receiving help was based on one criterion—the capitalist one of restoring Chrysler to profitability. In the name of profitability, it called for actions involving the loss of tens of thousands of jobs.

A key part of the plan called for Chrysler to make itself into a smaller company. It was to eliminate operations requiring large current outlays of money when profits were too far in the future and too uncertain. It was to sell assets that could bring large amounts of ready cash. This policy meant reducing Chrysler's product line, producing fewer types of cars. It also meant the divestiture of many Chrysler parts operations, especially if the parts could be obtained more cheaply abroad. The *Wall Street Journal* talked of Chrysler surviving, but as a "leaner" company. "Lean" meant that a large proportion of Chrysler's workers would permanently lose their jobs.

As one of the concessions for granting the loan guarantee, the government demanded that Chrysler workers scale down their wage demands. This had to do with more than Chrysler. It was part of the broad government-corporate strategy for reducing wages in general. Forcing Chrysler workers to accept what, given the inflation, amounted to a large cut in real wages, would be a useful precedent for coercing other workers into accepting wage cuts. In November, 1979, Alfred Kahn, the Carter administration's "inflation fighter," called a wage contract reached by Chrysler and the United Auto Workers "outrageous," adding that President Carter agreed with him and "may well refuse to authorize the loan guarantee unless we get more of a contribution." [28] Later—and more than once—the government, using the loan guarantee as a club, forced the union to reopen the contract and make large concessions to Chrysler on wages and benefits previously won.

THE STRATEGY of the monopolies for meeting the auto crisis can be summarized simply. Retool to be able to produce small cars, but use every opportunity to push big ones. Keep car prices high. Lower labor costs by whatever means possible. Where it promises to pay off in profits, retool the factories with the latest in automation and robots. Where the investment required for retooling is too great or the operation doesn't lend itself to automation and robots, get rid of it. Shut down the plant and get what it produces from nonunion suppliers or overseas. Move toward a world car to take advantage of the lower wages in many other countries and the possibility of playing off workers in one country against those of another. Use everything—the crisis, the imports, the threat of robots, shutdowns, and moving overseas—to wring concessions from the workers.

This strategy has been working. By the first quarter of 1983, the companies were again swimming in profits despite a weak car market. "GM Earnings Surge Fivefold In First Quarter," said one headline.[29] "A Record Quarter for Chrysler," said another.[30] Ford had the "best quarterly showing in nearly four years."[31]

But this strategy works only for the companies, not for the workers, the people at large, or the economy. It produces the all-holy of the monopolies—high profits. But it increases monopoly profits at the expense of the workers by increasing unemployment. It treats the workers as expendable.

Even government reports have had to admit that a large part of the job loss in the auto industry is permanent. The Department of Commerce report on the auto industry, for example, stated: "The probability of automotive employment ever recovering its 1978 peak is low. . . . The automotive industry . . . will employ 200,000 fewer workers in the mid-1980s. The supplier industry may suffer an employment loss in the range of 300,000 to 400,000 workers from the 1978 level."[32]

This loss, adding up to 500- to 600-thousand auto jobs, is by no means the worst that can happen. The process of robotization and the transfer of production to other countries will not have run their course by 1985, but will continue afterward, bringing with them further job loss. Another eruption of the oil crisis, with lines at pumps and hikes in prices, could also make the job loss go much higher than the government estimates.

The strategy of the monopolies is also the government strategy. What is happening in the auto industry is a major economic disaster, regardless of the restoration of the companies to profitability. What has the government been doing about this disaster? What has it been doing to help and protect not just the companies, but the workers, their communities, the economy as a whole? It is all very well for the government to provide statistical estimates of a permanent loss of over half a million jobs in the auto industry. But the important thing is action to meet the problem—to prevent the job loss from occurring, to get other jobs and training for the workers, to *do* something. But the government hasn't even recognized this problem as one it should do something about, much less actually grappled with it. It doesn't see the job loss as the core of the auto crisis, but rather as a means for dealing with that crisis; the key thing is to restore the profitability of the monopolies. The workers? They can be left to the mercies of the capitalist labor market in a stagnant economy.

THERE IS NO WAY under capitalism to bring about a full solution of the U.S. auto problem. We must keep this in mind in thinking about different possible measures that can be taken. We must not judge these measures by whether they will work perfectly. The test is whether they can bring about a significant improvement.

To begin with, the auto monopolies should be made to stop the transfer of operations and jobs abroad, either through general regulation of foreign investment or, failing that, through specific controls on the auto industry. Further investment by the U.S. auto companies in plants abroad must be prohibited. Captive car imports and the import of parts from U.S.-owned foreign plants should both be curbed. We ought not to sit by and watch as the auto industry goes abroad the way the consumer electronics industry did.

The government could also mount a large program for the development of mass transportation, with the required equipment to be produced by the auto industry. The country needs to have mass transportation developed, especially to be able to meet future tightness in oil supplies. A large transportation program would create many jobs for unemployed auto workers.

Although the possibility of converting auto plants to the production of mass transportation equipment has been raised in public discussion, the auto monopolies haven't uttered a peep about it. This is to be expected. These monopolies have a long history of fighting mass transportation.

It might be objected that the development of effective mass transportation would cut into the demand for autos and trucks and thereby further hurt auto workers. But the task of creating adequate mass transportation is so large that there would be a net addition to jobs even if auto sales were somewhat lower than they otherwise would be. And these new jobs would rest on a firmer basis than the jobs in auto production which are vulnerable to further eruptions of the oil crisis.

Mass transportation equipment is not the only possibility. The unemployed auto workers could be used in new factories, built and owned by the government, to produce many other things the economy and our people need. It is an enormous waste not to use the accumulation of skills that these workers represent.

Some will object that such ideas aren't feasible. But why not? They aren't "feasible" only because we allow our economy to be run according to the goal of accumulating profits rather than meeting people's needs. They aren't feasible only because working people and their allies haven't yet mobilized the political strength to make them feasible.

To the extent that the political strength necessary to guarantee new jobs for the unemployed auto workers does not yet exist, there remains a crucial measure: a program to provide all necessary assistance to these workers. What is required is a program geared to the problem of long-run structural unemployment, one that will provide unemployment insurance benefits for as long as these workers remain unemployed, that will retrain them for new jobs and pay for relocating them and their families if that is necessary for them to obtain such jobs.

Finally, another "unthinkable" thought—the auto industry can be nationalized and placed under democratic control. This one measure would greatly add to our ability to deal with the auto crisis. Take, for example, the dilemma that if we don't restrict auto imports, workers lose jobs; if we restrict them, the U.S. monopolies raise prices. With nationalization, we could restrict imports without suffering price increases. Nationalization would take away from the undemocratic and irresponsible monopolies the power they now have to shut down plants and move operations abroad, thereby weakening our whole industrial base. It would make it possible to make policy decisions for the auto industry not on the basis of what is good for profits, but what is good for the economy and the people.

11

Shrinking Steel

Our steel industry is also sick and this, too, means rot in our economic vitals.

Even if the steel industry doesn't hold the dominant position it once did, it remains a key industry. In the late 1970s, it accounted for one percent of the GNP, employed 450,000 people, and bought over $25 billion in materials and supplies—iron ore, coal, bricks, electric power, machinery, etc.[1]

Some talk glibly of allowing the steel industry to shrink, but shrinkage of the steel industry means widespread trouble.

Although the steel crisis has been building for decades, it became acute in 1975. Steel production plummetted that year and has never recovered to the levels of 1973 and 1974.

As in the auto industry, part of the monopolies' answer to crisis was a wave of plant closings. The following table, from *Steel at the Crossroads,* a publication of the industry's trade association, gives "recent" (as of January 1980) plant closings.[2]

Company	Location	Job Loss
U.S. Steel	Duluth (MN)	13,300
	Ellwood City (PA)	
	Youngstown (OH)	
	Torrance (CA)	
	Waukegan (IL)	
	Joliet (IL) and elsewhere	
Bethlehem Steel	Johnstown (PA)	12,000
	Lackawanna (NY) and elsewhere	
Youngstown Sheet & Tube	Youngstown (OH)	5,000
Alan Wood Steel	Conshohocken (PA)	3,000
Cyclops Corp.	Mansfield (OH)	1,300
	Portsmouth (OH)	
Phoenix Steel	Phoenixville (PA)	700

Additional closings have occurred since this table was prepared. Here is a list of some, gleaned from newspapers:

Company	Location	Job Loss
Bethlehem Steel[a]	Lackawanna (NY)	10,000
	Johnstown (PA)	
	Los Angeles (CA)	
	Seattle (WA)	
Armco Inc.[b]	New Miami (OH)	2,200
	Kansas City (MO)	
	Houston (TE)	
Crucible Steel[c]	Midland (PA)	5,000
Jones & Laughlin[d]	Youngstown (OH)	450
Republic Steel[e]	Cleveland (OH)	700

[a]*NYT* and *WSJ*, 12/29/82; [b]*NYT*, 1/11/83; [c]*NYT*, 10/16/82; [d]*NYT*, 1/22/83; [e]Cleveland *Plain Dealer*, 8/7/82.

On December 27, 1983, (just after Christmas) the U.S. Steel Corporation announced that it was closing three major plants and parts of more than a dozen others, eliminating 15,430 jobs. The closings reduced the company's steelmaking capacity by 16 percent. Here are a few of the plants:[3]

Company	Location	Job Loss
South Works (most of plant)	Chicago (IL)	3,103
Cuyahoga Works	Cleveland (OH)	1,105
Johnstown Works	Johnstown (PA)	790
Trenton Works	Trenton (NJ)	300

At least 70,000 workers have lost their jobs in the steel industry because of plant closings, but unemployment in steel is much larger than this. Between 1974 and January 1983, steel employment shrank from 487,000 to 246,000—a decline of one half. Three quarters of the laid-off workers will never get their jobs back.

The steel industry is concentrated in the same industrial belt as the auto industry, so the plant closings and job decline in steel, added to those in auto, devastate a whole region. Ohio, with heavy auto unemployment in Dayton and Cleveland has also been hit by the closing of steel plants in Youngstown, Mansfield, and Portsmouth. Buffalo, with heavy auto unemployment, has also been hit by the closing of the Bethlehem steel plant in the suburb of Lackawanna.

In steel, too, the job decline hits Afro-American, Hispanic, and other minority workers especially hard. They suffer a disproportionate share of the layoffs because they have lower seniority and are concentrated in those jobs—the coke ovens, for example—in which the biggest job slashes are occurring as the monopolies carry out modernization programs.

THE STEEL CRISIS has several causes: the working of monopoly and finance capital, the loss of technological leadership by the United States, the auto crisis, and the priorities by which the U.S. economy is run.

A small number of giant companies have traditionally dominated the U.S. steel industry. This industry came out of World War II as cock of the walk, the most advanced in the world and producing more steel than everyone else combined. It completely dominated the giant U.S. market. During the years 1950-55, U.S. steel imports were less than two percent of consumption.

The monopolies used this situation, not to advance the industry, but to charge top prices and rake in monopoly profits. They not only followed this policy during the early postwar years when they had no competition, but continued it even when steel imports began to rise. A report on steel to President Carter stated:

> Steel mill products price increases greatly exceeded the rise in other prices in the last half of the 1950s. . . . It was during this period that the industry first began to experience major problems with imports. . . .[4]

The companies could have fixed lower prices and prevented the Japanese and other foreign steel exporters from establishing a bridgehead in the U.S. market. But the companies analyzed the steel import threat just as the auto companies analyzed the small car import threat and came to a similar conclusion—to accept a certain amount of imports rather than cut prices. They calculated that high prices, even if they meant lower production and sales because of imports, would bring higher profits than the combination of lower prices, no significant imports, and greater production and sales.

It was not just in the late 1950s that steel prices rose faster than prices in general. As the report to the President points out: "During the 1960s, steel prices increased at a rate slightly above that of other industrial products. But, in the first half of the present decade [the 1970s], the rate of inflation in steel prices has again sharply outpaced inflation in the rest of the economy."[5]

Besides rising faster than other prices, "steel prices have also been the least flexible of industrial prices."[6] They rose fast during cyclical upswings, but didn't go down during recessions. Foreign steel prices have been more flexible, rising as steel demand rose and dropping as it fell.

Especially important are the periods of economic contraction, 1969-70 and 1974-75. As world prices for steel fell in this period, the U.S. domestic prices remained comparatively stable. This opened a large gap between U.S. and imported steel prices which inevitably caused imports to increase. It is no coincidence that imports rose sharply in 1971 and 1976-77, in light of the wide gaps that have opened up between domestic and foreign prices.[7]

High prices not only opened the door for imports but reduced the market for steel. They helped cause users of steel to shift to other materials: concrete, aluminum, plastics. The shift away from steel cost the steel industry millions of tons of possible sales each year.

THE WAY FINANCE CAPITAL works has also contributed to the steel crisis. The owners of the industry, not content with the rate of profit it provides, have been "diversifying"—pulling money out of steel to invest elsewhere where the profit rate is higher. This withdrawal of funds caused the U.S. steel industry to fall technologically behind that of Japan and other countries and become still less able to compete against imports. It also led to a shrinkage of the industry through reorganization and plant closings.

Milking the steel industry to diversify is not an accidental phenomenon limited to one or two cases like the Lykes-Youngstown Sheet and Tube operation described earlier. It is a basic steel owner strategy. As Paul Harmon, Research Manager of Armco Inc. once put it: "There's no divine law that says we were put on this earth only to make steel." And David Roderick, Chairman of U.S. Steel, has said: "We are no longer married exclusively to steel. Return on investment will dictate where the money goes."[8]

Steel at the Crossroads, presenting the owners' view of the steel crisis, frankly laid down what results from milking the steel industry and why it is done. First, on capital investment:

The American steel industry has made inadequate capital investments during the last 20 years. . . . As a result of inadequate capital

investment the replacement cycle of steel facilities has been too low
.... Many steel facilities are now quite old because capital expenditures have been inadequate. . . . Inadequate capital spending has
reduced steel's competitive edge.[9]

Then it explained the reason for the inadequate capital investment: "Steel companies and their stockholders have for too long
earned unacceptably low rates of return *relative to what could be
realized from alternative investment.*" (Italics added-E.B.)[10]

The monopolies are not saying that steel profits are low in
themselves, just low compared to other profits. The report presents
data showing that, during 1970-74, the average return on net worth
in the steel industry was 8.4 percent. But how could the finance
capitalist owners of the industry be content? For all manufacturing,
it was 12.6 percent.[11]

In 1982, U.S. Steel, the country's largest steel company, bought
Marathon Oil for over $6 billion. But well before this, U.S. Steel had
already gone a long way toward diversification. In the 1950s, steel
was the source of most of its operating income. Then it became a
conglomerate, branching out into chemicals, real estate, engineering services, barge lines, gas utilities, and other activities. By 1980,
steel accounted for only 11 percent of its operating income.[12] With
the acquisition of Marathon, steel became an even smaller part of
the company.

Other steel companies have also diversified. National Steel
bought banks: the Citizens Savings and Loan of California, the
West Side Federal in New York, and the Washington Savings and
Loan in Florida. The *New York Times* (11-19-81) reported that
"these acquisitions make National Steel . . . the fourth-largest
savings and loan company in the United States, with assets of $6.7
billion." Armco had diversified to such an extent that it decided to
drop the word "steel" from its name and call itself Armco, Inc. Even
Lukens Steel, a small company, announced in 1981 that it intended
to diversify. Its president, wrote the *New York Times* (11-30-81),
"said Lukens was 'in an excellent position' to diversify because of its
ability to generate cash even when business is slow."

BESIDES DIVERSIFYING from steel into other activities, U.S. finance
capital has also promoted a shift in steel operations from the United
States to other countries. U.S. banks have lent large sums to the very

foreign steel companies that have been competing with U.S. domestic steel. Steel monopolies in the U.S. have been moving toward importing partly processed steel from foreign companies for finishing in their plants in the United States.

Japanese steel companies, as well as those in a number of less developed countries, have received large loans from U.S. banks. In March 1977, for example, a series of U.S. banks—Citibank, Chase Manhattan, Bank of America, etc.—had more than $1 billion in loans outstanding to leading Japanese steel companies. During the years 1977-78, U.S. banks lent over $300 million to steel companies in Brazil, and $410 million to steel companies in Mexico, South Korea, and Taiwan.[13]

Even while denouncing imports (when they hurt profits), the steel monopolies are shamelessly moving to import steel themselves. In May 1983, the U.S. Steel Corp. announced that it was negotiating a deal with British Steel under which it would import three million tons of slab steel each year for finishing at its Fairless Works near Philadelphia. The idea was that U.S. Steel would shut down the operations for making raw steel at Fairless, while British Steel would end steel-finishing operations at its Ravenscraig, Scotland works which would produce the slabs. Three thousand jobs at Fairless would be eliminated.

In December 1983, U.S. Steel announced that there would be no deal with the British, but that it would continue to look for foreign suppliers of slab for its Fairless Works.[14]

Meanwhile, other U.S. companies have found foreign suppliers. The *Wall Street Journal* reports that "earlier this year [1983], little Lukens quietly joined what some economists are coming to call 'World Steel Inc.'" It signed a long-term agreement to buy slabs from Brazil. Besides Lukens, Republic Steel, Sharon Steel, McLouth Steel, and the Ford Rouge Steel unit have begun to buy semi-finished steel abroad for finishing at domestic mills.

The process of working with foreign suppliers is only beginning. "From Pohang, South Korea to Pittsburgh, and from the valley of the Amazon to the valley of the Ruhr, steelmakers big and small are exploring" the possibilities. The monopolies are erecting "a lattice-work of steel partnerships crossing oceans and continents."[15]

A continuation of this process will mean the end of the raw steelmaking industry in the United States.

ALONG WITH CONTROL of the industry by monopolies and finance capital, the second basic cause of the steel crisis is weakness in the demand for steel. U.S. steel consumption in 1980 was 20 percent or 37 million tons lower than it had been in 1973. At no time have imports increased by anything like this amount. The decline in consumption overshadows imports in explaining the steel crisis.

Recessions and low growth brought about part of the decline in consumption. The demand for steel is more sensitive than most goods to the general state of the economy.

The auto crisis also helped to reduce the demand for steel. Between 1975 and 1980, the average amount of steel going into a new car fell by 25 percent; cars had become smaller and manufacturers had also substituted aluminum and plastics for steel because they are lighter. The unprecedented slump in car sales that began in 1979, added to the decline in steel per car, drastically reduced the demand for steel by the auto industry. There is no prospect that the demand for steel by this industry will recover to past high levels. The Secretary of Transportation's 1980 report on the auto industry estimated that by 1985 it would take only 10 to 15 million tons of steel compared to 21 million tons in 1978.[16]

Finally, the distorted priorities by which the U.S. economy is being run reduce the demand for steel. The military budget, even the part that goes for hardware, requires little steel for the amount of money being poured into it. Some of this money, spent for building rapid transit systems or repairing our decayed bridges, could generate a large demand for steel.

WHAT HAVE THE MONOPOLIES been doing about the steel crisis besides milking the industry and laying off workers? They have raised a hullabaloo about imports and demanded curbs. They have complained about the cost of meeting environmental protection and occupational health and safety standards and demanded relief. They have undertaken plans to "rationalize" the steel industry.

The government responded to the demand for import curbs by setting up a system of so-called trigger prices; in effect, minimum prices on imported steel. Imports priced below a government price schedule can trigger an investigation into whether they are being sold below cost in violation of anti-dumping laws and this may lead to the imposition of additional duties.

How did the steel monopolies make use of this measure? Did they try to recapture some of their lost market from the foreign competition? No. They simply took advantage of it to raise their prices. Within weeks after an application of the trigger price system in early 1978, the monopolies had jacked up their prices more than they had the whole previous year. A Merrill Lynch analyst explained the result: "Second quarter profits of the six major steel-makers rose nearly 60 percent on a 0.6 percent gain in shipments despite big growth in imports; without trigger prices, I doubt earnings would have risen at all."[17]

Steel at the Crossroads complains that environmental protection laws "have led to very sizeable capital expenditures." Here is an example of the many types of relief it asks for: "Changes should be made in the Clean Water Act to eliminate the mandatory requirement that all streams must be fishable and swimmable and to eliminate the goal of zero discharge of pollutants."[18]

Actually, the U.S. steel monopolies have been spending too little rather than too much on environmental protection. The Carter steel report presents some interesting facts:

> The Japanese Iron and Steel Federation reports that pollution control expenditures have grown to more than 20 percent of investment in the most recent fiscal year. Pollution control outlays were nearly $600 million in 1976, *more than the U.S. industry spent in the same period* (italics added-E.B.).[19]

The story on occupational health and safety is the same. *Steel at the Crossroads* argues that

> To avoid unnecessary regulation and waste of irrecoverable resources, new and revised standards must reflect a clear need for increased employee protection. OSHA [Occupational Safety and Health Administration] must realize that overall improvement of occupational safety and health in the workplace can only be accomplished through the effective use of scarce resources.[20]

This is just high-sounding jargon to justify allowing the monopolies to continue with practices that cause cancer and accidents among steel workers.

How to "rationalize" the steel industry poses knotty problems for the monopolies. The monopolies can accomplish some "rationalization" at low cost. They can shut down the oldest, least efficient plants and concentrate production in the newer ones. Through modest investments in existing plants, they can often bring about large increases in efficiency.

But true modernization of the steel industry—building new, so-called greenfield plants from scratch or undertaking extensive overhauls of old plants—is in contradiction with the finance capital aim of the steel companies to invest where the return is greatest. To build greenfield plants and to make extensive overhauls would cost large sums of money. When a steel company considers laying out such a sum, it asks: Will this money bring us the maximum return if we put it into steel or will it bring a bigger return if we put it into oil, chemicals, banking, or real estate?

Even before the steel crisis became acute, the monopolies resolved this contradiction by putting large sums into diversification. That's why the steel industry ran down. Still, there was debate within the companies about the desirability of building greenfield plants and some people, like Edgar Speer, former Chairman of U.S. Steel, favored doing so: U.S. Steel proposed to build a multi-billion dollar greenfield plant on Lake Erie in Conneaut, Ohio.

But as the steel crisis got worse, enthusiasm for the Conneaut plant waned. With the retirement of Speer, whose background lay in steel production, and his replacement by David M. Roderick, who rose through the financial end of the business, the plan to build a plant at Conneaut was shelved. There were other uses for the money, such as the acquisition of Marathon Oil. A completely new plant, said Roderick in 1981, "is something for later in the decade," if at all.[21]

Concentrating on diversification, the steel companies have never tried to fight for the creation of a general economic environment in which the steel industry could prosper. They have never fought against the policy of fighting inflation with recessions, which lay the industry low, or against maintaining sky-high interest rates which paralyze the steel-using construction industry. They have never questioned the voracious military budget which sucks money from the economic sectors which require steel.

It goes without saying that the companies don't concern themselves with the problem of steel-worker jobs or the health of steel communities and regions. Their way of meeting the steel crisis is to put their capital into a position to earn the highest possible profits by diversifying, by shutting down plants and allowing the steel industry to shrink, by modernizing some of the remaining plants and equipment to slash labor costs, by destroying the jobs of hundreds of thousands of steel workers.

THE MONOPOLIES USE the steel crisis—the threat of shutdowns and layoffs—to blackmail steel workers into making concessions. However, labor costs are not the cause of the industry's sickness and cutting wages is not the cure.

The monopolies and their mouthpieces put out misleading statistics about steel workers' pay. For example, John M. Starrels writes in the *New York Times* (1-2-83): "Paradoxically . . . while employment was dropping by a disastrous 30 percent between July 1981 and July 1982, hourly employment costs in the American steel industry soared from $19.71 to $24.29." A later *Times* article (1-1-84) tells us that "in November 1982, the total cost, including fringe benefits, of employing a steel worker reached a record $26.29 an hour. . . ." Such statements were part of a campaign to make people, including other workers, believe that steel workers earn $25 an hour. Then the *Times* editorialized (12-30-83): "Taxpayers who average $15 an hour aren't about to underwrite the living standards of $25-an-hour steel workers."

But this is not what steel workers get. These figures are based on American Iron and Steel Institute statistics on "total employment costs per hour" which include not only wages and benefits paid to employed steel workers, but also the benefits of those laid off. When unemployment rises, the cost of benefits to the laid off rises temporarily and is spread over fewer working hours so the total "employment costs" increase. Direct wages and benefits, according to Bureau of Labor Statistics figures, were $12 to $14 an hour.[22]

Labor costs are not, as the monopolies would like us to believe, the industry's biggest cost. They account for little more than a third of total costs plus profits.[23] The figures on "labor costs" include not only workers' pay, but the remuneration of salaried employees and managers (some of whom earn six-figure salaries). Workers' pay accounts for much less than a third of total costs and profits.

Labor costs are not what causes the sharp profits declines that occur periodically in steel. It is the high fixed costs characteristic of a heavy industry, combined with recession-induced declines in output, that have traditionally caused them. These fixed costs, amortization of costly plant and equipment, etc., do not go down even when output declines, and this cuts sharply into profits.

Despite cyclical declines, the U.S. steel monopolies have done well on profits. The American Iron and Steel Institute states the following:[24]

Profitability of the American Steel Industry,
Although Very Low,
Is Higher Than Its Foreign Competitors
(1969-1977)

	Net Income as % of Net Fixed Assets
U.S.A.	6.7
Japan	1.7
West Germany	2.9
United Kingdom	-5.3
France (1972-76)	-8.3

In 1981, the rate of profit in the U.S. steel industry was 13.3 percent, the second highest in twenty-five years.[25]

What about the concessions from workers demanded by the companies? It is right to ask whether jobs might be saved by concessions. But the answer must be thought through carefully. The logic of the situation in steel is that the monopolies will grab the money that comes through concessions and still do what the principles of managing finance capital tell them will get the highest profits—diversify. In fact, by providing the steel monopolies with more money, the concessions may actually help them diversify.

The history of what has followed concessions by steel workers is eloquent. In February, 1983, the United Steel Workers negotiated a contract that accepted a wage cut of $1.25 an hour, a suspension of cost-of-living adjustments (COLA) for six quarters, cuts in vacations, and a reduction in Sunday pay.[26] According to the union, the concessions will save the industry $3 billion over 41 months.

What has been the response? Many companies, including U.S. Steel, have been exploring how to import slab steel and several have begun to do so. U.S. Steel announced the biggest batch of closings yet, idling 15,430 workers. Its Chairman Roderick says the company cannot guarantee that there will be no further closings.

To deal with the sickness in the steel industry, one must get at its causes, and cutting wages doesn't do this. The monopolies make a fuss about the supposedly high pay of U.S. steel workers compared to that of workers in other countries. Here, too, they put forth misleading statistics. They forget, for example, that while health care benefits are included in the remuneration of U.S. workers, in other countries they are not, because the workers are covered by government health care programs.

But the statistics are the least of it. U.S. workers don't have to apologize to the monopolies when their wages are higher than those in other countries. What are they supposed to do? Lower them to the level of Brazil or South Korea to stop the import of slabs? Such a solution is no solution and, besides, couldn't be carried out; other solutions must be found.

The solution of the problems of the peoples of Brazil and South Korea lies not in imperialist-sponsored trade patterns, but in true economic development under democratic, not dictatorial, regimes. The remedies for the sickness in the U.S. steel industry lie in understanding and attacking its true causes.

THE GOVERNMENT DEFENDS broader monopoly interests than just those of the steel companies. Its policies, therefore, differ a little from those of the companies, while fundamentally following the same basic finance capital logic.

The companies have been shameless in their price increases. If they were left completely alone, they would be even more shameless. However, the government cannot allow the steel companies to raise prices without limit. It has to be concerned about the steel-consuming industries, about inflation, about the economy as a whole. So while allowing the companies a free rein most of the time, it occasionally "jawbones" them (exerts pressure) to exercise a minimum of restraint.

Similarly, if the steel companies had the power to do so, they probably would cut out all steel imports except what they themselves choose to bring in. But the government has its whole foreign trade and investment policy to worry about, in particular its efforts to open up Japan more widely to U.S. trade and investment. So it resists strong curbs on steel imports, while using trigger prices or other selective controls to allow the companies to raise prices and profits. It is profits, not import curbs for their own sake, that the companies are really after.

Aside from a few such partial exceptions, government policy runs parallel to that of the monopolies. The government has done nothing to stop plant closings or the transfer of capital by the steel companies to other industries. One Carter administration official went so far as to call steel a "lemon" industry. There is no need, he said, to maintain more steel capacity than is required for defense purposes, so the industry should be left to decline. What about the jobs and communities of the steel workers? The official had an answer. "The transition will be painful. . . ."[27]

The Reagan administration lowered corporate taxes and eased the enforcement of environmental protection regulations, bringing great financial benefits to the steel industry. It was after these measures that U.S. Steel announced its intention to acquire Marathon Oil. What the government benefits to the steel monopolies have been doing is to help them finance their movement into other industries.

THAT THE STEEL PROBLEM can't be fully solved under capitalism is illustrated by the question of modernization. If the industry isn't modernized, it will be unable to meet the foreign competition and will shrink, which means a loss of jobs. If the industry is modernized, the modernization will cost jobs. Either way, workers are left unemployed.

Under socialism, this dilemma doesn't exist. Technological progress can eliminate jobs, and sometimes even plant closings are necessary. But those whose jobs are eliminated do not become unemployed. They get new jobs, along with the necessary reeducation and retraining. This doesn't mean that there are no problems. Sometimes older workers find it difficult to learn new skills. Sometimes workers have to be relocated. But they don't suffer unemployment or loss of income.

Though a full, or even adequate, solution of the steel problem isn't possible under capitalism, many useful things can still be done. The first is to run the economy in such a way as to increase rather than reduce the demand for steel—to stop fighting inflation with recession, to stop choking the construction, auto, and other industries with high interest rates, to slash the military budget and use the money saved to rebuild our cities, build rapid transit systems, and repair and replace our decaying bridges.

Another measure to increase the demand for steel would be to eliminate the restrictions on trade with the Soviet Union and other socialist countries. These countries are tremendous users of steel, especially the Soviet Union, with its intensive oil and gas drilling, and its giant projects for the construction of pipelines, railroads, ports, subways, and factories. U.S. restrictions mean the loss of many tons of possible sales of steel and steel products each year.

The logic of the situation now calls for nationalization of the steel industry. The inherent greed of the monopolies makes nationalization necessary. Unless we have nationalization, we cannot have import curbs without the monopolies taking advantage of the reduction in foreign competition to price gouge; we cannot have fair steel prices without the owners being dissatisfied with their profits and running the industry down to get money for investment elsewhere; we cannot prevent the steel industry from moving abroad in search of lower wages. Nationalization with democratic control is the key to the tangle.

No single measure can solve the steel problem. Running the economy better and eliminating the restrictions on trade with the socialist countries would help, but the steel industry would still be sick. Nationalization should be the main ingredient of action on the steel problem, but even with a nationalized industry, there would be trouble if the economy as a whole were sick or imports were excessive. A program comprising all these forms of action is necessary.

Such a program is worth fighting for, but even it could not solve all aspects of the steel problem so long as capitalism continues to exist. It does not, for example, answer the question of how to modernize the steel industry and still provide jobs, either in the industry or elsewhere, for all its workers. For this, socialism is required.

It is necessary, therefore, to add two additional elements to our steel program. Just like the auto workers, unemployed steel workers should be given jobs, if need be in specially built, government-owned factories. If the government does not provide all the unemployed steel workers with jobs, it should at least be forced to provide them with adequate unemployment benefits for as long as they are unemployed.

12

The Overall Crisis In Industry

There is more to the crisis in our industry than plant closings and permanent layoffs, important though these are. The closings and layoffs are part of a broader process which includes the switching of capital out of several of our basic industries, the erection of U.S. plants abroad, and an increasing dependence on imports for many goods formerly produced here. This process is changing the structure of our industry and economy. We must ask, where is this process leading and what does it mean for our economy?

Back in 1916, Lenin wrote about the connection between finance capital, imperialism, and economic decay:

> Imperialism is an immense accumulation of money capital in a few countries. . . . The export of capital, one of the most essential economic bases of imperialism . . . sets the seal of parasitism on the whole country that lives by exploiting the labor of several overseas countries and colonies.[1]

To illustrate where such parasitism, carried far enough, can lead, Lenin quoted the appraisal, by the English economist, J.A. Hobson, of what the partition of China might bring about:

> The greater part of Western Europe might then assume the appearance and character already exhibited by tracts of country in the South of England, in the Riviera, and in the tourist-ridden or residential parts of Italy and Switzerland, little clusters of wealthy aristocrats drawing dividends and pensions from the Far East, with a somewhat larger group of professional retainers and tradesmen and a larger body of

personal servants and workers in the transport trade and in the final stages of production of the more perishable goods; all the main arterial industries would have disappeared. . . .[2]

Lenin also noted that parasitism "manifests itself, in particular, in the decay of the countries which are richest in capital (Britain)."[3]

When Lenin and Hobson wrote their comments about parasitism and decay, they applied more to Britain than to the United States. Today, they apply with full force to the United States. Here is an excerpt from *U.S. Multinationals—The Dimming of America,* an AFL-CIO report:

[The] great exodus of American production to overseas plants has led economists, labor leaders, and even some farsighted businessmen to wonder whether we are witnessing the dimming of America. This greatest industrial power in the world's history is in danger of becoming nothing more than a nation of hamburger stands . . . a country stripped of industrial capacity and meaningful work . . . a service economy . . . a nation of citizens busily buying and selling cheeseburgers and rootbeer floats.[4]

What has changed since Lenin's day to bring full-scale parasitism and decay to the United States? A number of things. U.S. finance capital and imperialism are much further developed. Before World War I, Britain was the world's leading foreign investor, while foreign investments in the United States exceeded U.S. investments abroad. Today it is the United States that is richest in capital, that has the largest amount of foreign investment. Further, the uneven development of capitalism is working differently with respect to the United States. In Lenin's day, it was the United States that was forging ahead of the other capitalist countries. Today, the other capitalist countries are catching up and in some areas pulling ahead of the United States.

The process of decay is already well advanced here. We have lost a number of industries such as sewing machines, radios and cassettes, and big parts of many others such as shoes, shirts, work clothes, knitgoods, and glassware. The basic auto and steel industries are shrinking.

How far can this process go? To answer, we must consider the logic of the situation. Wages are lower in most countries than in the United States, and will remain so for a long time. In the underdeveloped countries, the abundant labor supply and general economic situation will insure this. But the monopolies can put up many types of industrial plants in these countries that are as modern and efficient as those in the United States, sometimes even more so. What is to prevent them from transferring more and more U.S. manufacturing abroad to take advantage of lower wages?

Historically, it was the technological lead of the United States, its greater productivity and ability to turn out superior products, that protected its manufacturing against excessive imports. But now that the U.S. lead is dwindling, what is to prevent imports from arriving in an ever-mounting flood that will swamp one U.S. industry after another?

For a long time, most U.S. industries faced little import competition and this enabled the monopolies to make colossal profits. As imports have risen in one industry after another, they have tended to reduce the rate of profit to levels the monopolies regard as unsatisfactory because colossal profits can still be made elsewhere. As illustrated by steel, one response of the monopolies is to pull their capital out of the industry. What is to prevent this withdrawal of capital from spreading to more and more industries as the United States becomes increasingly vulnerable to import competition? What is to prevent more and more capital from moving from industry to banking, insurance, real estate, services, etc. which are not as vulnerable to competition from abroad?

Even the theorists of finance capital can't deny the direction in which the U.S. economy is headed. *Newsweek* (5-16-83) asked Professor Robert Reich of Harvard, an expert on industrial policy: "It seems as if we're on an inevitable path toward a service-oriented economy. Will that continue?" The answer was, "Yes."

There is no clear limit to how far the industrial decay can go. It is de-industrializing the United States.

WHAT IS U.S. state monopoly capitalism's answer to the decay? What do those who speak for it say?

In 1980, *Business Week* devoted a special issue (June 6) to "The Reindustrialization of America," in which it laid out in detail the prevailing view and actual policy of finance capital. Here is the way it introduced the subject (p. 1): "A conscious effort to revitalize the U.S. economy is the only alternative to the nation's industrial decline. The necessary steps require nothing short of a new social contract between business, labor, government, and the minorities."

Early in the discussion, *Business Week* gave its underlying philosophy of reindustrialization (p. 56):

> The great danger is that the U.S. political system will translate reindustrialization into some brand of "lemon socialism" whose main focus will be to save the lemons—obsolete jobs and companies that are going bankrupt because they are too inefficient to compete in world markets.... A reindustrialization plan ... requires an industrial policy which chooses which industries, sectors, and product lines should be encouraged because they have a good chance in international competition and which should be abandoned as likely failures.

Among the industries to be "pushed" are aerospace, computers, machinery, machine tools, and energy. On the other hand, "a rational steel program calls for shrinking the industry somewhat through policies that encourage the elimination of the least efficient mills." Other targets for "selective shrinkage" are the apparel and industrial textile industry. "The attempt to compete head-on with the newly industrializing nations is ultimately self-defeating. . . ." (p. 122).

To support competitive industries, said *Business Week*, a number of things are necessary. Labor must get over "the illusion that the pie to be divided [will] never stop expanding. . . ." (p. 82). It must accept "wage restraint," and limitations on cost of living adjustments, medical and pension benefits, and the like. It must learn to collaborate on ways to improve productivity.

Business Week outlined the strategy for getting labor to go along. The government, when offering help to weakened industries, could say: "In exchange for job protection, you give us wage restraint." The corporations themselves can, of course, also use job security as a bargaining weapon. "The ability to guarantee job security appears to be one of the most important trade-offs that management can offer to induce worker cooperation in work-improvement projects" (pp. 100-101).

Workers, according to *Business Week*, are not the only ones whose illusions about the U.S. economy must be dispelled. After World War II, the idea took hold that the U.S. economy was limitless, that it could "support an ever-rising standard of living; create endless jobs; provide education, medical care and housing for everyone; abolish poverty; rebuild the cities; restore the environment; and satisfy the demands of Blacks, Hispanics, women and other groups" (p. 84).

This conviction that the U.S. economy could do everything engendered several other attitudes that "helped undermine growth." One is the notion of entitlement; that people "struggling for more jobs, more federal assistance, and a cleaner environment began to feel that these were rights to which they were entitled." Another was the notion that "society . . . should follow a 'principle of redress' in dealing with disadvantaged citizens." All this "helped spawn an enormous expansion in government programs aimed at correcting inequities" (p. 84).

These attitudes, said *Business Week*, "focus attention and resources on how the economic pie is divided [and] divert attention and resources away from how to make the pie bigger" (p. 84).

To make the pie bigger, *Business Week* proposed:

● Replacing class struggle with collaboration between capital and labor—"a partnership to build the new workplace" (p. 96).

● Recognizing that "the multinationals help rather than hurt" and avoiding any attempt to "rein [them] in . . . to force them to invest more in the U.S." (p. 112).

● Cutting down on regulations to protect health, safety, and the environment (pp. 122-23).

● Making a "determined . . . effort to promote exports" and pushing "an aggressive free trade policy. . . ." (p. 146).

● Understanding "the tonic role of new tax policies" and slashing taxes on the corporations (p. 127).

THE MOUTHPIECES of finance capital also present an additional and simpler argument. We needn't worry about the loss of "smoke-stack" industries. "High tech" industries will replace them.

On April 6, 1983, President Reagan gave a speech in Pittsburgh, while 4,500 steelworkers, mostly unemployed, were demonstrating outside with signs like "17.2% Unemployed In Western Pennsylvania" and "We Want Jobs." Reagan said he was sure high tech will solve the problems of the steelworkers. He goes into a favorite routine—the newspaper want ads. "The fact is that these laid-off steel workers have never had training to understand what these want ads mean . . . let alone apply for the positions." Afterwards, he is taken in his limousine to the Control Data Institute training center where all of seventy-five laid-off steel workers are receiving training in computer installation and repair.[5]

The *New York Times* carried a story (8-10-82) with a happy

ending, headlined "In Technology, Lowell, Mass. Finds New Life."
Here is an excerpt:

> When Theresa Aubut was 16 years old, she left school to go to work in
> a sprawling old red brick textile mill here, just as her father and
> grandfather had before her.
>
> But then the mill closed like almost all the factories that made
> Lowell one of America's first great industrial cities in the early 19th
> century. Lowell fell into apparently terminal decline, its buildings
> abandoned and its people jobless.
>
> But Mrs. Aubut's story and that of Lowell has a surprise ending.
>
> With the rapid growth of high technology industry in Massachu-
> setts over the past two decades, spreading from the laboratories of the
> Massachusetts Institute of Technology and Harvard University in
> Cambridge, Mrs. Aubut has found a new job assembling printed
> circuit boards for computers at Wang Laboratories, Inc. Wang Labs, a
> maker of automated office equipment, set up its headquarters in
> Lowell in 1978. . . .
>
> Lowell's plight and that of Massachusetts, before the advent of the
> high technology companies, was much like that of Detroit today. . . .

Other stories continue the theme.

> New York State's economy is going through a profound transition
> away from the brawn of steel mills, locomotive works, and shipyards
> into the brainy world of biomedical engineering, data processing, and
> microelectronics. . . . "High technology is begetting new companies in
> New York almost daily," said George G. Dempster, Commissioner of
> the State Commerce Department, which is seeking to capitalize on
> the shift to more sophisticated products through its "Made In New
> York" advertising campaign.[6]

THE *Business Week* PROGRAM is designed to further the interests of
finance capital, not to solve the problems of the people and
economy of the United States. The stories glorifying the high tech
industries are propaganda.

Finance capital, to serve its own narrow interests, milks such
industries as steel or sewing machines to obtain funds to invest in
banking, oil, aerospace, or overseas. *Business Week* elevates this
self-serving action into a general principle of how to reorganize the
whole economy—abandon the "lemons." Abandoning the
"lemons" means singlemindedly chasing the very highest profits
and disregarding what happens to the economy.

By what criteria, other than that it doesn't yield profits as outlandish as oil, is steel a lemon industry? Why is steel a good industry for Japan which is deficient in iron ore and coking coal, while it is a lemon industry for the United States which has a large supply of ore and the richest coal deposits in the world?

It's easy for a glib *Business Week* writer to dismiss the apparel industry as an "economic absurdity" that should be shrunk. But this industry employed 1.2 million people in 1981, over three-fourths of them women, over 18 percent "Black and other,"[7]* plus many Hispanic workers. Where would the workers who lost their jobs in a shrinkage go?

The defender of the finance capital line might ask: Haven't you forgotten about high tech and other growing industries? They will replace the jobs lost in our shrinking industries. Isn't that the way capitalism has always operated?

This argument is nothing more than a currently fashionable version of the old fairy tale that the market will automatically produce a happy ending to all our troubles.

First, how has capitalism operated? It has mercilessly thrown workers out of their jobs and often left them unemployed for years. Second, with the continuing development of finance capital, foreign investment, and parasitism, we are facing a new and still developing phenomenon. Never before have we had shrinkage and decay on the scale we are now experiencing. What we are facing cannot be understood with the mushy generality that some industries die while others grow and that's the way of the world. We must examine our economic situation concretely.

The United States has astronomical unemployment among Afro-American, Chicano, Puerto Rican and other minority youth; permanent depression-level unemployment among adult Black and other minority workers; heavy hidden unemployment among women and white youth; and an outrageously high level of plain, general unemployment. Our economy has proved itself incapable of generating all the jobs our people need. We can't afford to let industries shrink.

Even if the new industries did create enough jobs to absorb all the unemployed, which they will not come close to doing, this would not automatically solve the problems of those laid off in the older industries. Workers can't switch from one job to another as easily

---

*"Black and other" is a government statistical term. "Other" includes "American Indians, Alaskan Natives, and Asians and Pacific Islanders."

as—in Milton Friedman's textbook conception—"resources" flow around the economy. They lack the education and training required for the new job, or they are too old, or they are located in the wrong place, or racial or sex discrimination keeps them out. Unemployed apparel workers can't easily move into the technically-oriented aerospace industry which *Business Week* wants to promote. The coming of high tech to Lowell makes a nice story, but it doesn't provide jobs to unemployed steel workers in Buffalo or auto workers in Detroit and Flint.

There is also a problem of pay. Workers from such older industries as auto, steel, tires, locomotives, shipbuilding, etc. would face big pay cuts in high tech. The hype on high tech tries to give it glamor, the "brainy world" of microelectronics as opposed to the mere "brawn" of steel mills. The implication is that we will all be better off by the movement of our industry into the allegedly brainy world. But leaving aside the prejudice that sees only brawn in steel mill jobs, how do wages in the older and the high tech industries compare? Richard Gahey, an economist at the Urban Research Center at New York University, writes:

> Dazzling high tech factories are designed by highly paid professionals but are staffed by low-skilled, low-paid workers. Computer assemblers earn about 70 percent of the hourly wage of auto workers. . . . And unlike older unionized manufacturing industries with their promotion ladders, on-the-job training programs and collective bargaining agreements, the new industries do not offer much promise of upward mobility. . . .
>
> High tech industries produce polarized pay scales and working conditions—well-paid, securely employed professionals at one pole and low-paid workers in episodic labor-intensive jobs at the other.[8]

Now for the crucial question: How many jobs will high tech create? *Business Week* has looked into the question. It based its discussion on a Bureau of Labor Statistics definition of what constitutes high tech. Industries qualify for this designation when their Research and Development expenditures and the number of their technical employees run twice as high as the average for all U.S. manufacturing. The makers of drugs, computers, and electronic components, as well as such service industries as computer programing, data processing, and research laboratories are high tech. The BLS also has a second category of industries which it defines as "high tech intensive," in which expenditures and technical employment run simply above the average. This category includes such industries as chemicals and petroleum refining.

Here is what *Business Week* found (3-28-83, p. 85):

> Even when the broader BLS definitions are used, the number of jobs that will be created in high tech industries in the next 10 years is disappointing. Forecasts made by the BLS and for *Business Week* by Data Resources Inc., in fact, show that the number of high tech jobs created over the next decade will be less than half of the 2 million jobs lost in manufacturing in the past three years. . . . While high tech industries . . . will generate 10 times the number of jobs expected from the rest of industry, it will still amount to only 730,000 to 1 million jobs.

No matter how rapidly high tech grows, it will create relatively few jobs because the growth is from a small base. The high tech industries employed 3 million workers in 1979, less than 15 percent of those employed in manufacturing as a whole, while eighty-five percent were employed in the non-glamor industries such as steel, autos, textiles and apparel, rubber products, etc. If the non-glamor industries are allowed to decline, high tech can't make up the difference.

Out of the total nonagricultural work force of nearly 100 million in 1979, high tech employed only 3 percent. By the 1990s, this figure might rise to 4 percent. Even in regions with a heavy concentration of high tech, the figure would not be much higher. The *New York Times* reported (2-27-83): "A study by the State of California estimated that even though employment in the state's high technology industry would grow almost twice as fast as overall employment, by 1990 high technology would account for only one of every 14 jobs in the state [7 percent]."

Finally, the same phenomena that have been causing problems in the older industries are also happening in high tech. The high tech industries are automating. They are moving abroad. And they are increasingly feeling the heat of foreign competition.

The low-skill nature of many high tech jobs makes them vulnerable to automation. *Business Week* reported (3-28-83, p. 86) that many companies are using the very products they make to replace labor in their plants. "Hewlett-Packard Co., for one, estimates that several thousand of its computers are now being used throughout the company."

In February 1983, Atari Inc. announced that it was shifting the bulk of its manufacturing (the production of home computers and video games) from California to Hong Kong and Taiwan, eliminating 1,700 U.S. jobs.[9] Many Massachusetts-based high tech companies, including Wang, the hero of the *New York Times* story on Lowell, have established plants in Ireland.[10] Hewlett-Packard has predicted that its overseas work force will grow faster than that in the United States.[11]

The challenge to U.S. high tech industry from abroad is already characterized as "strong" by the Department of Commerce. Inevitably, it will grow still stronger. Not only has Japan been gaining ground, but new countries are entering the fray.

"Taiwan Developing High Technology," said a *New York Times* headline (9-7-82). To move its economy into high tech, such as computers and semi-conductors, Taiwan has set up a big industrial park. The park is near two of Taiwan's best science and engineering schools. It "has all the ingredients of Silicon Valley 20 years ago," said its director, who holds a doctoral degree from Stanford University. Several U.S. companies, including Wang Laboratories and Control Data Corporation, have set up operations in the park.

The *Times* article points out that Taiwan is being pushed into high tech because the older industries are no longer able to sustain its growth. "The same challenge," the article says, "is now confronting eastern Asia's three other industrializing economies—those of South Korea, Singapore, and Hong Kong."

Advanced technology does not provide more than temporary sanctuary from the forces now operating in the capitalist world market. With time, decline and decay will spread from the older industries to the newer ones.

THE *Business Week*-FINANCE CAPITAL industrial policy means not only the destruction of millions of U.S. jobs, but also a systematic reduction in U.S. wages. Again, we must look at the logic of the situation. The key finance capital test of whether an industry is worthy of surviving is its "competitiveness." Industries must be able to compete, to "make it" against industries abroad without benefit of tariff or other "artificial" government protection. But what does it mean for U.S. industries to be in ever-increasing competition with foreign industries, precisely at a time when the U.S. technological lead is disappearing? It means not only the shrinkage and disappearance of U.S. industries, but also steady downward pressure on U.S. wage rates.

In the struggle over wages, the monopolies can use foreign competition as an argument and a weapon. Workers are told they must restrain their wage demands, must even agree to givebacks, or the company will not be able to compete and there will be layoffs or even worse—the whole company may go under.

Business Week presents the monopoly strategy in a subtle, well-thought-out form. When it says that "the ability to guarantee job security appears to be one of the most important trade-offs management can offer," it doesn't really mean that. The monopolies don't guarantee job security. What it really means is that the ability to threaten job loss is one of the monopolies' strongest weapons.

Business Week proposes to use the threat of foreign competition and declining industries to obtain "the new social contract" it says is necessary. "Increasing numbers of labor and business leaders and workers—especially in declining industries such as steel, autos, and electrical equipment—are beginning to recognize that the survival of their institutions and jobs is threatened."[12] *Business Week* wants to use the threat to survival to force workers to collaborate with the monopolies in the solution of "mutual problems." It wants the "class struggle notion" to give way to a "collaborative relationship." It neglects to mention that what it wants are concessions from the workers.

It would be a mistake to underestimate the effectiveness of the weapon that unchecked foreign competition provides for the monopolies. The monopolies often exaggerate the competitive threat and hide what they themselves could do to meet it by lowering prices or investing more in modernization. But after allowing for this, the fact remains that foreign competition can threaten companies with a big decline in business and even bankruptcy. Since this does threaten jobs, it provides the monopolies with a strong weapon; one they are using with increasing effectiveness to exert pressure on wage rates.

WHEN *Business Week* PRESENTS the idea that the U.S. economy is not "limitless," it is talking "objective" economics, but defending finance capital interests. Because the economy is not limitless, it says, workers, minorities, women, the poor, and others struggling for jobs, education, medical care, the abolition of poverty, and a clean environment must recognize that these are not rights to which they are entitled.

But who is really guilty of forgetting that the U.S. economy is not limitless? It is U.S. state monopoly capitalism, with its sky-high military expenditures.

It doesn't take a limitless economy to meet the demands of our people. They are reasonable, one could even say modest, demands. Creating jobs for the unemployed doesn't weaken the economy, but strengthens it. Good education is essential for the economy; it is absurd to talk of the wonders high tech will perform, while maintaining a miserable educational system. Our economy is rich enough to afford adequate medical care; many poorer countries have better health care systems. The cost of good environmental protection is only a fraction of what now goes to the military, but the monopolies see this cost as cutting into their profits, and they are infinitely greedy.

But it does take a limitless economy to meet the demands of the military budget because they have been made limitless. Carter and Reagan undertook a big arms buildup to attain military superiority over the Soviet Union. They thought they could be sure of achieving this aim because the United States is richer and could therefore spend more. The logic of such a policy is to squeeze out as much as can be gotten away with for the military. Whenever the government thinks it can get away with more, it squeezes more.

MILITARY EXPENDITURES aren't even mentioned by *Business Week*. But the swollen military budget has been a key cause of the decline of U.S. competitiveness. Historically, the movement of military expenditures helps explain both the emergence of a U.S. economic lead and the later cutting down of that lead.

For decades, beginning in the final quarter of the last century, the United States bore a far smaller burden of military expenditures than the leading imperialist countries of Europe. While the European powers were pouring resources into preparations for World War I, the United States was investing them in economic growth. But after World War II, the situation reversed. Now it was the United States that had the largest military rathole.

It is no accident that two of the countries with the highest postwar rates of economic growth have been Japan and West Germany. For years after World War II, restrictions on the rearming of these countries left them with little or no military expenditures. Even after they began to rearm, their per capita military burdens remained tiny compared to that of the United States.

In 1979, Japan's per capita military expenditure equaled 16 percent that of the United States.[13] Would Japan have been able to outstrip the United States in growth if the per capita military burdens had been reversed? The answer is no.

The enormous, parasitic U.S. military budget eats at the sources of growth in productivity. It gobbles up resources that could be going into investment. It pre-empts resources for military Research and Development (R&D) that could be going into civilian R&D.

Many observers have noted the low rate of investment in the United States. Here is what C. Jackson Grayson, Jr., chairman of the American Productivity Center, found:

> During the quarter century after World War II, roughly one third of Japan's growing national product flowed directly into new machinery and equipment in its factories. For [West] Germany, France, and Italy, fixed capital investment ranged from one fifth to one fourth their GNP during the same period. In sharp contrast, U.S. industrial investment was dead last among all major industrial nations, with a capital to GNP ratio only half that of Japan.[14]

The Machinists' study of *The Costs and Consequences of the Reagan Military Buildup* compared the ratio of fixed capital investment to gross domestic product for thirteen capitalist industrial nations: "The United States investment level ranks *last*. . . ."[15]

The study found that "Military spending negatively correlates with fixed investment as a share of [GNP] in our comparison. . . ." In other words, the higher the military spending, the lower the level of investment.

The United States has also fallen behind in the effort to promote the advance of knowledge, another key factor in the growth of productivity. West Germany and Japan now lead the United States in the percentage of gross national product devoted to civilian Research and Development, and in some recent years, France and Britain have also been ahead.[16]

Here, too, the parasitic military budget eats up resources. Since 1955, military and space R&D has accounted for 30 to 57 percent of total U.S. R&D expenditures.[17] The percentage is far smaller for

West Germany while Japan, until recently, spent virtually nothing on military and space R&D.

While other countries have been concentrating on the development of better civilian products and more efficient ways of producing them, the United States has been devoting an enormous effort to the creation of ever more advanced weapons of mass destruction. The results are inevitable. One example: While U.S. military electronics leads the world, Japan has been catching up and moving ahead of the United States in the international markets for civilian electronic products.

As with the total military budget, the problem is more than just a waste of resources for a few years; it is the cumulative damage caused by a military hogging of R&D prolonged over decades. Between 1955 and 1982, the United States spent over $300 billion on military and space R&D. If this sum had been added to civilian R&D expenditures, they would have been 80 percent larger than they actually were. Think what might have been discovered and developed with an additional $300 billion!

U.S. INDUSTRIAL DECAY goes hand in hand with a weakening of the U.S. balance of trade and payments.

The gigantic economy established abroad in the form of a network of affiliates not only weakens U.S. industry, but reduces exports and increases imports. Computers provide an example of potential exports lost to foreign affiliates. "Over two thirds of all computers that have been installed in Europe originated with American-owned firms," according to a 1981 report of the Office of Technology Assessment. But originating with American-owned firms doesn't always mean U.S. exports. "In addition to exports from the United States, American computer manufacturers have large sales through foreign subsidiaries."[18]

Then there is the flood of goods produced by the U.S. affiliates abroad and imported into the United States: sewing machines, TVs, radios, cassettes, calculators, cameras, watches, glassware, typewriters, knit goods, shirts, work clothes, men's suits, shoes, office equipment, auto parts, automobiles, etc.

U.S. trade policy, the insistence on a high degree of free trade despite the decline in the U.S. technological lead, also results in a large flow of imports into the United States. As different U.S.

industries have lost their lead in technology and productivity, imports from their foreign competitors have increased.

A few figures illustrate the connection between the decay in U.S. industry and the worsening of the balance of trade: In 1981, the United States ran a balance of trade deficit of $32 billion. Among its imports were: autos, buses, trucks, and parts—$26 billion; iron and steel—$11 billion; telecommunications apparatus—$9 billion; clothing—$8 billion; footwear—$3 billion. Imports of just these few categories totalled $57 billion. Exports of these same items totalled $25 billion, so that the trade deficit for them equalled $32 billion, the same as the overall trade deficit. In 1960, exports of these items exceeded imports, which then totalled only $2 billion.[19]

If the United States were not suffering from industrial decay, it would not have a trade deficit. And if the industrial decay gets worse, the deficit will get still bigger.

THE STATEMENT BY *Business Week* that "the U.S. should push an aggressive free trade policy" expresses the view held by most representatives of U.S. monopoly capitalism, except when their own industries are being hurt by imports. Many others have swallowed the free trade line and also act as though any demand for protection against imports is immoral. Don't our economic textbooks teach us that if each country specializes in the goods in which it has a "comparative advantage" a rational international division of labor will result and all countries will benefit?

The talk about "comparative advantage" and a "rational international division of labor" is textbook prattle which doesn't have anything to do with the real world. In the real world, the kind of international division of labor we get depends on which class is organizing it. What we get in the capitalist world is not the rational division of labor depicted in the never-never land of the textbooks, but a division of labor set up by finance capital in its own interest.

This division of labor operates not only through trade, but investment; foreign investment is a crucial element of the system. When *Business Week* propagandizes for "free trade," it is working not only to promote the "free movement of goods," but also (and even more), the penetration of other countries by U.S. capital.

"Free trade" involves losses for some parts of U.S. finance capital; for example, the auto and steel industries. Yet U.S. finance capital's basic line is to defend "free trade." Why? Because the value of a good part of U.S. foreign investment is tied to the ability to ship the goods produced from such investment back to the United States. Because the whole system of foreign investment, yielding U.S. finance capital enormous profits, is tied to a so-called open international economy.

The assertion that the "open trade and investment system" makes for an efficient division of labor is hogwash. What is efficient about closing down an auto parts factory in Michigan and importing the parts from faraway Mexico just because the workers there can be exploited even more than they are here? It has nothing to do with efficiency, just higher profits. What the monopoly-dominated "open" international economy produces is not an efficient but an imperialist division of labor.

This economy enables the U.S., European, and Japanese monopolies to exploit the raw materials, markets, and labor force of the underdeveloped countries to their own advantage. While the monopolies may create a few jobs in these countries, their stranglehold constitutes the chief cause of underdevelopment.

Moreover, the system is one of only partially free trade. U.S. finance capital manages the system selectively. It pushes toward free trade when it is profitable or necessary to get concessions from other countries. But it also maintains countless protectionist "exceptions," using not only tariffs, but also subtle, indirect barriers including complex administrative procedures, health and technical standards, etc.

While U.S. finance capital benefits from the system, the underdeveloped countries and the U.S. working class do not. The underdeveloped countries, for all the vaunted "free trade," get only the amount and type of access to the U.S. market that U.S. finance capital chooses to give them, not what they need. U.S. working people get an aggravation of unemployment.

The trade problem of the underdeveloped countries, one of the most important in the world economy, is knotty. These countries must be given access to the U.S. market, yet without aggravating unemployment here or further deforming the U.S. economy. To do this requires comprehensive planning by both the underdeveloped countries and the United States.

International working class solidarity is highly important. Workers should not fall for chauvinist campaigns against workers of other countries. These only divert them from a true understanding of their problems and the united struggles necessary to solve them.

But true solidarity does not mean going along with finance capital's rules of trade and investment which bring workers unemployment, help the monopolies beat down their wages, and offer the underdeveloped countries not salvation but entrapment. Solidarity cannot be interpreted to mean that U.S. workers must sit idly by as thousands of U.S. factories move abroad and ship their products back to the United States. It cannot mean that U.S. workers must never fight for import curbs regardless of the number of jobs at stake.

It was the big technological lead of the United States that enabled it to become the world's greatest promoter of "free trade," just as Britain's lead enabled it to occupy a similar position earlier. But with modern technology spreading rapidly, joined in most countries to wages lower than in the United States, "free trade" will inflict ever-greater damage on the U.S. economy.

WHERE IS THE U.S. industrial crisis leading? It is leading toward high structural, long-run unemployment among industrial workers, toward the decay of many formerly leading industrial areas, toward making our economy excessively dependent on foreign trade. It is leading toward a lopsided economy in which it will be difficult to provide all the jobs our people need and to deal with the balance of trade and payments problems.

To fully solve the overall crisis in U.S. industry is even less possible than to fully solve the problems of the auto or steel industry. A full solution would require comprehensive planning guided by the needs of society; and greedy, anarchic capitalism isn't capable of such planning. But even under capitalism, programs that are worth fighting for can be developed and won.

Healthy industry cannot exist in an economy operating at a low level of capacity. The precondition for effective action to ease the crisis in industry is a government policy aimed at maintaining a high level of economic activity, a policy which fights the inflation by slashing the parasitic military budget, not by deliberately intensifying recession.

The curbing of foreign investment is a fundamental requirement for an effective attack on the industry crisis. The AFL-CIO has talked about the problem. In a 1971 study of foreign trade policy, it recommended that the President be given authority to supervise and curb the outflow of U.S. capital. . . . Authority within the President's hands should include consideration for the kind of investment that would be made abroad, the product involved, the country where the investment would be made, the linkage of the investment to the flow of trade and its effect on U.S. employment and the national economy.[20]

Given what has been happening since this report appeared—the epidemic rise in plant closings, the plans of such industries as auto to move abroad in a big way—the time has come to mount a vigorous campaign to back up the demand that foreign investment be curbed.

The abandonment of the "free trade" system is another requirement. No matter what else is done to meet the crisis, imports can still often make too much trouble to allow them to be managed according to finance capital's rules of the game.

But what about the argument that moves toward import curbs will set off a trade war? The argument about trade war is glibly used—one would almost think that every import restriction will set off such a war. Actually, there is a long stretch between import regulation and trade war. Take the case of restrictions on auto and steel imports from Japan. Japan has such an enormous trade surplus with the United States that even severe import curbs would only reduce, not eliminate it. What interest would Japan have, with its continuing surplus, in starting a trade war against the United States? Speaking more generally: The United States has been the world's most aggressive promoter of trade liberalization since World War II. It has a lot of room to step back.

The most fundamental requirement for an attack on the industry crisis is the nationalization of industries in trouble. What would nationalization do? It would at one swoop take care of a number of specific problems. Decisions about plants closings, investment, prices, etc. could be made according to what is best for the people rather than what is best for monopoly profits. No longer would plants be closed down here so they could be set up abroad. No longer would an industry be run down because its owners wanted to extract capital to invest for higher profits elsewhere. No longer would an industry given import protection gouge us with exorbitant prices. There would still be problems, but far fewer, because one big source of difficulties would be gone.

The monopolies howl at the threat of nationalization. The government can't run anything well, according to their propaganda. The answer to this is simple: Look who's talking. If the monopolies run things so well, how come industry is in such a crisis? Representatives of the public, the workers, and the government could run the nationalized industries. They couldn't run them as badly as the monopolies have done.

A final note: The crisis in industry basically stems from the imperialist system and one manifestation of this system is U.S. support of dictatorships in many countries such as El Salvador, Guatemala, Haiti, South Korea, Taiwan, etc. These countries outlaw or severely curb unions and keep wages super low; then, on the basis of the super low wages, they attract plants out of the United States and export cheap goods back to it. The U.S. support of dictatorships is not only vicious in itself, but costs U.S. workers dearly in reduced wages and lost jobs. As Marx once noted, a people that lends itself to the oppression of another is forging its own chains. An effective attack on the industry crisis requires a struggle by workers and all other Americans who believe in democracy to end U.S. support of repressive, often murderously fascist regimes.

PART V

ONE RESULT OF THE CRISIS—DECAY

13

Decaying Cities

Most U.S. cities in the Northeast and Middle West and many others are suffering from decay. They have become concentration points for many of our society's most virulent ills: unemployment, poverty, racism, slum housing.

The roots of the urban crisis lie deep in capitalism, especially its present monopoly stage. Cities reflect the society of which they are a part. Under capitalism, they reflect class division and racism; they have rich neighborhoods, poor neighborhoods, ghettos. They also reflect capitalist anarchy. For a city to work well, many things have to mesh—its economy, finances, population, housing, transportation system, etc. Anarchic monopoly capitalism cannot produce the necessary meshing.

The development of giant corporations subjects cities to anarchic forces more powerful than ever. The fate of cities lies in the hands of a small number of companies which form part of an international finance capital network. The decisions of a few companies to transfer operations to another part of the network can doom a city by destroying its economic base.

THE WRITINGS OF Marx and Engels show vividly how capitalist cities, from the beginning, have reflected the ills of capitalism. Engels wrote in *The Condition of the Working Class in England*, published in 1845:

Every great city has one or more slums, where the working class is crowded together.... The houses are occupied from cellar to garret, filthy within and without, and their appearance is such that no human being could possibly wish to live in them. But all this is nothing in comparison with the dwellings in the narrow courts and alleys between the streets. . . . Scarcely a whole window pane can be found. . . . Heaps of garbage and ashes lie in all directions. . . . Here live the poorest of the poor . . . the majority Irish, or of Irish extraction. . . .[1]

Analyzing the position of the Irish, Engels made a point basic to the understanding of cities under capitalism: the need of the capitalists for a reserve army of labor.

The rapid extension of English industry could not have taken place if England had not possessed in the numerous and impoverished population of Ireland a reserve at command. . . . There are in London, 120,000; in Manchester, 40,000; in Liverpool, 34,000; Bristol, 24,000 . . . poor Irish people.[2]

Then, as now, unemployment plagued the working class. During the economic crisis of 1842, "the starving workmen, whose mills were idle . . . besieged the sidewalks in armies. . . ." Millions of people had to apply for relief under the Poor Laws.[3]

Marx in *Capital* carried the analysis further. Capitalism was producing great cities:

Except London, there was at the beginning of the 19th century no single town in England of 100,000 inhabitants. Only five had more than 50,000. Now there are 28 towns with more than 50,000 inhabitants.[4]

Capitalism, by bringing about an agricultural revolution and the use of machinery, was driving people off the land:

As soon as capitalist production takes possession of agriculture . . . the demand for an agricultural laboring population falls absolutely. . . . Part of the agricultural population is therefore constantly on the point of passing over into an urban or manufacturing proletariat. . . .[5]

The accumulation of capital in the industrial and commercial towns was drawing a "stream of exploitable human material" to them.[6]

THE FLOW OF immigrants from abroad into cities was repeated on a vast scale in the United States. Between 1860 and 1914, 27 million immigrants poured in—waves of British, Irish, Germans, and Scandinavians and later, Italians, Jews, and Slavs.

Except for a small proportion who settled on the land, these immigrants, mostly from rural or semi-rural backgrounds, were packed into ghetto slums and relegated to the lowest-paying, most unattractive jobs. Around them they found prejudice.

Yet for all the misery, there were also favorable circumstances. Cities were growing, their industry and commerce expanding, their populations increasing. In good times, they were able to provide jobs for the immigrants. The economy then wasn't nearly as much in the grip of monopoly as later; there was far greater room to open a small business, and some immigrants did. The children of the immigrants were usually able to improve their economic situation over that of their parents.

The cities were not in a state of long-term stagnation. They had problems, but they were moving with, not behind, the economy as a whole.

LARGE-SCALE MIGRATION into U.S. cities continued during and after World War I, but now it mainly consisted of Afro-Americans, Mexicans and Chicanos, and Puerto Ricans.

In 1910, 90 percent of the Afro-American people lived in the South, most in rural areas. In all, 6.5 million Afro-Americans migrated between 1910 and 1970. By the latter year, almost half the Black population lived outside the South, most in cities of the Northeast and Midwest.[7]

Between 1910 and 1979, over two million Mexicans migrated to the United States, according to the official statistics; an unknown, but large, additional number came without documentation.[8] Over 600,000 Puerto Ricans migrated here between 1950 and 1970.[9]

The racism which met these new migrants to the cities was incomparably more ferocious than the discrimination that the earlier ones had to contend with. The job discrimination against them was far more fierce. They were locked into much more rigidly segregated ghettos and barrios.

The landlords carried their greed and viciousness to new extremes. They fomented, spread, and exploited racism. They divided the housing market—one part for whites, others for Black and Hispanic people. Blocking the access of the minorities to an open choice of housing helps the landlords gouge, so that housing in the ghettos and barrios commands higher rents than comparable housing outside them.

The new ghettos are not only more segregated than the earlier ones but more durable. This applies especially to the Black ghettos. Instead of showing signs of breaking up with time as the earlier ones did, Black ghettos have been expanding.[10]

THE BASIC FACTOR in the crisis of the cities is the flight of industry to the suburbs, the South, and abroad. A movement of people and commerce from city to suburb has also contributed.

Just driving around the United States gives an idea of the extent of the industrial flight. The areas surrounding our cities are dotted with the one-story factory buildings adapted to automated operations. Before World War II, the development of automation, and the spread of auto and truck transport, most of these factories would have been located in cities.

The movement of people from city to suburb has also been massive. The auto made this movement possible, but doesn't explain its magnitude. The government promoted the movement. It subsidized private home ownership by providing government-supported mortgage credit and by allowing income tax deductions for home mortgage interest payments. It subsidized highway construction.

Many cities have grown smaller. Of the twenty-four largest cities, fourteen—including New York, Chicago, Philadelphia, Detroit, Baltimore, Cleveland, Milwaukee, and San Francisco—declined in population between 1960 and 1973.[11]

Employment has declined in many cities while in the surrounding suburbs it has risen. One analyst comments that to appreciate the size of the shift from city to suburb, "it is important to look at individual [cases]. . . . Between 1960 and 1970, Detroit lost nearly 20 percent of its jobs (roughly 2.1 percent per annum), while the number of jobs in the surrounding area grew by an average of 4.7 percent. . . . St. Louis, Cleveland, Buffalo, Chicago, New York, and Newark are among the cities that had a similar experience."[12]

Not only has the number of jobs in most large cities declined, but their nature is changing. New York is an example. "The New York City economy is growing to be more white-collar and professionally oriented than ever," said the regional commissioner of Labor Statistics in a 1982 report. While jobs in knitting mills, clothing factories, and department stores declined, those in research, consulting, legal services, and data processing increased. The Commissioner expected that seven out of ten job openings in the years ahead would be white collar, with 30 percent in the professional, technical, managerial, and administrative groupings.[13]

Racism helps lock the minorities into unemployment in the stagnant cities. While employment opportunities were declining in New York City, they were growing in surrounding Long Island and Westchester County, but no cheap mass transport system to the suburban areas exists. And the construction of low income apartment housing in these areas is restricted by racist zoning regulations.

STAGNATION, UNEMPLOYMENT, and poverty, coupled with racism, create a setting favorable to a process of general decay.

Housing abandonment is now a widespread disease, scarring numerous cities. A study put out several years ago estimated that there were 150,000 abandoned units in New York City.[14]

What causes the spread of abandonment? The poverty which afflicts a large proportion of city people limits the amount of money that even the most rapacious landlords can squeeze out of them. So the landlords turn to making their money by cutting down services and maintenance. The banks, noticing that buildings are becoming decrepit, "redline" the whole area—make it ineligible for mortgage loans. Buildings ineligible for mortgage loans cannot be sold. The possibility of sale is a main reason for holding a building— a high proportion of landlord gains comes from the resale of buildings at higher prices. With this possibility eliminated, the landlord switches to an alternative, ceasing to turn in property taxes and perhaps also mortgage payments; this multiplies profits quickly. When the city or bank gets after the landlord, he abandons.

Most arson today is part of the same phenomenon as abandonment. The *New York Times* interviewed Robert May of the International Association of Arson Investigators after members of an arson ring were arrested in Boston. Mr. May

> feels that the Boston situation could be duplicated in virtually every city in the country. [He] gave what he said was a common scenario of arson for profit, starting with the acquisition at "distress prices" of property in inner city neighborhoods. The landlords, he said, "do little in the way of maintenance and frequently blame the tenants." The property continues to deteriorate, he said, and then come the first fires which cause the tenants to vacate the property. . . . Finally, the

authorities order the building condemned as uninhabitable, and the landlord collects his insurance.[15]

THE FISCAL CRISIS of the cities stems from several factors—the corrupt way they are run, their general decline, the condition of the U.S. economy as a whole, and the system of public finance through which the federal government skims the cream of the county's tax potential and then pours the money into the military budget.

U.S. cities have always been the object of wholesale looting by businessmen and politicians. The banks have a juicy business in municipal bonds: for example, they buy a bond issue for $295 million and then in one day sell it for $300 million, realizing a quick, cool, $5 million profit.[16] Giant real estate operators make campaign contributions to city politicians, and the tax assessments on their properties are reduced. Those who sell to cities pad their costs, construction companies inflate their expenses. Billions of dollars in legal fees, insurance premiums, public relations retainers, etc. go to companies to which city officials are connected. Countless political hacks receive cushy city jobs.

The flight of industry and the movement of higher income people to the suburbs has reduced the cities' tax base. At the same time, the problems stemming from unemployment, poverty, and decay have caused their need for funds to balloon.

The overall condition of the U.S. economy has been hurting the cities financially. The inflation has been biting into a main source of revenue—property taxes; it is hard to keep property assessments for tax purposes rising as fast as inflation. The series of frequent and severe recessions that started in the early 1970s has done great damage, especially to cities which, like New York, depend on a sales tax.

Still, the cities would be able to help themselves more and get more help from the states, if it were not for the huge proportion of taxes preempted by the federal government. And the federal government would be able to undertake a large-scale effort to help the cities were it not for the voracious military budget.

The very system of public finance—the way finances are divided between cities, states, and federal government—is being used as a device to channel money to the military while starving the cities. While grabbing off the bulk of the country's tax revenues, the federal government leaves responsibility for dealing with social problems and for maintaining highways, bridges, and other items of infrastructure with the states and cities. The shortage of funds in which the states and cities are kept acts as a check on their expenditures. Demands that they do more meet with the argument that there is no money. But there *is* money. It is just flowing elsewhere because of the way public finances are arranged.

THE URBAN FISCAL CRISIS is widespread. New York, with its virtual bankruptcy, and Cleveland, with its default, are the most widely known examples. But Chicago, Philadelphia, Detroit, Boston, St. Louis, Yonkers, and other cities have also suffered financial crunches. A survey of 594 cities by the Joint Economic Committee of Congress found that over 50 percent reported deficits in 1979 and 1980.[17]

The consequences of the cities' financial troubles have been several: wage cuts and layoffs for municipal employees, reductions of municipal services, and long-term damage to the cities' infrastructure due to failure to maintain and replace it properly.

The Joint Economic Committee survey tells what happened to wages. "While wage and salary increases in other size cities were frequently below the rate of inflation, in the largest cities they didn't even approach it." Large layoffs accompanied the pay cuts. From 1979 to 1980, 400,000 out of a total workforce of 14 million in the largest cities (2.9 percent) lost their jobs.[18]

The layoffs meant slashes in municipal services. The authorities cut police protection, shut down fire stations, clinics, hospitals, and day care centers; reduced school staffs, decreased the frequency of garbage collection and street cleaning, and slashed park services and library hours.

The neglect of infrastructure is an insidious consequence of the cities' fiscal crisis, one which is piling up damage and problems for the future. Deferring expenditures on infrastructure is a painless way of meeting financial stringency and easier to get away with politically than raising taxes or laying off employees and cutting services. If you put off painting a bridge or replacing a decrepit water line, the bridge won't collapse and the water line won't burst immediately. By the time these things happen, other politicians will be in charge.

"The deterioration of the capital plant in many cities has reached a critical stage," said another Joint Economic Committee report.

"Capital expenditures, therefore, may be deferred in the future, only at the risk of physical collapse."[19]

IN 1975, NEW YORK CITY's finances collapsed. But the New York crisis is more than the fiscal crisis to which the banks and the government paid the most attention. The fiscal crisis was simply one expression of the more general crisis.

Manufacturing industry has been leaving New York for a long time. In 1948, employment in apparel—the city's largest manufacturing industry—stood at a peak of 350,000 workers. By the time the fiscal crisis erupted, this industry had lost 200,000 jobs. Employment in printing and publishing—the second largest manufacturing employer—was down 40,000 from its peak.[20]

Until 1969, growth in private nonmanufacturing employment helped counteract the effects of the decline in manufacturing. Then this employment also began to decline. Many company headquarters left the city. In 1956, 140 of *Fortune*'s 500 largest industrial corporations were headquartered in New York. By 1976, the number had shrunk to 84.[21]

Automation also cut down jobs. Computerization reduced the demand for clerical personnel in brokerage houses and banks. Containerization eliminated thousands of port jobs.

A report by the Congressional Budget Office states that "New York's immediate [1975] crisis has been precipitated by its inability to borrow in the municipal bond market."[22] This seemingly factual statement is a subtle lie. The crisis was not precipitated by the ordinary workings of that anonymous entity, "the municipal bond market." It was precipitated, as a matter of deliberate policy, by New York's bankers.

The bankers started dumping billions of dollars in city bonds months before the crisis broke out. William Haddad, Director of the Office of Legislative Oversight and Analysis in the State Assembly, described the actions of the banks in a memorandum to the Chairman of the Assembly Banking Committee:

> They began to rapidly and quietly (and, perhaps improperly and illegally) unload their New York City bonds *and thus saturated the market*. You recall they claim the market was saturated and hence they could not sell their bonds. This seems to be untrue. In fact, it appears that Chase unloaded two billion dollars worth of bonds in a very short time![23]

The banks were concerned by New York's weakening financial situation and the danger it posed to the value of the bonds they held. They also had long been disturbed by the growth in the number of municipal employees, the level of wages and pensions won by the municipal unions, the free tuition at the City University. These things threatened bank interests. They could cause the city to try to raise taxes on the banks themselves and on the insurance, real estate, and other businesses with which they are connected.

The banks understood that there were only two ways of dealing with the city's financial problems—either attacking the interests of the banks and their partners or attacking the interests of the municipal workers and the people of the city. To make certain that their interests would not be the ones attacked, the bankers wanted themselves to be in charge of dealing with the problems. They wanted to put New York through a financial wringer, much as the International Monetary Fund does with underdeveloped countries. How could they get themselves in charge so they could put New York through the wringer? By precipitating a crisis.

The crisis, in the form of a "danger of default," need not have broken out. Not only could the banks have refrained from dumping New York bonds, but they could have worked out with the city a long-term plan for stretching out the repayment of the city debt they held. Whether to force a debtor into default is not a technical matter, but a matter of policy. The banks often renegotiate the debt of foreign countries, stretching out payments, and they would have done so with New York if it had been to their interest or they had been forced to do so. But how could they compel the city to fire municipal employees, freeze municipal wages, and slash municipal services? By raising the specter of default.

The federal government allied itself with the strategy of the bankers. Not only does it represent bankers, but it had its own reasons for squeezing New York. It wanted the city's finances put into a condition which would make federal financial help unnecessary. Federal help would set a bad precedent for other cities in trouble. The precedent to be set was that cities must learn to "live within their means."

New York's municipal unions have a history of class collaboration. Their leaders pride themselves on their "realism" and their ability to work out backroom arrangements with their friends, the officials of the city. This history left both unions and leaders unprepared for the offensive of the banks and federal government. It was easy for the bankers, President Ford and his Treasury Secretary, William Simon, to outwit, outmaneuver, and outbluff them.

The unions' strength lay in acting as one, and in mobilizing the people of the city behind them. But the unions were disunited and didn't negotiate as one. Their leaders didn't develop a common strategy and public relations policy.

The unions should have done everything possible to unmask the phony line of the banks and federal government that "there is no money" to help the city. There was money. The banks, the real estate interests, and the federal government had it.

The unions never worked out and publicized a program of their own for handling the crisis—one which could have contained a debt moratorium by the banks, the collection of the enormous backlog of unpaid real estate taxes, the raising of real estate assessments on large properties, the assumption of welfare costs by the federal government, and large-scale federal aid and loans. Instead the leaders of the unions let people be bamboozled by the claptrap the banks and the federal government were handing out.

The banks took over full control of the city's finances through a Municipal Assistance Corporation and an Emergency Financial Control Board—corporate juntas which, in effect, supplanted the elected government. The key officials on these bodies were people like Felix Rohatyn, partner in the investment banking firm of Lazard Freres, and William Ellinghaus, president of the New York Telephone Company, a director of Bankers Trust, and a Trustee of the Union Dime Savings Bank.

The unions not only caved in one by one on wages and layoffs, but they also invested almost $4 billion of union pension funds in emergency financing. The pension funds took up the loans that were not good enough for the banks. This was not only a poor financial practice, but weakened the union position in future nego-tiations. If the unions did not agree to layoffs, wage freezes, etc., they might be endangering their pensions.

The juntas put through a program that was a banker's dream—massive layoffs which reduced the number of city jobs by 60,000, or one out of eight; a wage freeze for city workers; an increase in the subway fare from 35 to 50 cents; an end to free tuition at the City University; large cuts in services and outlays for infrastructure.

Jack Newfield and Paul DuBrul describe some cuts in services:

People bled to death in the emergency room at Lincoln Hospital in the Bronx for want of plasma, a nurse, an empty bed. Wood-frame houses burned to the ground because eight firehouses were closed. Twenty-eight day care centers closed, displacing 1800 children of working parents. A new school—P.S. 390 in Crown Heights—was 80 percent completed, but construction stopped. Eleven eye clinics treating 10,000 children closed down. Coney Island Hospital closed four of its seven operating rooms. Garbage collection on the Lower East Side dropped from six times a week to three. The Child Health Station on DeKalb Avenue, in the Fort Greene neighborhood of Brooklyn, shut its doors. The 70th police precinct in Brooklyn lost one-quarter of its force.[24]

WHAT HAPPENED in New York's fiscal crisis was of national significance. The attack against New York's municipal workers opened a general offensive against labor. From New York, the attack spread to municipal workers throughout the country, to the workers of Chrysler, General Motors, and Ford, to workers in general.

The federal government's refusal to provide the money that New York City needed set the tone for its treatment of other cities in distress. The cooperation between the banks and the federal government to force New York City to slash its municipal services sprang from the same philosophy as the later Reagan budget cuts.

WHAT HAS BEEN the government's answer to the urban crisis? Hot air plus a few limited measures to soften the edges of some of the worst problems.

Carter pledged a "comprehensive" urban policy and issued reports with high-flown titles like *A New Partnership To Conserve America's Communities, A National Urban Policy.*[25] These reports abounded in empty generalities which made it obvious that his administration had no urban policy.

The most fundamental cause of the urban crisis is the power of the monopolies to decide where to locate plants and other operations, their power to move out of cities. Since this power is sacred for the monopolies, the Carter urban policy didn't touch it.

The Carter administration provided "Supplementary Fiscal Assistance" to distressed cities, but the amount was piddling. It provided money to state and local governments under the Comprehensive Employment and Training Act (CETA) to create jobs for so-called hard core unemployed. But again the amount was piddling, and, besides, many cities, instead of hiring additional workers, used the CETA money to pay for old jobs that had previously been financed by local taxes.

Reagan slashed even the limited aid that Carter was providing the cities, eliminating three hundred thousand CETA jobs. Reagan's program for the cities consisted in establishing "enterprise zones" in them. The enterprise zone concept is a more windy version of the idea put forth by Carter that the problem of the cities can be solved by providing "incentives" for private business to locate in them, a variant of the general capitalist idea of how to solve all problems from the oil crisis to the shrinking steel industry—by giving the monopolies more.

A TRUE ATTACK on the problems of the cities would:

● Mount massive programs that could serve both to create jobs and rebuild the cities, such as the large-scale construction of public housing, the rehabilitation of the urban infrastructure, and the building of mass transit systems in those cities and metropolitan areas that require them.

● Mount a large-scale job training program to prepare the unemployed, especially minority youth, for jobs in the rebuilding program and elsewhere.

● Take a series of measures to put the cities on a strong financial footing; for example, the assignment to them, as a matter of right, of a fair proportion of federal revenues and the assumption by the federal government of all welfare costs.

● Mount a strong program against racism, including the removal of all barriers to the residence of minorities in all city and suburban areas, and affirmative action to deal with the specific job problems of the minorities.

● Prohibit bank "redlining" by federal law.

● Get at the root cause of the urban problem by curbing the freedom of corporations to move around wherever they like without regard to anything other than profits.

14

Crumbling Infrastructure

The U.S. infrastructure—streets and roads, bridges, water mains, sewers, subways, etc.—is crumbling. Undermaintenance is widespread and in addition, many facilities (especially in older parts of the country) are ancient and need replacement. It is much cheaper to keep up current maintenance than to undo the damage later. An enormous problem is being allowed to build up— one that will eventually cost trillions of dollars to resolve.

NO COMPREHENSIVE inventory exists of infrastructure facilities. This is a further example of capitalist disorder. It helps explain how the decay of the infrastructure was able to sneak up on us without the people becoming quickly aware of its magnitude and meaning.

While a comprehensive inventory would show an even worse picture, here are some highlights of what the scattered available data show:

● A pothole plague afflicts the streets of New York, Chicago, Cleveland, and many other cities. New York had to pay out so much money in negligence claims for damage caused by potholes, that several years ago, it enacted a law exempting itself from responsiblity for accidents caused by any street defect not reported at least fifteen days earlier.[1]

● The 42,000-mile Interstate Highway System has been deteriorating at a rate requiring reconstruction of 2,000 miles per year. By 1981, a backlog of 8,000 miles in need of reconstruction had accumulated.² Conditions on the larger network of primary and secondary roads are even worse.

● Forty-five percent of the country's 558,000 bridges were classified by the Department of Transportation in 1982 as structurally deficient or obsolete; that is, seriously deteriorated or unable to handle the traffic because of narrow lanes, low load capacity, etc.³

● The capital plant of the New York subway system is in a state of advanced decay; those of the Philadelphia, Boston, and Chicago subways have also deteriorated. Decades of deferred maintenance have caused a deterioration in the roadbed of the railroads. Brock Adams, Carter's Secretary of Transportation, contended that half the 8,000 train derailments in 1977 were caused by improperly maintained roadbeds.⁴

● In older cities, many water lines are decrepit and need replacing; in newer ones, many are suffering from a lack of proper maintenance. Boston's system loses half its water through leaky pipes at a cost of several million dollars a year. The Urban Institute, in a survey of 28 cities, found that ten cities were losing more than ten percent of their treated water. Each year there are thousands of water main breaks in the United States. Even a small break can mean the disruption of an entire city block. Some breaks are big. In July 1982, an aqueduct serving Jersey City ruptured and the water supply for the city of 300,000 was shut down for six days.⁵

● The sewage systems of many cities are also time-worn, undermaintained, or inadequate. In some places, the Chicago area, for example, sewer systems overflow regularly, flooding raw sewage into lakes, rivers, and basements. Other localities suffer from a less severe though still difficult problem—ground water flows into leaky sewer pipes, adds to the volume of sewage, and increases the cost of treating it.⁶

● The Army Corps of Engineers, in an inspection of 9,000 dams in highly populated areas, found one third to be unsafe, and over one hundred in danger of imminent collapse.⁷

● Many other elements of the infrastructure—parks, schools, hospitals, fire houses, prisons, and ports—are rundown, inadequate, or both. A small example from the testim ny of the City Engineer of Hot Springs, South Dakota before a congressional committee in 1919:

In the city of Hot Springs, there are approximately 150 fire hydrants; 30 percent of these are mechanically defective, unreparable antiques, only decorating the street corners; another 30 percent have such low flow output due to constricted mains that [they are] totally ineffective for fighting fires.[8]

THE INFRASTRUCTURE is in especially bad condition in those of our older cities which have suffered acute financial crisis, such as New York and Cleveland.

Harrison Goldin, New York City's Comptroller, testified before the same congressional committee:

For years, the city deferred maintenance of [its] magnificent public property; the fiscal crisis abruptly and effectively brought our capital program, including both new projects and reconstruction or replacement of old plant, to a virtual halt. The result of these years of neglect, combined with the fiscal crisis, is a rising number of collapses of rundown facilities. . . .[9]

A look at New York's infrastructure shows that the word "collapse" is not an exaggeration:

● Half of New York's elevated West Side Highway had to be closed and torn down after a truck fell through it in 1976. In his book, *The Future of New York City's Capital Plant,* David A. Grossman writes that this "collapse . . . [has] been attributed to maintenance neglect . . . as simple an omission as failing to paint the elevated supports to prevent rust."[10]

● New York's chief engineer, George Zaimes, talked to the *Wall Street Journal* (8-11-82) about New York bridges:

At last count, Mr. Zaimes had been forced to close 19 bridges. At least 100 others aren't receiving the immediate attention they need. Dozens more are getting at best only "Band Aid" repairs, such as the application of plastic sealants to retard erosion or the installation of wooden supports to reinforce cracked concrete columns. . . . The Manhattan Bridge is a textbook case of physical decay. . . . Years of neglect have resulted in the hopeless clogging of the drains that once siphoned rainwater and melting snow off the bridge. As acid from the salt spread on the pavement collects, it eats into the steel structure.

● In the late 1960s, the city and state of New York decided to build a new Second Avenue subway line with connections to Queens and the Bronx to relieve congestion on the city's east side lines. The city's fiscal crisis brought construction of this line, already well under way, to a halt. Now the city owns a useless tunnel under the East River and empty subway passages under Second Avenue for which it has been vainly trying to find some sort of commercial use.

● The fiscal crisis also struck hard at the existing subway lines. *Business Week* wrote (10-26-81):

The Metropolitan Transportation Authority of the State of New York "literally stopped preventive maintenance in 1975," when the city's fiscal crisis hit, says City Council President and MTA board member Carol Bellamy. The results were stark: the number of serious break-downs en route rose to 12,291 in 1977 and tripled to an estimated 36,000 this year; and the number of miles travelled by the average subway car before having to be laid up for major repairs dropped from 13,627 in 1977 to 6,500 in 1981.

● Between 1947 and 1978, the number of water main breaks per year in New York City doubled—from 234 to 469. "There is a huge backlog of repairs and replacements," according to the city department in charge of water supply.[11]

● David Grossman writes, "New York is estimated to lack adequate sewerage in about 1,500 miles or 25 percent of its total street length. In addition, an estimated 40 percent of the existing system is more than 60 years old."

In the Williamsburg-Crown Heights section of Brooklyn, the 80-year-old cement pipes are decaying. In many areas of Queens and Staten Island, the sewers flood after heavy rains. The fiscal crisis halted the city's sewer construction program.[12]

● A *New York Times* headline (10-13-80) reads, "New York City Park System Stands As Tattered Remnant of its Past." The article goes on:

The city was once internationally famous for its parks system. . . . Perhaps no other municipal facilities have suffered so much in recent years. . . . Parks supervisors recently rated the system and concluded that only 26 percent of the city's parks and playgrounds were in good condition. The decay has come when more and more New Yorkers appear to be using the parks. . . . The poor complain that because the parks have increasingly become their oases, the parks are no longer taken care of. . . . In the 1930s . . . as many as 30,000 civil servants— gardeners, monument keepers, plumbers, carpenters, laborers, zoo keepers—worked in the city parks. Today, an even larger and more complex system is tended by an aging permanent work force of 2,779 and a revolving crew of 1,458. . . .

The story is the same for the rest of New York's infrastructure. The Department of Corrections, Board of Education, New York Public Library, Department of Sanitation, Health and Hospitals Corporation—all reported to the Office of the State Comptroller in 1982 that they needed more money than they were getting just to prevent further deterioration of their facilities and many times more to be able to attack their big backlogs of deferred maintenance.[13]

CLEVELAND's infrastructure also suffers from long-term neglect, topped by a fiscal crisis. "The city has not paved any streets for a year except for a handful of blocks chosen for special care," said the *New York Times* on Feb. 15, 1981.

- An Urban Institute study, *The Future of Cleveland's Capital Plant*, states that

Thirty percent of the 163 bridges for which the city has full maintenance responsibility are in intolerable or unsatisfactory condition, requiring replacement or major repair and rehabilitation. . . . Neglect and deferral of maintenance on aging structures are key factors in explaining the critical bridge problem in Cleveland today. . . . Such preventive maintenance activities as painting had to be eliminated more than five years ago.[14]

- Cleveland's water distribution system also has "major deficiencies." Deposits in pipes have reduced flow capacity. Water pressure often falls too low, and during periods of peak demand some customers don't get water. The poor condition of its water system threatens Cleveland's ability to provide adequate fire protection.[15]
- The flooding of sewage into basements happens often in Cleveland. Eighty percent of the sewer system consists of combined sanitary and storm sewers, but its capacity for handling storm water runoff is inadequate. Even moderate rains push the rate of flow to levels higher than the system can handle. Some flooding results from clogged pipes. Many cities carry out a regular pipe cleaning program, but Cleveland doesn't—it cleans only in response to complaints of flooding.[16]

THE PROBLEM of infrastructure is most acute in the older cities, but not restricted to them. As *Business Week* put it (10-26-81):

Even cities in the Sunbelt, which have newer physical plants and rapidly expanding tax bases, face problems with their infrastructures. Fast-growing Dallas must raise some $700 million for water and sewage treatment facilities over the next decade and more than $109 million to repair deteriorating streets. And booming Denver has begun informally delaying its repair and maintenance schedules. . . . If growth continues at the present rate, without the development of a mass transit system, cities like Dallas and Houston could eventually be paralyzed.

IT IS IMPOSSIBLE to measure the full toll taken by infrastructure decay.

Here and there partial estimates exist. *Newsweek* (8-2-83) tells of a government study which "found that spending an extra $4.3 billion to fix dilapidated bridges and roads could save 480,000 injuries and 17,200 lives over fifteen years." *Business Week* reported in 1981 (Oct. 26th) that U.S. Steel was "losing $1.2 million per year in employee time and wasted fuel rerouting trucks around the Thompson Run Bridge, in Duquesne, Pa., which is posted for weight restrictions because it is in such disrepair." An economist of the Federal Reserve Bank of New York estimated in 1980 that every five minute average delay per subway ride cost New York City workers and companies $166 million per year.[17]

But how can one measure the human cost of having to contend with an inhuman subway system? Or the total human and economic cost of all the decay—everything from collapsing highways and bridges through dilapidated schools, hospitals, parks and jails to the pollution of the environment with raw sewage?

The economic consequences of infrastructure decay go far beyond the immediate, visible damage. The decay cuts productivity and increases costs. It reduces U.S. competitiveness and acts as a growing drag on U.S. economic growth.

WHAT HAS BEEN CAUSING the decay of the infrastructure? The main immediate cause is the financial crisis afflicting city and state governments—it is these governments that bear responsibility for most of the infrastructure.

The federal government is a key part of this crisis, hogging the tax revenues and dumping responsiblities on the cities and states. To boot, it has recently been cutting financial aid to local governments while increasing the military budget. The military budget is a basic cause of infrastructure decay.

The federal government aggravates the problems by fighting inflation with high interest rates. The cities and states depend heavily on borrowing to meet many infrastructure needs, and the high interest rates caused by the Federal Reserve Board often make the cost of borrowing prohibitive.

Besides preventing the cities and states from properly taking care of those portions of the infrastructure that they are responsible for, the federal government has been neglecting what is under its own jurisdiction—national parks, for example.

Some infrastructure decay results from neglect by private owners. Many unsafe dams, for example, are privately owned.

To fully understand the infrastructure problem, we must view it broadly. Our infrastructure is decaying regardless of jurisdiction— and not just our infrastructure, but our cities and many of our industries. What accounts for so pervasive a decay?

More than ever before, the capitalist system in the United States is harnessed to finance capital and a gigantic military machine. Finance capital is far removed from the material basis of the economy. It finds that the highest profits come from financial manipulation, not from maintaining the physical plants and carrying out the material processes which provide the goods and services from which we live. The basic system and the priorities of the government combine to channel resources to whatever makes the highest profits and to the military machine designed to protect the profit system. Everything else—people, industries, cities, infrastructure—is bound to suffer.

ELEMENTS OF THE establishment have become concerned about the state of the infrastructure. Several years ago, a congressional committee looked into it. The Council of State Planning Agencies, an affiliate of the National Governors Association, published a book on the subject entitled *America In Ruins. Business Week* ran a Special Report subtitled, "Deteriorating Infrastructure in the Snowbelt, Unfinished Infrastructure in the Sunbelt." *Newsweek* carried a cover story entitled, "The Decaying of America." The Morgan Guaranty Trust Company included an article in its monthly survey entitled, "Rebuilding America's Infrastructure."[18]

But what results come from all this concern? A collection of examples of decay plus a bewailing of the situation, not a meaningful program for dealing with it. In *America In Ruins*, the most original and serious of the studies, the authors lose themselves in long, semi-technical discussions—the need to reduce delay, administrative waste, and fraud in public works, to put better trained personnel in charge of the infrastructure, to set up a national capital budget. Some of the ideas are good; we could use a capital budget with which construction and maintenance of the infrastructure would be planned systematically. But the book doesn't discuss the main thing required to reverse the decay of the infrastructure; money, an enormous amount. It doesn't discuss the connections between the infrastructure, the urban crisis and the military budget.

The Morgan Guaranty Trust Company does have a proposal for raising the money. Congress should "set up a public construction trust fund, financed by excise or other consumption taxes." In other words, Congress should squeeze more money from the hides of the people, and do so through a regressive tax that would weigh most heavily on those with low incomes. Apart from the injustice of this proposal, it is not practical. Congress couldn't pass a regressive tax that would provide enough money to dent the infrastructure problem; the people wouldn't allow it.

How much money is required for the infrastructure? *U.S. News & World Report* (9-27-82) turned for an answer to Pat Choate, co-author of *America In Ruins*:

Choate estimates that local, state, and federal governments would have to spend from 2.5 to 3 trillion dollars this decade—slightly more than all planned defense outlays in the same period—just to maintain today's level of service on public facilities. At present spending levels, he says, less than a third of that renovation can be done.

The most costly items Choate presented to a congressional group:
* Highways and bridges outside urban areas, 1 trillion dollars.
* City streets, 600 billion.
* Municipal water systems, 125 billion.
* Ports and inland waterways, 40 billion.
* Constructing and renovating up to 3,000 prisons and jails, 15 billion.
* Water pollution controls to meet current standards, 100 billion.

"Rebuilding the nation's public infrastructure," concludes Choate, "promises to be the single most expensive government challenge of the 1980s and 1990s."

What we need is a massive public works program that would

both reverse the decline in our infrastructure and put our unemployed to work. A massive public works program is a quick way of bringing about a large reduction in unemployment among Afro-Americans, Hispanics, and other minorities, youth, and especially minority youth.

But we must beware of oversimple analogies to the 1930s. We are facing a more tangled economic problem. We cannot simply forget about inflation and an unstable dollar and finance a public works program with budget deficits. A public works program should be properly financed, and the financing can be obtained only by increasing taxes on the monopolies and the rich and slashing the military budget.

Until the military budget is slashed, we can never get an adequate public works program. All we can get are a few bandaid measures which would allow the decay to continue and to undermine the whole U.S. economy.

PART VI

EFFECTS ON THE PEOPLE

15

The Retirement System in Trouble

The sickness of the economy as a whole has put the retirement "system" of the United States in trouble. *System* is in quotation marks because we don't have a comprehensive retirement system, but rather a crazy quilt of more than 500,000 separate systems. Hundreds of thousands of private corporations, several thousand state and local governments, a host of federal agencies including the military, the foreign service, the CIA, etc., have separate "plans." Finally, there is Social Security.

Those who defend the U.S. retirement setup refer to it as a "three-legged stool." They claim that Social Security provides basic protection which is supplemented by private pensions and personal savings. This is bull. For most working people, two of the three legs on which the stool is supposed to stand aren't there.

Few working people accumulate enough savings to provide significant retirement income. In 1980, the Social Security Administration published a report showing that only 12 percent of those 65 and over received more than $5,000 a year in "asset income"—income from savings accounts, bonds, stocks, etc. Forty-four percent did not have asset income. Among Blacks, eighty-five percent had none.[1]

The main asset of retirees is the equity in their home and millions don't have even this. The savings that some senior citizens have is mostly money put aside for a rainy day and, as one pension expert has put it, only a few such days would use it up.

PRIVATE PENSIONS* are also a weak reed for a retirement stool to rest on. Whether one will get a pension and how much it will be worth is no more certain than playing the horses. The pension setup misses a large fraction of the working population and it is unable to protect pensions from the ravages of inflation.

Half of private wage and salary workers have no pension coverage; in 1979, thirty-five million workers were not covered. Coverage is correlated with earnings; among those with lower earnings, fewer are covered. Coverage is lower for women than men and for Blacks than whites.[2]

Further, a large proportion of workers will not receive benefits from plans under which they are covered. Until 1974, a person covered by a private pension plan who left his job before retirement usually lost all pension benefits under that plan. As a result, there are countless people who, having lost or switched jobs, find themselves with no benefits from plans in which they had long participated. In 1974, a federal law that was supposed to deal with this problem provided that those who participated in a pension plan for ten years were "vested"—they had a right to their accrued pension even though they left the job before retirement. This still means that workers with less than ten years' seniority hit by plant closings lose not only their jobs but their pension credits.

Inflation cuts into the real value of benefits, both as they accumulate during working years and after retirement. A common type of plan relates benefits to length of service and annual earnings; for example, a person earns a pension credit of two percent a year and after thirty years is entitled to benefits equal to sixty percent of annual earnings. In some plans, annual earnings means the average for the whole working life. For a worker who retired in 1983, the calculation would include earnings from the 1950's and 1960's when the dollar was worth more and wages were correspondingly lower. In the dollars of 1983 and beyond in which the pension will be paid, average earnings are being grossly understated and this drags down the benefits. Many pension plans are based on average earnings during the last five years of employment. This lessens the inflation damage, but doesn't eliminate it.

---

*The American Council of Life Insurance defines private pension plans as "those established by private agencies including commercial, industrial, labor and service organizations, nonprofit organizations, and nonprofit religious, educational and charitable institutions."

After cutting into the value of pension benefits before retirement, inflation continues its robbery afterwards. Even an inflation at the comparatively low rate of three percent per year reduces the value of the pension dollar to 74 cents in ten years. An inflation of ten percent cuts the pension dollar to 62 cents in five years and 39 cents in ten. For millions of people, a high rate of inflation means that in the last years of their lives their pensions will amount to peanuts.

Some companies give cost of living increases, but they usually fail to keep up with inflation. According to Consumers Union: "A 1980 survey by Bankers Trust Co. found that companies increased benefits to employees who retired in January, 1975 an average of 8 or 9 percent (depending on the type of plan) over the period 1975 to 1979. But the Consumer Price Index for that period rose by 48 percent."[3]

While private pensions don't meet the needs of the mass of the people, they serve the executives of the monopolies very well. Take Harold S. Geneen, former chairman of ITT. When Geneen retired in 1979, he was scheduled to receive a pension of $243,097 plus consulting fees of $450,000 in 1980 and $250,000 a year through 1985; plus life and disability insurance, office space, security protection, secretarial aid and limousine service.[4]

BY FAR THE MOST important element in the retirement setup is the Social Security system which now covers almost the whole working population. Three-fifths of those 65 and over get more than half their income from Social Security.

Social Security credits accumulate to one's account regardless of job change. Benefits are now adjusted for inflation, even if belatedly and inadequately. The main weakness of Social Security is that the benefits are inadequate. The average monthly benefit in 1983 was $427.[5]

The way to a good retirement system lies in strengthening Social Security. Only Social Security can provide a rational retirement system, one which covers everyone, instead of a favored few, and is reliable and adequate. But since the crisis in the U.S. economy erupted in the early 1970's, the Social Security system has been under attack.

The establishment media worked hard to prepare us for action against Social Security. The business magazine *Forbes* asked on its cover: "America's Elderly—Can We Afford Them?" The *New York Times* in one editorial after another told us that the Social

Security system was in "deep financial trouble."

Did the media give us a full, honest analysis? Their usual argument ran like this: Social Security is a pay-as-you-go system. There is no large capital reserve backing the obligation to pay benefits. The money paid out in benefits each year comes essentially from the money received in payroll taxes that year. But because the proportion of senior citizens in the population is growing, Social Security—as the *New York Times* put it—has to "collect from a shrinking work force for a growing number of pensioners."[6] Today, there are three workers contributing to Social Security for every one collecting benefits; by the year 2025, the ratio will be two to one.

Obviously, something must be done, we were told. Then different ideas were tried out to see how people would accept them: Payroll taxes should be raised; benefits should not be fully adjusted to compensate for the rising cost of living; benefits should be made subject to income taxes; the retirement age should be raised.

Part of the attack on Social Security consisted of insidious propaganda designed to win over younger people for action against it. There is a limit, we were told, to how much the young can be expected to contribute to the support of the old.

Finally, the press used scare tactics. It raised the spectre of the Social Security system going broke, being unable to meet its obligations. This was an attempt to make the planned attack on Social Security look like a program to save it. As David Stockman said in his *Atlantic* interview, the purpose of the scare campaign is to generate pressure to "save" Social Security. This pressure "will permit the politicians to make it look like they're doing something *for* the beneficiary population when they're doing something *to* it which they normally wouldn't have the courage to undertake."[7]

THE EXPLANATION that Social Security's troubles are due to the aging of the population is an attempt to snow us under with technicalities. Population aging does have a long-run effect on the system, but it is not the cause of the troubles the media and government have been talking about since the mid-1970's. The cause of these troubles is the general economic crisis with its high unemployment, rapid inflation, and reduction in real wages.

John A. Svahn, Commissioner of Social Security, stated in 1982: "Every time the unemployment rate rises 1 percentage point—or approximately 1.1 million people—it costs us about two billion dollars a year in lost payroll tax revenues."[8] The official unemployment rate in 1982 was 9.7 percent, or 5.7 percent above the 4 percent level that even capitalist economists used to consider full employment. This meant a loss for the year of over $11 billion in payroll tax revenues.

Inflation also hurts the Social Security system. Benefits are adjusted for inflation—not to do so would destroy the system. But payroll taxes have not kept up with inflation since wages have gone up less than prices.

Without the high unemployment, rapid inflation, and big lag in wage rates that set in during the early 1970's, we would not have had the troubles we have been having with Social Security. In 1973, Social Security actuaries were not expecting the system to run into financial difficulty. In December of that year, according to a Senate Committee report, "the Social Security Administration informed Congress that income to the cash benefits program . . . would be more than outgo for the period covered by the short term estimates" [through 1978].[9] The estimates went wrong because the economy went wrong.

The population projections bandied about by the press not only did not explain Social Security's immediate troubles, but even gave an oversimplified picture of the long-run situation. No one—actuaries, statisticians, etc.—can predict the population in 2025 with any certainty. All they can do is lay down assumptions and say, if these assumptions are met, this is what will happen. Often (one could almost say usually) the assumptions are not met and what happens is different from what was projected. The *Report of the 1979 Advisory Council on Social Security* warned that "the history of the official population projections illustrates the need for caution in basing policy on long-run projections."[10]

TO PROMOTE THE IDEA of the Social Security system going broke and out of business the way a private company sometimes does is to deliberately distort the situation. The concept of going broke in this way doesn't apply to a federal institution like Social Security. As Alicia H. Munnel, a vice-president of the Federal Reserve Bank of Boston and leading Social Security expert, put it: "A private pension plan must have sufficient assets to meet all prior and current commitments because it cannot be certain of receiving future premiums. But the Social Security System is a mandatory and permanent program, which can rely on the government's taxing power to meet its obligations. . . ."[11]

Under the guise of saving Social Security, the government could put through increases in Social Security taxes and cuts in benefits. It wanted these not because of long-term population projections, but to counterbalance the Reagan military expenditures and budget deficits. Democrats accused Stockman, said the *Atlantic* article, of trying to balance his budget at the expense of Social Security recipients, which, of course, he was. "The Social Security problem is not simply one of satisfying actuaries," Stockman conceded. "It's one of satisfying the here-and-now of budget requirements."[12]

To help fool the people on Social Security, Reagan appointed a "bipartisan" commission to agree on proposals for him to carry out. Reagan didn't need the commission to provide new ideas—ideas for "saving" Social Security had been floating around for a long time. What he needed was a procedure that seemed to be above politics, a "rescue plan" worked out and backed by both Republicans and Democrats.

In April, 1983, Reagan signed into law the plan worked out by the commission. It included the following:

- An increase in the Social Security payroll tax.
- A six month delay in the adjustment of benefits for the increase in the cost of living, originally scheduled for July, 1983.
- A gradual rise in the retirement age to 67.

The bipartisan plan served Reagan well. At a time when his administration was lowering taxes on the corporations and the well-to-do, it raised taxes on workers, the self-employed, and small businesses. It helped push the United States toward an increasingly unfair, regressive tax system.

By delaying the cost of living adjustment, it bites into the most important source of income for most senior citizens. It reduces benefits which are inadequate to begin with. It brings increased hardship to the millions of seniors who are living in poverty.

Raising the retirement age will hurt many millions of people. As Professor Merton Bernstein has pointed out, "many—very possibly a majority of retirees—*cannot* continue work until age 65, let alone some higher age. For them, a normal retirement age above 65 would constitute a deprivation . ."[13] Even with the previous retirement age, a certain proportion of workers, higher among

Black people than white, never received Social Security benefits because they didn't live beyond 65 years.

Tip O'Neill, the Speaker of the House, proclaimed that with the new plan, "Social Security is secure for the next 25 or 30 years."[14] Jimmy Carter made a similar statement in 1977, only to have a crisis erupt within two years. Actually, the Social Security system could be in trouble again before long, depending upon the level of unemployment and inflation.

A TRUE SOLUTION to the Social Security problem would provide that it be financed from general revenues of the federal budget rather than through the present payroll tax. General revenues come largely from the income tax, which is progressive, at least in theory; that is, the higher the income, the higher the proportion which should be paid in taxes. The payroll tax is strongly regressive; not only does it have an even rate for everyone, but salaries above a certain level are not subject to the tax, and dividends, interest, and other unearned income are not taxed at all.

Tying Social Security to the payroll tax serves several purposes for the powers that be. It is a key part of the strategy of splitting those still working from the retirees and using the split to hold down or cut back benefits. It helps preserve the maximum amount of general revenues for those expenditures to which our rulers assign the highest priority, especially the military budget. In the jargon of some of the writings on Social Security, the tie-in to the payroll tax "helps preserve fiscal discipline." What this means in plain English is holding down benefits, even cutting them back, on the threat that otherwise the payroll tax would have to rise.

There are several possible ways of using general revenues to support Social Security. Several years ago, Representative James A. Burke, Chairman of the House Subcommittee on Social Security, introduced a bill to finance one-third of Social Security from general revenues. Another method, recommended by the 1979 Advisory Council on Social Security, would be to insulate Social Security from recessions—whenever unemployment rises above a specified level, automatic payments would go into Social Security trust funds from general revenues. At the very least, Social Security could be allowed to borrow from general revenues whenever its reserves fell to less than three months' outlay.

The establishment propaganda often tries to make it sound as though the use of general revenues to help support Social Security—even just to help out in an emergency—would be a sin, a violation of the principles of sound finance. This is nonsense. Many European countries use general revenues to help finance Social Security retirement benefits. The percentage of benefits financed from general revenues was as follows in 1977—the Netherlands, 8 percent; France, 10 percent; Switzerland, 15 percent; Sweden, 19 percent; Belgium, 23 percent; West Germany, 24 percent; and Austria, 35 percent.[15]

THE STRUGGLE AROUND pensions and Social Security has to be many-sided. Those with pensions that are not indexed to the cost of living must fight to have them indexed. Those receiving pensions from funds that run into financial trouble should fight to have the federal government bail these funds out. The main cause of the problems the pension funds are facing is the inflation produced by the policies of the federal government.

But the broadest, most important struggle is that around the Social Security system. This struggle should be waged not just to defend that system, but to advance it; to raise benefits; to provide better options for early retirement at 62 or even 60; to index benefits quarterly for inflation; to improve the lot of minorities and women in retirement—for example, by establishing a higher minimum benefit and by providing extra increases in the benefits of those who received low pay during their working years.

The movement supporting Social Security has great political power and will gain even more as the proportion of seniors in the population increases. It is important not only to mobilize and use this power, but to counter the tactics by which the powers that be try to divide older people from the rest of the population.

Younger people also have an interest in Social Security. They are paying into a system which will benefit them when their turn comes. If Social Security were weakened or dismantled, the older people would still have to be supported one way or another—with a great and often unmanageable burden falling on their children.

By the same token, seniors have an interest, even apart from just plain humanity, in the unemployment problem of those who are still of working age.

The key to a good strategy for the fight over Social Security is to see it as part of the broader struggle for slashing the military budget, reducing unemployment and inflation, improving the living standards of working people, and guaranteeing economic justice to Black, Hispanic, and other minority people—for the creation of a broad, strong, anti-militarist, anti-monopoly people's movement.

16

The Health Care Crisis

The U.S. health care "system" is also in deep, growing trouble. On the one hand, it doesn't do the job; tens of millions of people do not receive adequate care. On the other, it imposes enormous financial burdens and risks on the people.

Again, as with retirement, we don't have an arrangement for systematically providing health care to those who need it. What we have is a profit-making apparatus which sells health care as a commodity like apples or shoes. Health care is a vital need which people should receive as a matter of right. But the health care market doesn't operate on this basis. It operates on the basis of profits. Though it deals with services which can determine the future of children, the welfare of families, and life or death, the health care market shows the same greed and anarchy as all capitalist markets.

What we have in the United States is a state monopoly capitalist health care apparatus made up of several elements: doctors, hospitals, and nursing homes; giant monopolies that produce and sell drugs and medical equipment; vast financial companies that sell health insurance; and the government that provides Medicare and Medicaid programs as well as funds for medical education and research.

A HUNDRED YEARS AGO, health care was a cottage industry, based on the individual doctor, an independent professional, who worked from an office in his home. This doctor made a small investment in equipment and supplies, most of which he carried in his little black bag. Hospitals were few and were used far less often than the doctor's office or the patient's home.

But just as industry in general outgrew the cottage stage, so did the health care industry. The advance of medical science and technology brought changes in the structure of the industry. The development of surgery as a specialized skill is an example. Surgeons needed special facilities which the individual surgeon could not personally provide. Hospitals could provide such facilities for groups of surgeons, and the use of hospitals grew rapidly.[1] The provision of health care was shifting from an individual to a social basis.

How to pay for medical care was less a problem when doctors couldn't do much and hospitals hardly existed. But as advancing medical science increased what doctors could do and as hospitals became necessary for surgery, cost began to loom large for most of the population.

The problem was met simply. A large part of the population did not get all the health care it needed; only the rich did. The delivery of health care increasingly reflected the class structure and racism of U.S. capitalism.

Hospital financing was a problem from the beginning. Hospitals couldn't maintain themselves from patients' fees alone. Fees couldn't be raised high enough to cover costs since most people couldn't pay such fees. Beyond a certain point, higher fees would simply mean fewer patients. Hospitals had to depend on philanthropy. Even so, they did not provide service to many who needed it but could not pay.

So the growth of health care out of the cottage industry stage created a gap, one that was to grow ever larger, between the care that advancing science made possible and that which the people could actually get.

THE GREAT DEPRESSION shook the health care industry. Hospitals and doctors often couldn't collect their bills. Philanthropies, hit by the stock market crash, cut their contributions. Hundreds of hospitals had to shut down.

The difficulties led to two developments: Private health insurance began to grow and the federal government began to increase its financial support of health care. The first big increase in private insurance came through hospitals. To help meet the problem of delinquent bills, groups of hospitals began in the early 1930s to organize prepayment plans under the name Blue Cross. Plan members paid a monthly sum to Blue Cross, and it paid the bills. Later, state medical associations promoted plans called Blue Shield for the payment of doctors in the same way.

As philanthropic contributions to hospitals fell, government contributions rose to avoid a complete collapse of the hospitals. In 1927, private contributions accounted for more than seventy percent of capital investment in hospitals, government contributions for less than thirty percent. By 1937, the percentages were reversed.[2]

During World War II, when trade unions had to settle for fringe benefits instead of wage increases, private insurance grew rapidly. Not only did the number of people covered by Blue Cross greatly increase, but life insurance companies—such as Aetna, Metropolitan, and Prudential—seeing the success of Blue Cross, jumped into the hospital insurance business.

The postwar years brought gigantic strides away from what was left of cottage industry. Prewar health care revolved around the solo practitioner. But the individual practitioner could no longer furnish his office with the equipment or employ all the technicians required to examine and treat patients. The doctor had become dependent on the hospital.

The drug industry developed into a gigantic business, dominated by a handful of transnational monopolies—Johnson & Johnson, American Home Products, Warner-Lambert, Bristol-Myers, etc. The sales of these four companies totalled $14 billion in 1979.[3]

The business of selling supplies and equipment to hospitals is also gigantic. American Hospital Supply, which sells thousands of products—bed pans, surgical gloves, heart valves, blood-typing serums, etc.—employed 30,000 people and had sales of $2 billion in 1979.[4] Hewlett-Packard, the electronics company, has a giant, highly profitable medical electronics division which makes such equipment as electrocardiogram machines, bedside patient monitors, and systems that monitor the fetal heartbeat.

Private health insurance has grown to proportions undreamed of in the 1930s. In 1979, 78 percent of the population had some form of private hospital insurance. Large, though lesser percentages, had some form of coverage for surgical benefits and major medical expenses. Health insurance premiums for the year totalled $56 billion.[5]

But private health insurance, no matter how much it grew,

couldn't solve the problem of paying medical bills. There were too many gaps in its coverage. It especially couldn't solve the problem for non-unionized workers, the unemployed, the poor and the elderly, who couldn't afford to buy insurance and didn't acquire it through their jobs.

Since the 1930s, there has been pressure for national health insurance. The growth of private insurance, especially the acquisition of insurance as a fringe benefit in union contracts, weakened this pressure but by no means eliminated it. This pressure resulted in the enactment of two government programs in 1966: Medicaid which provides medical services to some of the poor, and Medicare which provides hospital and medical insurance to senior citizens. Medicaid and Medicare increased the government's already big involvement in health care. Government—federal, state, and local—provided 42.7 percent of the money spent on health care in 1981.[6]

But the government trod carefully in instituting the new programs. It arranged to pay Medicaid and Medicare bills not directly but through Blue Cross, Blue Shield, and the commercial insurance companies. This arrangement not only gave these organizations additional revenues, but also great power over the programs. It is they who administer controls over whether care is necessary and charges are reasonable.

The arrangement also satisfied the doctors and hospitals. Just after Congress passed Medicaid-Medicare, President Johnson met with leaders of the American Medical Association. An official present reported afterward: "He explained that Blue Cross and private insurance companies who are the administrative middlemen under the law, would determine the bill's definition of 'reasonable charges'. Naturally, the doctors went for this because they have great influence with most of these outfits."[7] The hospitals also went for it. When they negotiate with Blue Cross, they are dealing with organizations on whose governing boards they are strongly represented.

HOW WELL DOES the health care system work? The first, most basic point is that it provides poor, inadequate care for a large part of the population.

Even apart from medical care, health is related to income and whether one is white or a member of an oppressed racial or national minority. Because of the conditions under which they have to live, poor people and oppressed minorities tend to have poorer health to begin with than those with higher incomes. On top of this, the poor and the minorities get less preventive care. Finally, when they fall sick, they get poorer medical care—they need more and they get less.

Professor Barbara Starfield, MD, Head, Division of Health Care Organization, Johns Hopkins University, has studied the relation between income, health, and medical care, and writes:

> Poor children are 75% more likely to be admitted to a hospital in a given year. They have 30% more days when their activity is restricted and 40% more days lost from school due to acute illness. They are also more likely to be reported by their parents as having one or more chronic problems and much more likely to be reported by their teachers to have a chronic condition interfering with their school work. . . . Illness, when it occurs, is more severe among poor children than among the non-poor.[8]

Professor Starfield discusses the medical care received by poor children:

> Poor children . . . still receive less medical care than non-poor children. The discrepancy between poor and non-poor children is most evident when their greater need is taken into account. Sick day for sick day . . . poor children have many fewer physician visits. . . . Poor children also receive a different kind of care from non-poor children. Three times as many have no regular source of care, over four times as many report a place rather than an individual doctor as their regular source of care. . . . [9]

Official reports of the U.S. government also provide evidence of the relation between income, minority status and health care. Here are a few items from a publication called *Health of the Disadvantaged:*

● Persons in the lowest income group experience three times more disability days than those in the highest income group.

● Persons from families with lower incomes had more problems securing medical care than those from families with higher incomes.

● The infant mortality rate in 1977 was almost twice as high for Black infants as for white.

● In 1975, the tuberculosis case rate for minorities was five times the rate for whites.

● Members of minorities had higher death rates than whites from leading chronic diseases in 1977.

● Minorities experienced the greatest difficulty in acquiring and regularly using medical services.[10]

Discrimination by income and race shows in many things, beginning with the location of doctors. It is a commonplace that doctors concentrate where the money is—in the well-to-do areas of the cities and suburbs. You can find one doctor after another along the ritzy Park Avenue of New York, but it is hard to find them in the ghettos of the Bronx. Thirty percent of the U.S. population lived in rural areas in 1979, but only seventeen percent of primary care doctors were to be found there.[11]

The problem is more than just being far away from doctors. Those in the "underserved" areas find it hard to get doctor appointments. They are compelled to accept inadequate medical care—to do without regular checkups, to overlook ailments for as long as they can, to get no prenatal care at all or only in the last months of pregnancy. When a severe illness does force them to seek care, they have to do so at the outpatient clinic or emergency room of a hospital where they face long waits, difficulty in seeing the same doctor twice, and the chance that they will be used as teaching and practice material.

Just getting into a hospital can be hard for those who are poor, Black or Hispanic—and often for many others as well. Many hospitals demand proof that the bills will be paid. Even while the emergency patient is waiting at the door, they check finances.

The people in the ghettos often can't get into nearby hospitals, but must use others farther away that will accept them. Professor Seymour Harris wrote in his book, *The Economics of Health Care:* "In Chicago, the Cook County Hospital serves half of all the city's Black patients. Blacks must travel eight times farther for hospital care than they would have to go, if the nearest facilities were available to them."[12] The poor, the Afro-Americans and other oppressed minorities get the worst hospital facilities and treatment. They are dumped into the overcrowded, run-down city and county hospitals. Or they are assigned to the "charity" clinics and wards of the private hospitals.

WHERE PROFITS ARE SMALL, our health care apparatus provides poor, inadequate care. Where there is money to be made, it often provides what is not necessary and may even be harmful—unnecessary surgery, hospital stays, drugs, and sophisticated equipment.

Several years ago, a congressional committee investigated the problem of unnecessary surgery. Here is a quote from its official report:

> The Subcommittee found that surgical payments by the fee-for-service mechanism encourages surgery in questionable situations. . . . [The report] estimates that there were approximately 2.4 million unnecessary surgeries performed in 1974 at a cost to the American public of almost $2.4 billion, and it further estimates that these unnecessary operations led to 11,900 deaths that year.[13]

The literature on health care abounds in discussions of unnecessary removal of the uterus, the appendix, the tonsils, and other types of operations that are not needed.

Unnecessary hospitalization is also widespread. It arises because hospitals make money by keeping their beds occupied and because most health insurance will cover certain services (for example, lab tests) only when performed in hospitals. There is an incentive to put and keep patients in hospitals just to get the services paid for by the insurance.

Drugs are overused. Again the health care literature is rich in examples. Doctors prescribe potentially harmful drugs for the relief of minor muscular ailments, dose patients with antibiotics for colds that would go away by themselves, and overprescribe tranquilizers.

But the main cause of the problem is not the doctors, it is the drug industry. The drug monopolies make their money by advertising drugs to patients and doctors, not by pointing out that people would often be better off without them.

The power of the drug companies over the flow of information about drugs shows up in the following comment from the foreword of an AMA study: "The study emphasized the importance of pharmaceutical advertising in physician education. It showed that physicians receive a large proportion of their postgraduate medical education from advertising and detail programs of pharmaceutical companies."[14]

U.S. medicine is geared to high technology, which has spectacular achievements to its credit, but is overemphasized at the expense of simpler, less costly methods which are often more important in providing the care that large numbers of people need. Dr. John Knowles, for many years Director of the Massachusetts General Hospital of Boston, once recalled an occasion in which he was making the rounds of the hospital with a group of medical students and they saw patients who "had intravenous lines, and central venous pressure catheters and tracheotomies, and positive pressure respirators, and all the rest." Knowles said that, despite the high cost of the treatment, the patients deserved it. "But you can't help reflecting," he added, "as you look at all this stainless steel and tubing and sophisticated equipment, that right outside your door there are people with TB who aren't getting antibiotics, and kids who aren't getting vaccinations, and women who aren't getting prenatal care."[15]

As with the overuse of drugs, the main responsibility for the overemphasis on technology lies not with the doctors, but with the monopolies, this time the medical equipment companies. Again we have company influence on the education of doctors—and of those who control and administer hospitals. The monopolies establish connections with leading medical centers and hospitals. They get prestigious doctors to write articles in the medical journals which, in effect, promote their equipment. They work to create an atmosphere in which hospitals and doctors demand the equipment as a matter of prestige.

In sum, the reason the Massachusetts General Hospital had the sophisticated equipment while right outside there were women who weren't getting prenatal care, is that the big profits come from the sale of equipment.

HOW WELL DOES the medical care system work financially? The problem of financing is significant from several angles. What kind of health insurance people have helps determine the adequacy of the medical care they get. The problem of the money drained out of people by medical bills is important in its own right—medical bills are a heavy burden, a leading cause of personal bankruptcy. Finally, with the government paying over 40 percent of total health care expenditures, health care financing has become a major problem in public finance.

Like the retirement setup, health insurance is also a crazy quilt. Many people have no insurance. Some have it at one time, but not at others. What insurance will pay for varies. Only a small proportion of the population is fully covered, so that most people can still be hit by large medical expenses.

In 1977, the government found that twenty-six million people—12.6 percent of the civilian population—had no health insurance. Eighteen percent of racial minorities had no insurance as against twelve percent of the white population.[16]

Since 1977, the percentage of uninsured has increased because of higher unemployment. The *New York Times* reported on Oct. 31, 1982: "More than 16 million Americans have lost health insurance coverage as a result of unemployment . . . according to health officials. The principal source of coverage for most workers is the group health plans offered by employers. For that reason, workers generally lose health insurance when they lose their jobs."

Laid-off workers cannot usually continue health insurance on their own because the cost is prohibitive—equal to one-quarter of the payments they get from unemployment insurance.

What do workers and their families do when they lose their health insurance? The *Wall Street Journal* reported (4-6-82) from Detroit:

> Margie Wilde, who had a kidney removed back in 1950, has stopped having the recommended regular blood and urine tests since her husband was laid off as an auto-supply worker two years ago.
>
> Thomas Arnold, laid off by Chrysler Corp. two years ago, is putting off a needed hernia operation. His wife, Karen, says the Arnolds are putting off something else as well. "We would probably have tried to have children by now," she says, "but the hospital bill would be sky-high. . . ."
>
> Without income or insurance, "people are deferring all activities except the most necessary ones," says Stephen Blount, a medical consultant with the Detroit Health Department. Detroit-area doctors say visits have declined as much as 30% as people dose themselves with home remedies, phone to wheedle prescriptions from reluctant physicians, or simply tough out illness they once would have had checked.

But having health insurance is no guarantee of adequate coverage. Most health insurance is full of gaps, leaving pre-existing illness, out-of-hospital doctor care, dental care, preventive medicine, and many other things uncovered.

Even for what is covered, there are many limitations on what insurance will pay: *deductibles,* the patient must pay a certain amount before the insurance benefits begin; *coinsurance,* the patient must pay 20 or 25 percent of the charges even after the benefits start; a *cut-off point,* a maximum benefit beyond which the insurance does not go.

The protection that insurance does provide can sometimes be reduced or nullified by the greed of doctors. Here is an old story that still applies today, though the sums of money involved would be larger:

> The child of a San Franciscan came down with appendicitis. The family physician called in a surgeon who performed a successful, uncomplicated operation and rendered a bill for $150, which the father paid. Later the father and his coworkers joined a health insurance plan which provided cash allowances for surgery. The man noticed that the allowance for an appendectomy was $150 and wished he had been covered by the insurance when the child was ill. In a few weeks, however, the insurance paid off. The child's twin came down with appendicitis. The same family physician called the same surgeon, who performed the same successful, uncomplicated operation in the same hospital. This time the surgeon's fee was $300.
>
> When questioned the surgeon explained that he was merely conforming with the tradition that requires the physician to adjust his fees to the patient's financial status. "If that man could pay $150 for an appendectomy a couple of months ago," said the surgeon, "he can still pay it."[17]

Less clear than the greed of some doctors, though more important in shaping the health care system, is the role of the insurance companies. To begin with, the insurance companies are not interested in insuring everybody—only those from whose insurance they can get a satisfactory profit. When Blue Cross started, it charged everybody the same for the same coverage. When the commercial companies entered the field, they needed a way of competing with Blue Cross. They found it by offering lower insurance rates to those less likely to need hospital care—the young, those in safe occupations, and the better paid. To avoid losing the business of those being offered lower rates, Blue Cross had to lower its rates to them—which meant that it had to raise rates for the rest of the population. This differential method of fixing rates has caused many employers whose workers are poorer risks to resist providing them with insurance. It works to keep health insurance from those people who need it most.

The companies are also not interested in whether their insurance results in adequate health care for those insured. They prefer certain types of insurance over others, not because they mean bètter care but because they are more convenient and profitable to them. They prefer, for example, to insure for big events like hospitalization rather than ordinary visits to the doctor—checking whether every little visit is justified is too troublesome. Because of this insurance company preference, many parents can't take their children to see the doctor as often as necessary. The type of insurance promoted by the companies helps mold the whole health care setup, helps explain the de-emphasis on ordinary primary care in favor of fancy hospital-oriented care.

The insurance companies are a main cause of rising health care costs. As critics have pointed out, they have an interest in rising costs. When medical costs rise, they can increase their premiums, have more money to invest, and obtain higher profits. The companies are unwilling to force confrontations with doctors and hospitals over high costs, unnecessary surgery, or excessive use of hospitals and costly equipment. They are allied with the doctors and hospitals in a lucrative business in which the interest of all lies fundamentally not in fighting each other but in having the flow of money to the business as a whole rise.

A RECENT DEVELOPMENT in medical care is the swift growth of corporate, for-profit hospital chains. These chains already owned 15 percent of the country's general hospitals by 1983 and some experts predict that the figure will jump to 30 percent by 1990. As usual, monopoly prevails—five large companies own more than half the for-profit hospitals.

There are profits, of course, even in the "non-profit" hospitals—medical equipment companies, insurance companies, banks and others make profits through them. But the hospitals themselves are not supposed to be working directly for profits.

The hospital corporations claim that by good business management—bulk purchasing, the use of computers to bill patients, etc.—they can both provide necessary services and pull out a healthy profit. "The same ingredients that propelled such companies as Sears, McDonalds, and Exxon are applicable to the institutional health care sector," asserts an official of the Hospital Corporation of America.[18]

However, the key to the profits of the hospital corporations does not lie in efficiency, but in something else—skimming the financial cream of the market in the same way that insurance companies do.

The corporate hospitals provide care only to those from whom satisfactory profits can be made. Everyone else they send away.

The *New York Times* (5-29-83) described how the Hospital Corporation of America operates:

> H.C.A. makes no bones about the fact that it wants dollars and not promises from patients. Pre-admission checking is done to see if patients have deep enough pockets. Deposits are often demanded....
>
> You won't find H.C.A. in downtown Detroit or Newark. The settings it favors are advantageous in insuring black bottom lines. It skirts the inner cities, with their heavy concentrations of poor. . . . It likes communities where younger people, with private insurance, settle.

As *U.S. News & World Report* explained (8-17-81), "Most for-profit hospitals are in the fast-growing communities of the sunbelt states and in prosperous suburbs. Few are in the Northeast and Midwest, where a strong tradition of nonprofit hospitals exists, or in states with effective hospital-rate-setting commissions."

Several studies disprove the claim of the for-profit hospitals that they are more efficient than the others. One study, published in the *New England Journal of Medicine,* compared different types of hospitals in California and found that "both costs and charges were higher in for-profit than not-for-profit hospitals. . . ." The for-profits generate their high profits not through lower costs produced by the much-touted economies of scale, but by charging more, especially for non-routine "ancillary" services.[19]

The growth of the for-profit hospital chains represents a harmful, dangerous tendency. These hospitals will make enormous profits for their owners but will weaken other hospitals by taking the best-paying patients away from them. They themselves will not treat patients who cannot pay their high charges and they will weaken the ability of the non-profit hospitals to treat them. They will make the U.S. hospital system even more of a class system than it already is—one that provides inferior care, and often no care, to a large part of the population.

MEDICAID AND MEDICARE constituted an advance, though a limited one. They do nothing for the bulk of the population, and even for the poor and elderly, are shot through with holes.

Under Medicaid, the federal government matches the state and local funds to set up programs for medical assistance to the poor. Despite the federal contribution, most states have severely restricted eligibility for Medicaid. Professor Richard Brown, of the University of California School of Public Health at Los Angeles, writes: "Somewhere between 40 percent and two thirds of all poor persons in the United States are ineligible for Medicaid because of [maximum income and other] requirements. In eight states, Medicaid recipients totalled less than 20 percent of the poverty population in 1970."[20]

Professor Brown also states that Medicaid has not solved the problem of poor people having "to travel longer and wait longer to see a physician" and of being forced more than others to rely on hospitals and clinics for care. "One reason why . . . people with Medicaid are less likely to have a private physician is that most doctors treat few, if any, Medicaid patients." Medicaid fees average less than Medicare and Blue Shield fees and "Medicaid requires physicians to accept the 'assigned' fee. . . ."[21]

Medicare does cover almost all the elderly, but it suffers from other weaknesses. It has the same rigmarole of deductibles, co-insurance, and cut-off point as private insurance. A hospital patient in 1984 paid the first $356 of the bill as a deductible. From the 61st through the 90th day, there is a co-insurance charge of $89 a day. To cover further hospitalization, there is a lifetime reserve of 60 days at a charge of $178 a day—once this reserve is used up, a patient must pay in full for all further hospitalization.

Insurance for doctors' services is optional; those who enroll for it must pay a monthly premium. Even for persons enrolled, Medicare does not pay for certain services—among them, immunizations, physical examinations, eye examinations and eyeglasses, and dental care. Again, there is a deductible and co-insurance—after paying the deductible, the patient must pay 20 percent of the remaining bill. Further, Medicare only pays its percentage on "reasonable" charges; the doctor is allowed to charge more and the patient must pay the difference.

The net result is that the elderly still have to meet whopping medical expenses. In 1977, Medicare paid for only 44 percent of the health care costs of the aged, while Medicaid paid for another 14 percent.[22] The 42 percent left was an oppressive burden. Skyrocketing costs have more than counterbalanced the effects of Medicare and Medicaid. Older people are paying more in real dollars for medical care than they did before Medicare and Medicaid.[23]

BETWEEN 1965 AND 1980, the price of a hospital room rose 450 percent, three times the increase in the consumer price index. The price of physicians' services rose 205 percent, a quarter more than the consumer price index.[24] During the latter half of this period, the real income of the U.S. working class and many other people was not going up, but down.

Soaring medical care costs mean hardship to many people. A one-day hospital stay can eat up half the monthly unemployment insurance check of a laid-off auto or steel worker or the average monthly retirement check of a person on Social Security.

The capitalist press has been bombarding us with articles on health care costs, but almost always with a different focus—a focus on the high-sounding theme of *national* health expenditures. These expenditures, the articles tell us, have been running away.

The reason for the difference in focus is simple—the capitalist press is concerned with the rising cost of health care, not to the people, but to the government. As the *New York Times* put it (3-28-82), there is a danger that "The cost of medical care, which annually consumes a tenth of the country's wealth, will claim an even larger share of the national resources in the years ahead, draining money from other vital needs."

What vital needs? The military budget.

Besides making rising *national* health expenditures the central problem, the press and government try to blame them on the people. Here is an example from a government publication: "In 1981, two thirds of personal health care expenditures were made by the government or by private health insurance. To that extent, consumers of health care are isolated from the true price of health care, and tend to consume more care than they would were they to pay directly the full price of the goods and services they receive."[25]

Some capitalist propaganda puts the blame on Medicare and Medicaid. Actually, health care costs were soaring long before the introduction of these programs.

Some blame the increased pay of hospital employees. This also doesn't hold water. Hospital wages have traditionally been miserably low. They have risen, but payrolls have constituted a declining proportion of total hospital costs.[26] The bulk of the increase in these costs in due to expenses other than wages.

The increase in the price of health care results from several factors: the general inflation; the increasing use of costly technology; the opportunities opened up by insurance, both private and government, for hospitals and doctors to charge more. Capitalist anarchy helps raise costs and charges. Often, for example, several different hospitals in the same area will insist on duplicating expensive equipment when all that is necessary, given the number of potential patients, is to have the equipment available at one hospital.

Of course the increasing cost of health care helps increase national health care expenditures. And Medicaid and Medicare, for all their limitations, have widened access to health care.

We should not allow ourselves to be hoodwinked by the capitalist media. National health care expenditures have been rising in many countries, and in some, such as West Germany and Sweden, constitute a higher proportion of the gross national product than here. An increase in these expenditures is natural, given the advance of medical science and an aging population which needs more health care. Despite the fuss in the press over expenditures, a large proportion of our people do not get adequate care.

But the rise in the price of care, especially when it has to be paid directly by the people, does pose a serious problem—one that along with the problem of inadequate care calls into question the very nature of our health care setup.

HOW CAN WE CONTROL the rise in medical care costs without reducing needed services?

The government has been talking "cost containment," but what it has been doing is to cut services and increase charges. It has been cutting Medicaid benefits since shortly after that program began. Various states, at the prodding of the federal government, have tightened eligibility requirements, imposed charges for drugs previously provided free, and limited the length of hospital stays.

The Reagan administration not only accelerated the pace of cutbacks in Medicaid, but began to lay hands on Medicare. It eliminated some benefits, reduced reimbursement rates to hospitals, and increased the deductibles and co-payments that come from the patient's pocket.

In 1983, the Reagan administration introduced a "cost-cutting" idea inherited from Carter—Medicare will pay hospitals the same amount, fixed in advance, for any patient with a particular diagnosis. Each patient will be placed in one of 467 "diagnosis related groups" and the hospital paid accordingly—so much for a heart attack, so much for a gall bladder removal, etc. If a hospital can hold its costs below the payment, it can keep the difference; if its costs exceed the payment, it has to absorb the loss. The trouble with this system is that hospitals can benefit not only by improving efficiency and eliminating unnecessary services, but also by cutting down care that is necessary.

The new system will subject medical treatment to inflexible bureaucratic rules. Not all heart attacks and gall bladder removals are equal. The same illness, depending on its severity and whether the patient is suffering from other diseases, can require different treatment. In many cases, the bureaucratically fixed fee will not be enough to pay for the care the patient really needs—so that the hospital will be under pressure to reduce the care.

Some hospitals will turn away Medicare patients whenever they have enough patients covered by private insurance which will still be paying on the old basis of simply covering all costs. The differences in hospital care provided different sectors of the population will be further sharpened, with the elderly, like the poor, having access only to inferior care.

Given the private health care system, there is no way out of the dilemma—either inflated costs or a decline in care. As between the two, it is better to have the government overpay than to open the door to a degeneration in care.

OVER THE LAST hundred years, the process of providing health care has become increasingly social. To prevent and cure illness now requires the combined effort of many people and institutions—not just doctors and nurses, but all sorts of specialists and technicians, as well as hospitals and producers of equipment and drugs. But the system of health care remains privately run for private profits.

With the scientific and technologic advance of health care, the private nature of the setup more and more distorts the way it is delivered. New methods and types of care are developed which are beyond the ability of many, often almost all, individual families to pay for. The purveyors of health care gravitate to those specialties that provide big profits to the neglect of other areas that are more important for the health of large numbers of people.

The private profit nature of the setup makes it impossible to take full advantage of advancing science. Science develops modern systems of prenatal care, but many women can't get it—they can't afford to pay so there is no profit in providing it to them.

To meet some of the problems thrown up by the private health care setup, adjustments have been made. The growth of insurance is one. But the insurance is dominated by private companies interested only in profits, and brings its own distortions.

Increased government involvement in health care is another adjustment. But the government involvement has been grudging and piecemeal, designed not to create a rational system of providing care, but to prop up the private setup for doing so. It has not been able to halt the development of a health care crisis.

Today, the poor, the unemployed, the aged, and a growing proportion of those with middle incomes cannot cope with rising medical bills. Inability to pay, in a private profit system, means inability to get proper care. Medicaid and Medicare, the programs designed to mitigate the problems, are under attack because the government sees them as a threat to the military budget.

To appreciate the damage to health care inflicted by the military budget, one must consider the potential progress lost because of increased military spending. Were it not for the growing demands for the military, we would by now probably have national health insurance. The movement for such insurance was gathering force after the end of the Vietnam War until the proponents of increased military spending succeeded in sidetracking it.

National health insurance would be an important step forward, especially if it were financed from general budget revenues, provided full coverage for all medical and dental care, had no deductibles or co-insurance to be paid by the patient, and was run by the government without the participation of the private insurance companies.

Yet even national health insurance would be no more than a prop to a fundamentally flawed system. Health care would remain a commodity to be sold for profit in an anarchic capitalist market, not something planned to meet a basic human need. The combination of privately sold care and comprehensive insurance would give rise to an even bigger constant hassle over costs than there is now.

The social nature of health care calls for eliminating the private aspect of not only its financing, but its delivery. It calls for a *national health service* which would own and run the country's hospitals and other health facilities, employ doctors, nurses, and other health workers for a salary, and provide everyone with all the health care they need—free. Ronald Dellums, joined by nine other Congressmen, introduced a bill for a national health service in 1981.

A national health service would be democratically organized, with representatives of labor and various racial and ethnic groups on the local, regional, and national bodies that run it. Financing would come from general revenues.

Such a service would mean a basic change. Everyone—without regard to income, race, sex, ethnic origin, or age—would have a right to the health care they need. The health care system would be planned. The distribution of doctors, hospitals, clinics, and costly equipment would be rationalized. With doctors paid by salary, the incentive for unnecessary operations would be gone. With all health services free, there would be no incentive to keep people in hospitals just to get the insurance to pay for services that could be performed outside. In sum: a national health service would provide health care more adequately, more fairly, more efficiently, and at less expense than the present system.

THE STRUGGLE OVER health care has many levels. There are local struggles—for example, to prevent an inner city hospital from being closed. There are broader struggles—for example, against cutbacks in Medicaid and Medicare. But while the struggle over health care has its specific features, it is at bottom part of the overall economic and political struggle in the United States.

Some people stress the reactionary role of the American Medical Association as the main obstacle to progress in reforming the health care system. But the doctors are only junior partners in a coalition that includes hospitals and the drug, medical equipment, and insurance companies. Moreover, with the increase in the proportion of doctors who work for a salary and with the developing health care crisis, the outlook of an increasing number of doctors has been shifting in a progressive direction.

The main obstacles to progress in health care are, therefore, the same as the obstacles to progress in the solution of our other economic problems—the military budget and the monopolies. Unless we succeed in slashing the military budget, we can only fight defensive, rearguard actions over health care. We cannot make strategic advances without capturing the resources which the military budget now devours. And we cannot remold the health care system unless we lay hands on the vested interests of the giant insurance companies. Those who fight for a better health care system are part of a broad anti-military, anti-monopoly coalition.

17

Jobs and the Quality of Life

The many-sided economic crisis afflicting the United States is bound to have cruel effects. Unemployment and inflation, plant shutdowns, the decay of cities and infrastructure, cuts in public services, and monopoly greed have all been taking a great and painful toll. The damage has been especially severe for the working class, the Afro-American, Chicano, Puerto Rican and other oppressed peoples, and the youth.

The broadest effect is on the quality of life. Even those not suffering direct economic hardship are being hurt in countless ways. People feel greater anxiety and tension, uncertainty about the future. They have to live in the midst of pervasive deterioration and decay.

GOVERNMENT STATISTICS show that the goal of reducing the American people's standard of living, expressed by leading officials of both the Carter and Reagan administrations, has been realized. Median household income*, measured in constant 1981 dollars, was eleven percent ($2,440) lower in 1981 than in 1973.[1]

The drop in household income has meant a rise in poverty. The poverty rate according to official figures was eleven percent of the population in 1973. By 1982, it had climbed to fifteen percent, the highest figure since 1965, when President Johnson announced his "War on Poverty." Thirty-four million Americans were officially classified as poor.[2]

*The median income is the mid-point of household incomes. Half get more than the median and half get less.

In the official definition, a family of four was poor in 1982 if its income was below $9,862, an unrealistically low figure. Some experts think that $15,000 would have been more reasonable. If $15,000 had been used as the cutoff, the number considered poor would have been 55 to 60 million, a quarter of the population.

With poverty goes hunger. "Once Again Hunger Troubles America," says a *New York Times* headline. The article tells of a family of two—Frank and his wife—living in suburban Bergen County, New Jersey:

> Although Frank was taking home $824 a month (or $9,888 a year) as a machinist, he found himself with little money for food, clothing, and gasoline, because his rent and utilities (more than $500 a month) and medical bills usurped most of his income. His 44-year-old wife can't work because she has impaired vision.
>
> On several occasions last year, Frank and his wife were unable to buy food. A priest referred them to the Center for Food Action, a five-year-old privately funded agency that rents its basement office space from the West Side Presbyterian Church. At times, Frank and his wife had nothing to eat except the canned goods the center gave them—Spam, macaroni and cheese, spaghetti.[3]

"U.S. Hunger on Rise Despite Swelling of Food Surpluses," was another *Times* headline. The story said:

> Hunger is emerging again as a national issue even as Government stocks of surplus dairy products rise to record levels. . . .
>
> After the hearings this year, Mr. [Leon E.] Panetta, who is chairman of the House Agriculture Subcommittee on Nutrition concluded: "This country faces a very serious problem with regard to hunger. Everywhere we went, whether it was Cleveland, Ohio, Birmingham, Alabama, or Los Angeles, California, we heard the same story. The use of soup kitchens, food pantries, and hunger centers is up dramatically in the past two years, in some areas by 400 and 500 percent.[4]

Capitalism by its nature breeds poverty, and in addition, U.S. government policy has been promoting it. Nobody in the government would ever assert that it was following a policy of deliberately increasing poverty. But the Reagan cuts in government aid to those with low incomes and the policy followed by both Republican and Democratic administrations of trying to fight inflation with recession and unemployment have as their inevitable effect an increase in poverty.

THE WORKING CLASS, of course, bears the brunt of the economic crisis. Average real hourly earnings reached a peak in 1972 and then began to decline. In 1982, they were eight percent below the peak. Real weekly earnings declined even more sharply. They were fifteen percent lower in 1982 than in 1972. To find a lower level of weekly earnings than in 1982, one must go back to 1961.[5]

Unemployment has struck a large part of the working class, much larger than appears from the official unemployment rate. In 1973, this rate was 4.9 percent. By December, 1982, it had soared to 10.8 percent, representing 12 million people. But, in addition, there were over 1.5 million workers so discouraged that they had stopped looking for work—unemployed though not counted in the official figures. There were also six million workers involuntarily employed part-time who wanted a full-time job, but couldn't get it, many living in the same cruel circumstances as the fully unemployed. The officially unemployed plus the discouraged and involuntarily part-time totalled 20 million, equal to 18 percent of the labor force.[6]

Further, there is turnover among the unemployed—the number of workers hit by unemployment over a year is much larger than the number of unemployed at any given time during that year. Referring to the turnover, the *New York Times* disclosed in October, 1982: "It is estimated that fully a fourth of the labor force has been officially unemployed for some period during the past 12 months . . . ."[7] The proportion of really unemployed, as opposed to just officially unemployed, was larger still.

What are the human consequences of unemployment? Those who have ever been unemployed know that there is no way of fully measuring the misery and damage inflicted by this curse of capitalism. But here is a glance at what unemployment does, taken from an article by Jane Brody, the *New York Times* writer on health:

> The unemployment problem . . . affects many people who had never before thought they would be involuntarily jobless. A growing number are family men in their 50s who see a quarter century of hard-won equity dissolve before their eyes, with few prospects for restoring what they have lost. In many families, wives who previously had not worked outside the home are being forced to take unskilled jobs. The results are often an undercurrent of resentment and anger, disruption of personal and family routines, and a growing sense of desperation and fear.

> Dr. Harvey Brenner, a sociologist at Johns Hopkins Univer-

sity, has been a longtime student of the health and social consequences of recession and unemployment. His data show that for each 1 percent rise in unemployment, suicides increase 4.1 percent; homicides, 5.7 percent; deaths from heart disease, cirrhosis of the liver and stress-related disorders, 1.9 percent; and admissions to mental hospitals, 2.3 percent for women and 4.3 percent for men. . . .

Dr. Ramsey Liem, psychologist at Boston College, examined the consequences of job loss among 40 blue-collar and 40 white-collar families. He found that within a few months, the wives of unemployed men became significantly more depressed, anxious, phobic and sensitive about interpersonal relationships than did the wives of employed men.

Dr. Louis A. Fermen of the University of Michigan's Institute of Labor and Industrial Relations found that children in unemployed families commonly experience digestive problems, irritability, and retarded physical and mental development. . . .[8]

WITHIN THE WORKING CLASS, the economic crisis has been striking hardest at the oppressed minority peoples—Afro-Americans, Chicanos, Puerto Ricans, Native American Indians, peoples of Asian origin and others. For them, the crisis has halted and reversed the process—weak to begin with—of economic improvement. In 1960, the median income of Afro-American families was 55 percent of the white family median. During the latter half of the 1960s, this percentage began to rise, reaching 61.5 in 1975. Then, *despite a decline* in white income, it began to fall, dropping to 55 in 1982, back to where it was in 1960.[9]

Statistics on the income of Hispanic families are not available before 1972, but the figures since then show that Hispanic people have also suffered a sharper drop in income than whites. Whereas the median income of white families dropped by 10 percent between 1973 and 1982, that of Hispanic families fell by 14 percent.[10]

The chief cause of the deterioration in the position of minority families is their proportionately greater unemployment. By the last quarter of 1982, the official unemployment rates for white, Black and Hispanic people were as follows:[11]

The average rate for all workers, 10.3%. Black, 19.9%; Hispanic origin (average), 14.8%; white, 9.1%. Among the Hispanic unemployed: of Mexican origin, 15.4%; Puerto Rican origin, 19.5%; Cuban origin, 13.2%.

The official figures, we must remember, understate. The true unemployment rate among Afro-Americans and Puerto Ricans was over 30 percent.

This rise in unemployment and decline in real income caused a big increase in poverty. Between 1974 and 1982, the percentage of Black people living below the official poverty line rose from 30 to 36, the percentage of Hispanics from 23 to 30.[12] With a more realistic definition of poverty than the official one, over fifty percent of Blacks and Puerto Ricans would have been classified as poor in 1982.

EVEN IN "GOOD TIMES" unemployment and poverty among Native American Indians are astronomic. A 1973 Bureau of Indian Affairs survey of Native Americans living on or near federal reservations found an unemployment rate of 37 percent among them.[13]

The general economic crisis has made things even worse. Here is a quotation from a *New York Times* story on January 31, 1983:

> Some 1,600 San Carlos Apaches, nearly 70 percent of the tribe's total labor force . . . are without work this winter. That is twice as many as two years ago, a time the tribal leaders recall as a period of relative prosperity. Meanwhile, welfare payments on the reservation have increased by 25 percent over the last two years as tribal members who have lost jobs on the outside return home. At the same time, Federal money available to the tribal government for job training and development programs has declined more than 30 percent over the same period. . . .

HOW ABOUT THE GROWTH of a "middle class" among the Black and Hispanic people? Back in 1968, the *Report of the National Commission on Civil Disorders* discussed the question:

> It can be argued that a rapidly enlarging Negro middle class would promote Negro out-migration and thus . . . would open up an escape hatch from the ghetto. . . . [But] even if enlargement of the Negro middle class succeeded in encouraging movement out of the central city, could it do so fast enough to offset the rapid growth of the ghetto?[14]

This report did not conclude that the growth of a Black middle class would solve the problems of the ghetto, even at a time when the proportion of middle class Blacks was growing. In recent years, the proportion has declined. The proportion of Black families with incomes above $25,000, in constant dollars, has declined since 1978. It was lower in 1982 than in 1972. The proportion of Hispanic families with incomes above $25,000 was also lower in 1982 than in 1972.[15]

One must be careful in drawing conclusions from the number of Hispanics of Cuban origin who are in the middle class. Many Cuban families were already middle class—headed by business-men and professionals—when they arrived in the United States. For the bulk of Hispanic people, the possibility of joining the middle class is no more of an escape hatch than it is for Afro-Americans.

WHY DOES THE ECONOMIC crisis strike with special force at the oppressed minority peoples, so that they lose ground relative to whites? Why does unemployment among them rise even more than among whites? The answer lies in the working of capitalism—in the discrimination fostered by capitalism, in the special position cap-italism has assigned the oppressed minorities in the economy.

The use of racism and national and ethnic prejudice to divide the working class and squeeze out superprofits goes far back in U.S. history. Here is a comment on Chicago in the 1880s:

> The columns of the *Tribune* and *Times* were filled day after day with cruel and senseless attacks upon the foreign-born. A 'communist' was always a 'German communist.' Strikes and labor demonstrations were always mobs composed of foreign scum, beersmelling Germans, ignorant Bohemians, uncouth Poles, wild-eyed Russians.[16]

The average wages of the foreign-born were, of course, kept far below those of the native-born workers. The corporations followed a conscious policy of exploiting ethnic and racial differences. An 1884 report on the coke regions of Pennsylvania tells how the operators were "pitting the English against the Irish, and vice versa, and the Germans against both . . . keeping up a constant war of the races. . . ."[17]

The monopolies do the same today. They try to pit white, Black, and Chicano, Puerto Rican, and other workers against each other. They promote a division of the labor force by race and national background and use it to force large sections of the working class to accept lower wages and worse conditions, thus gaining tens of billions in additional profits each year. They force the minority peoples to function as the main source of their reserve army of labor.[18]

The oppressed minorities are concentrated in jobs that are most vulnerable to the downswings of the business cycle and unemployment. For example, in 1981, unemployment among managers and administrators was 3 percent, while among non-farm laborers, it was 15 percent. Twelve percent of whites were managers and administrators, but less than half that percentage of Afro-Americans and Hispanic people, while for laborers, the relationship was reversed.[19]

Unemployment runs lower for white collar than blue collar workers. A higher percentage of white workers are white collar. Among blue collar workers, unemployment is lower in the skilled crafts than among ordinary operatives. A higher proportion of white workers are in the skilled crafts.[20]

The oppressed minorities hold a disproportionate share of the jobs in industries most likely to be transferred abroad. Take apparel. This industry has been a traditional source of jobs for low-paid immigrant workers. In recent years, a large proportion of its labor force has consisted of Afro-Americans and Hispanics and in some places, like New York City, newly-arrived Chinese immigrants. The transfer of apparel factories abroad illustrates how U.S. capitalists have internationalized their reserve army of labor. They have incorporated workers in many other countries into the reserve, at the expense of jobs for U.S. workers.

As is illustrated by the apparel, steel, and auto industries, the oppressed minorities are concentrated in the manufacturing industries which have been suffering the most from imports. They are only slightly represented in the production of high technology goods—computers, aerospace, scientific instruments, etc.—where the U.S. competitive position is strong.

Finally, only a small share of the jobs in military industry are of the type that usually go to minority workers. A much higher proportion of jobs in military than civilian industry are for engineers and other professional and technical people and for craftsmen. A much lower proportion are for production workers.

What is the future of the multiracial, multinational U.S. working class in our crisis-ridden economy? An important lesson emerges from the struggle of the last thirty years. The fight for civil rights and against discrimination is vital to the unity of Black and white workers, and to Black liberation, but it is not enough, even when accompanied by affirmative action. It is just not true that if the oppressed minorities achieve formal legal and political equality, capitalism will do the rest. Capitalism will *not* do the rest.

Even when not beset by crises, capitalism works against the solution of the economic problems of the minorities because the monopolies gain superprofits by paying lower wages to minority workers and by using the differential to reduce the wages of all workers. The economic crisis stymies the economic advance of the minorities. Economic inequality makes it impossible to achieve real legal and political equality.

How must the problem be dealt with? It requires, on top of affirmative action, a full-scale battle over how the economy is run, a fight to have it run in a way that guarantees jobs for all. Such a battle is now crucial for all elements of our multiracial, multinational working class, and only by the unified action of all working people and their allies can it be waged successfully.

HOW DOES THE ECONOMIC crisis affect the youth? The figures on youth unemployment tell their own story. In the second quarter of 1983, according to the official statistics, unemployment among 16- to 19-year-olds was as follows: Afro-American—51 percent; Hispanic—30 percent; white—21 percent.[21]

Again: the offical statistics understate. No one knows what the true youth unemployment rates are—probably between 70 and 90 percent for the Afro-American and other minority youth in our central cities.

Black teenage unemployment has been rising since the mid-1950s. For white youth, it began to go up in the 1970s. The problem is still deepening. Youth unemployment afflicts not only the United States, but most other leading capitalist countries.

What accounts for the high and growing youth unemployment? Several things: the flight of factories from the cities, the decline in unskilled jobs as a result of automation, the general stagnation and high unemployment. When unemployment in general rises, youth unemployment rises even more. Young workers are also a labor reserve and suffer especially from slack labor markets. For Black and Hispanic youth, hiring discrimination is, of course, also a key factor.

Black youth are as eager to work as white youth and tend to stay on the job longer, according to a 1983 study by a research organization created by the Ford Foundation. Dr. Judy Gueron, Vice President of the organization, states: "The problem is not that [Black youth] have unreal wage expectations, a preference for crime, or lack of motivation, but rather an absence of jobs."[22]

Astronomic youth unemployment inflicts terrible wounds. It causes some youth to feel that they are excluded from society. The problem is more than economic. The insecurity created by the growing militarization and the danger of war has a special meaning for youth.

UNEMPLOYMENT OF PEOPLE 55 and older is lower than that for the population as a whole, but still reached a record level of 5.8 percent in December, 1982. When the elderly lose their jobs, they tend to remain unemployed much longer than average. Many, even though they are desperately looking for jobs, will never find work again.

As an article in the *Wall Street Journal* states:

Joblessness, always a bitter pill, strikes older men and women especially hard. Their lives sour at a time when they expected to begin reaping the fruits of their labor. They question their long-cherished work values of honesty, loyalty, and service. . . . When their jobs disappear, they feel that they have lost "their place in society," and they make comments such as "I've been raped. I have nothing left. . . ."

The article cites a House Aging Committee report:

It says older workers' typically longer siege of unemployment makes them more prone to develop alcoholism, depression, insomnia, and stress-related illnesses, including ulcers and high blood pressure. . . . To cover the treatment of such ailments, the older unemployed must buy health insurance at high rates, aggravating their money woes.

One worker who lost his job as a food-concession manager after 32 years put it simply: "When people let you go when you're in your 60s, they're practically ringing the death knell for you."[23]

The inflation has, across the years, been robbing almost everyone, but especially the senior citizens. No one will ever be able to calculate the billions stolen from pensions by the inflation. Soaring health care costs also hit the seniors particularly hard.

Finally, we have the government's attack on Social Security, Medicare and Medicaid. Here, too, there is a lesson about the value of struggle. The attack would be stronger, were it not for the government's fear of the senior citizens' political clout.

THE AVERAGE WEEKLY earnings of women are 65 percent those of men. They can ill afford the reduction in real earnings of the last ten years. In 1982, 9.5 million families—15 percent of the total—were classified in the government statistics as headed by women.[24] In many more families, women contribute to the joint family income, sometimes earning more than the men.

What lies behind the changing position of women? The traditional claim about woman's place being in the home has never been true for many sectors of the population. Black women, immigrant women, and poor women have always worked. But since World War II, the percentage of working women has increased dramatically from 30 percent of all women in 1947 to 52 percent in 1981.[25]

In 1982, 36 percent of families headed by women were below the official poverty line—a higher percentage than in any year since 1965. In this category, there were 1.8 million families headed by white women, 1.5 million headed by Afro-American women and 425,000 headed by Hispanic women.[26] For these families, the struggle to do away with the Reagan budget cuts has special urgency.

WITH ALL THE DAMAGE and suffering it has inflicted on the quality of life so far, the crisis is still developing. Allowed to continue unchecked, it can do much more damage. We Americans find it hard to imagine how much more.

We have grown up in the tradition that our country is the economic leader of the world, the one that provides the highest standard of living. The first reaction of many of us to these problems is that they are temporary—that they will go away either by themselves or with a few changes in government policy.

Some of us tend to measure our economic difficulties against the crisis of the 1930s. We rationalize that the present troubles haven't developed as suddenly as the white-hot emergency we had in 1931-33 and, therefore, don't really constitute a crisis.

But because what we have today is different from the 1930s does not make it any less a crisis—one that is in fact in many ways more comprehensive, more unyielding, more durable. Given high military budgets and a failure to curb the power of the monopolies, this crisis will not end. It will go on indefinitely. We will have continued balance of payments deficits and inflation, frequent recessions and high unemployment, further shrinkage and disappearance of industry, futher decay of cities and infrastructure, and further human losses.

We could easily get something still worse. One of the attempts to contain the balance of payments deficit or inflation through recession could set off a big, prolonged depression. A new eruption of the oil crisis, whether in the form of an acute shortage or a longer-run tightening of supplies could wreak further havoc on the auto industry and the economy.

The working class faces high unemployment indefinitely—unemployment that could easily climb even higher than the peak reached during the 1981-82 recession. Workers face constant pressure on wage rates and benefits as the monopolies carry through their policies.

What will the situation be if the crisis is allowed to gnaw away at the U.S. economy for another twenty years? More countries that are less burdened by military expenditures than the U.S. will catch up and surpass the United States technologically and economically. More U.S. industries will vanish. The U.S. economy will be more deformed. The time when the United States provided the highest standard of living will be only a memory.

The economic crisis involves more than economics. The political process in the United States evolved during the golden days of the U.S. economy and bears the imprint of this period. With an economy that, for all its faults, was rich compared to others, the ruling class was often able to make politics revolve around secondary issues, to set up the tweedledum-tweedledee, Democratic-Republican two-party trap. But now the developing economic crisis as well as the problem of preventing nuclear war makes it crucial that we have a political process that is a more effective means of solving the problems that plague us.

18

The Struggle Ahead

Why is it that the Democratic and Republican parties are so bankrupt in the face of the crisis? The answer is that to make a dent on the crisis requires measures that would cut deeply into monopoly capitalist-imperialist interests—and these two parties exist to promote and defend those interests, not to damage them.

We must be careful about drawing conclusions from the experience with the crisis of the 1930s. Roosevelt represented monopoly capitalism, yet was able to soften the worst of the crisis through mild reforms. Far less can be accomplished today by such reforms. Now it is necessary to lay hands on basic, not just secondary, monopoly interests.

Moreover, it took a world war to get the United States fully out of the crisis of the 1930s. The present crisis is different—a war would make it worse. A nuclear war would mean the end of the human race.

Even Roosevelt's mild reforms provoked fierce opposition from the monopolies. Against the measures required to deal effectively with the present crisis, the opposition would be many times more fierce. How far would a President who represented monopoly capitalism be willing to go? How far would the monopolies allow him to go?

Effective action against the present crisis requires an independent people's movement—one whose focus is the needs of the people, not how to get by with concessions that do the least damage to the monopolies. Effective action requires mobilizing the people into a grand coalition: workers—white, Black, Hispanic, other minorities; men and women; youth; farmers and other small business people, professionals, and seniors; and any others hurt by economic crisis and decay or worried about war.

Trade unions, as the organized sector of the working class, have a leading part to play in the attack on the crisis. But to play this part, they must recognize that their problem is not limited to individual companies, but extends to state monopoly capitalism as a whole. They must broaden their range of activity. They must develop and fight for their *own comprehensive program* for dealing with the crisis. They must fight against the ruinous military and foreign policy of the United States. They must engage in political action on a far greater, more comprehensive scale than they do now.

Political action has its own logic. To be done with full effectiveness, it requires an organization specifically adapted to the purpose. The Communist Party of the United States has long advocated an independent, anti-monopoly political party led by labor and committed to a program of radical reforms. Only the people, mobilized, can provide the strength to deal effectively with the crisis we face. A coalition against the monopolies would fight for changes along the following lines:

1. End the arms race, sharply reduce the military budget, and strengthen peace.

2. Institute a comprehensive set of measures for improving the economic position of Afro-American and other minorities so that within a reasonable time, there is no "income gap."

3. End the practice of fighting inflation and a weak dollar by using economic slowdown, recession and higher unemployment.

4. Renew our infrastructure, rebuild our railroad system, construct mass transit systems where necessary, renovate and build schools and hospitals, and create public housing on a mass scale—thus providing millions of jobs.

5. Establish at least a national health insurance system and preferably a comprehensive national health service.

6. Carry out a tax reform that will eliminate tax loopholes, raise taxes on the corporations and the rich, lower them for working people and provide a truly progressive tax structure.

7. Strengthen our social security system by providing for support from general budget revenues and reversing the recent government actions to raise the retirement age and limit benefits.

8. Attack the problem of plant closings and shrinking industries through government regulation of closings and of investment abroad.

9. Nationalize the steel, auto, railroad, energy and electric power industries, as well as any others that the monopolies show they cannot or will not maintain in a healthy state.

This list is not exhaustive; many other items could be added.

BY THE STANDARDS propagated by U.S. state monopoly capitalism, this program is "radical." But we must judge radicalism in relation to the problems we face. These problems are such that only with so-called radical measures can we make a dent.

How can we think through to solutions to our problems if at the very start we must reject certain measures which the monopolies want us to regard as radical? The test we must apply is not whether a measure is radical, but whether it makes sense.

We must think through the issue of peace and disarmament. In our own interest, we must try to arrive at an accurate answer to the question of who—the United States or the Soviet Union—is responsible for the arms race.

Who started the arms race shortly after World War II? The last thing the war-devastated Soviet Union needed was an arms race.

Who was the first to develop and deploy all the main weapons, including the atom bomb, the hydrogen bomb, the intercontinental ballistic missile, the ballistic missile submarine, the MIRV missile with its multiple warheads? The United States. It is still the first today in pushing ahead with such weapons as the cruise missile, the neutron bomb, and space weapons.

Who, as part of its military doctrine, maintains the possibility of fighting "limited" nuclear war? Who still refuses to renounce first use of nuclear weapons? The United States.

Those who don't want to end the arms race try to make it appear as though this can't be done. But it can. It requires honest negotiations with the Soviet Union.

We must also think through the question of curbing the monopolies. The monopolies work to create an atmosphere in which regulation of plant closings and investment abroad, to say nothing of nationalizing whole industries, are unthinkable. But following this monopoly line makes our problems insoluble. Plants close, industries shrink and disappear, and people watch bewildered—it seems as though nothing can be done. But something can be done. It requires laying hands on the monopolies.

Actually, if we free ourselves from the point of view the monopolies try to implant, the above program is moderate. What's immoderate about wanting peace and effective action against our economic ills?

We are approaching the twenty-first century and we must bring our economy more into line with the possibilities and requirements of the times. We must fight to democratize our economy and to establish an economic bill of rights.

Such a bill would guarantee everyone the right to a job, an adequate income and decent housing, a good education, proper health care, adequate retirement benefits and comprehensive free or low-cost child care for all who need it.

The material forces of society are sufficient to make such a bill of rights a reality. Why, then, shouldn't we establish it?

TO PUT THROUGH an effective economic program, to establish a people's economic bill of rights, requires struggle. Where, ultimately, can the struggle lead?

To answer this question requires a proper perspective on the crisis now afflicting the U.S. economy. The economic crisis is not just a cyclical crisis of the type that has afflicted industrial capitalism from its beginnings. It is a comprehensive crisis affecting all aspects of the economy, a developing crisis that keeps getting deeper with time. On top of the classical ailments of capitalism, we now have new ones flowing from the development of monopoly finance capitalism and imperialism and the world wide struggle against them. The U.S. economic crisis is part of the general crisis of capitalism, tied to the desperate attempts of the United States to preserve world capitalism by military means. Not just the economy is in crisis, but all of U.S. society.

In crises, society doesn't mark time—it either goes forward or back. The choices become sharper. The choice now is to move forward or sink further into crisis.

We have already witnessed a great degeneration in U.S. society. Nothing in our economy works right. Since World War II, we have suffered two wars and live under the constant threat of others, including a nuclear war. Administrations from Truman to Reagan have used varying degrees of domestic repression to put down opponents of their policies. The U.S. ruling class is in deep trouble and there is the danger that one of these days it will feel compelled to try to establish an American brand of fascism to preserve its interests.

But there is also another side. A big struggle is now a-building in the United States, one that revolves around elemental issues: jobs; the escape of the Afro-American and other minorities from the economic morass; the future of our youth; the quality of life; and not simply war or peace, but the survival of humanity.

Struggle has more than one aspect. It is crucial for lowering the danger of nuclear war. It can win important economic concessions. But struggle is also a process in which one thing leads to another; it is what propels society forward. In periods of heightened struggle, we learn especially fast. We learn what has to be done and who stands in the way—and then what more has to be done. Because of the depth of the crisis and the power of the issues involved, the struggle now developing can propel our society far.

No one can predict how far, how fast, but the basic point can be made: While immediate action is indispensable to preserve peace and can do a great deal of good on our economic problems, a full solution of the crisis requires the building of socialism. What we are dealing with is not a partial crisis, but the general crisis of capitalism, which only the elimination of the whole rotten system can fully resolve.

Historical development and concrete fact are bearing out the theories of the great founders of Marxism-Leninism. Marx and Engels pointed to the contradictions inherent in capitalism, to the clash between the social nature of production and private capitalist ownership and control. Capitalist economists sneered, either denying the existence of the contradictions or claiming that capitalism would somehow resolve them. But today we see capitalism writhing in contradictions more acute than ever.

Lenin developed the theory of imperialism as the final stage of capitalism, as parasitic, decaying capitalism. Back in 1914 he wrote: "Imperialism sets at hazard the fate of European culture. this war will soon be followed by others. . . ."[1] The salesmen for capitalism try to ignore Lenin. But whom does the crisis in U.S. society show to be right?

Some will say that talk of socialism is unrealistic; that the majority of Americans don't believe in socialism. True, they don't; but in growing numbers they know something is wrong and they want it corrected. Without socialism, it cannot be corrected.

Socialism in the United States will be a response to the crisis here. It will be born in the struggle of the American people to deal with their problems. It will be shaped in line with the traditions of our people. We will make our own mistakes and our own contributions to the building of socialism in the world.

Stormy struggles and great opportunities lie before the American people.

NOTES

I

1. In 1980, there were over 50 million people in the U.S. who could be classified as members of racially and nationally oppressed minorities. These included Afro-Americans; Chicanos, Mexicans, Puerto Ricans, Dominicans, Haitians, Jamaicans, and others of Caribbean, or Central or South American origin; Native American Indians and Native Alaskans; Chinese, Filipinos, Japanese, Asian Indians, Koreans, Vietnamese and other Asian peoples; Palestinians, Yemenis and other Arabs; Iranians, and others. The two largest minorities are the "Blacks" and "Hispanics" (as they are often designated in government statistics), together accounting for three-quarters of the total members of minorities. (Statistical Abstract of the U.S., 1982-83, p. 32). Hereafter cited as *SA.*

2. V.I. Lenin, *Collected Works* (Moscow: Progress Publishers, 1964), IV, 311.

3. Karl Marx, *Capital* (Chicago: Charles H. Kerr & Co.), 1926, I, 652.

4. Lenin, op.cit.

5. For a fuller discussion, see Gil Green, *What's Happening to Labor* (New York: International Publishers, 1976), Ch. 4, "Exploitation, U.S. Style;" also Karl Marx, *Wage-Labour & Capital/Value, Price & Profit* (New York: International Publishers, 1976).

6. Paul Samuelson, *Economics,* 7th ed. (New York: McGraw-Hill, 1967), p. 40.

7. Milton and Rose Friedman, *Free to Choose* (New York: Harcourt, Brace, Jovanovich, 1979), pp. 14-15.

8. Ibid., 14, 17.

9. Samuelson, op.cit., 41.

10. Marx, op.cit., III, 292. See also Ch. XV, "Internal Contradictions."

11. Alfred Marshall, *Principles of Economics,* 8th ed. (London: Macmillan and Co., 1938), 711.

12. Samuelson, op.cit., 239, 255.

13. Frederick Engels, *The Condition of the Working Class in England* (Moscow: Progress Publishers, 1973), 123.

14. U.S. Dept. of Commerce, *Historical Statistics of the United States, Colonial Times to 1970* (hereafter cited as *H. Stat.*); (Washington: U.S. Government Printing Office, 1975 (hereafter, Govt. P.O.) I, 135.

15. Samuelson, op.cit., 581.

II

1. Editors of *Fortune, The Conglomerate Commotion* (New York: Viking Press, 1970), 7. Italics in original.

2. *New York Times,* 4-24-83.

3. *Conglomerate Mergers—Their Effects on Small Business and Local Communities,* Report of the Committee on Small Business, House of Representatives, 96th Congress (Washington: Govt. P.O.), p. 25.

4. John F. Winslow, *Conglomerates Unlimited, The Failure of Regulation* (Bloomington and London: Indiana University Press, 1973), 134-136.

5. Lenin, op.cit. XXII, 105.

6. Ibid., 240. Italics in original.

7. *H. Stat II,* 870, and U.S. Dept. of Commerce, *SA,* 1981, p. 836.

8. William K. Chung, "Sales by Majority-owned Foreign Affiliates of U.S. Companies," *Survey of Current Business,* March, 1978.

9. Sidney Rolfe and Walter Damm, eds., *The Multinational Corporation in the World Economy* (New York: Praeger Publishers, 1970), 9.

III

1. John Maynard Keynes, *The General Theory of Employment, Interest, and Money* (New York: Harcourt, Brace and Co., 1936), 28.
2. Ibid., 377-78.
3. Ibid., 378.
4. Ibid., 129.
5. Ibid., 380.
6. John Kenneth Galbraith and Nicole Salinger, *Almost Everyone's Guide to Economics* (New York: Bantam Books, 1979), 19.
7. Calculated from data in Council of Economic Advisers, *Economic Report of the President 1981* (Washington: Govt. P.O., 1982), Appendix B. Hereafter cited as *ERP*.
8. Calculated from SA, 1981, p. 545.

IV

1. Calculated from gross national product (GNP) statistics in *ERP*, 1983, 164.
2. *H. Stat. II*, 1104-05.
3. William F. Mueller, *A Primer on Monopoly and Competition* (New York: Random House, 1970), p. 111.
4. Quoted in John Blair, *Economic Concentration* (New York: Harcourt, Brace, Jovanovich, 1972), 436.
5. Ibid., 424.
6. Ibid., 470-95.
7. "The Inflationary Impact of Unemployment: Price Markups During Postwar Recessions 1947-70," prepared for the Joint Economic Committee, U.S. Congress, in *Achieving the Goals of the Employment Act of 1946* (Washington: Govt. P.O., 1976), p. 2.
8. "Inflation in the United States," John Blair, et al, *The Roots of Inflation* (New York: Burt Franklin & Co., 1975), 48.
9. *ERP* 1982, p. 291.
10. *ERP* 1973, 267-68.
11. *ERP* 1982, 233, 318.
12. J.K. Galbraith, *The New Industrial State* (New York: Signet Books, 1968), 256-57.
13. *ERP* 1982, 276.
14. Friedman, op. cit., 270-71.
15. 44th Annual Report, June 10, 1974, p. 38.

V

1. "State of the Union Message," 1981, *New York Times*, Feb. 19, 1981.
2. *New York Times*, 2-19-81.
3. *New York Review of Books*, May 14, 1981.
4. William Greider, "The Education of David Stockman," *The Atlantic*, Dec. 1981, 47, 51.
5. AFL-CIO Dept. of Economic Research, *Reagan Economics—Behind the Rhetoric*, August, 1981, II-4.
6. Ibid., see also Americans for Democratic Action, *The Reagan Watch, the First 100 Days*, Spring, 1981.
7. Ibid.
8. Derived from figures in "Excerpts from a White House 'Fact Sheet', Describing the Economic Program," *New York Times*, 2-19-81.

9. *New York Times*, 2-7-82.
10. *New York Times*, 6-16-82.
11. *New York Times*, 2-14-82.

VI

1. Robert DeGrasse, Jr., with Paul Murphy and William Ragen, *The Costs and Consequences of Reagan's Military Buildup*, a Report to the International Association of Machinists and Aerospace Workers (IAM), AFL-CIO; and the Coalition for a New Foreign and Military Policy, Council on Economic Priorities, New York, 1982, pp. 24, 26.
2. Ibid., 26-29.

VII

1. SA, 1971, 444.
2. Howard S. Piquet, *The Balance of Payments and International Monetary Reserves* (Washington: American Enterprise Institute for Public Policy, 1966), 93.
3. *1980 Supplement to Economic Indicators*, prepared for the Joint Economic Committee, U.S. Congress (Washington: Govt. P.O. 1980), 134; *H. Stat.* II, 885.
4. *ERP* 1982, 346.
5. SA, 1981, 852.
6. *ERP* 1981, 343.
7. 1978 Annual Report, International Monetary Fund, (Washington), 39.
8. U.S. Dept. of Labor, Office of Foreign Economic Research, *Report of the President on U.S. Competitiveness* (Washington: Govt. P.O., 1980).
9. Press release accompanying report, 1.
10. See n.8, Ch.1, p.2.
11. Fact sheet accompanying report, 2.
12. See n.8, Ch.3, p.21.
13. Ibid., Ch. 4, p.1.
14. Ibid., p.30.
15. Statement accompanying report by Director, Office of Foreign Economic Research, 10.

VIII

1. *American Ground Transport*, Part 4A, Hearings before the Subcommittee on Antitrust and Monopoly of the Committee on the Judiciary, U.S. Senate, 93rd Congress (Washington: Govt. P.O. 1974), 43-45.
2. *Ground Transportation Industries*, Part 3, Hearings, (see n.1), p. 1919.
3. See n.1, p.32.
4. Robert Stobaugh and Daniel Yergin, eds., *Energy Future: Report of the Energy Project at the Harvard Business School* (New York: Ballantine Books, 1979), 18.
5. Anthony Sampson, *The Seven Sisters* (New York: Bantam Books, 1976), 144.
6. John Blair, *The Control of Oil* (New York: Pantheon Books, 1976), 117.
7. Stobaugh, op.cit., 23.
8. Ibid., 25.
9. Sampson, op.cit., 253-54, 269, and Stobaugh, op.cit., 25-27.
10. SA, 1977, 596.
11. Estimated from the OPEC price increase, the proportion of U.S. oil consumption covered by imports, and the retail price increase.
12. "1980—Financial Analysis of a Group of Petroleum Companies," *The Petroleum Situation*, January 1982.
13. Office of Technology Assessment, U.S. Congress, *World Petroleum Availability 1980-2000* (Washington: Govt. P.O., 1980), p. 33 ff.; Exxon Corp., *World*

Energy Outlook, December 1980 (New York: 1981), p.22; Stobaugh, op.cit., pp. 47, 50.

14. SA, 1982-83, 712; American Petroleum Institute, *Basic Petroleum Yearbook* (Washington: 1980), Sec. II, Tables 1, 1a.

15. Stobaugh, op.cit., 47-48.

16. *Basic Petro. Yearbook*, Sec. II, Table 1.

17. *See OTA*, n.13, p.33.

18. *New York Times*, 9-5-83.

19. Special Energy Message to Congress, 1-23-74; in Congressional Quarterly, Inc., *Energy Policy* (Washington: 1981), 244.

20. Address to Congress on Energy, 4-20-77; in ibid, p.256.

21. U.S. Dept. of Energy, *Securing America's Energy Future, The National Energy Policy Plan* (Washington: Govt. P.O., 1981), p.2.

22. Op.cit., n.20.

23. Op.cit.,n.21, p.13.

24. *New York Times*, 11-9-82.

IX

1. (Washington: A Progressive Alliance Publication, 1980), p.59; *see* also Barry Bluestone, Bennett Harrison, and Lawrence Baker, *Corporate Flight: The Causes and Consequences of Economic Dislocation* (Washington: A Progressive Alliance Book, 1981), p.13.

2. Edmund S. Whitman and James Smith, *Plant Relocation, A Case History of a Move* (New York: American Management Association, 1966), 13-14.

3. North American Congress on Latin America (NACLA), *Capital's Flight, the Apparel Industry Moves South* (New York: March, 1977), pp.11, 25.

4. NACLA, *Electronics: The Global Industry* (New York: April, 1977), 10.

5. Ed Kelly and Lee Webb, *Plant Closings, Resources for Public Officials and Activists* (Washington: Conference on State and Local Policies, 1979), 38.

6. Milton Moscowitz, Michael Katz and Robert Levering, eds., *Everybody's Business, The Irreverent Guide to Corporate America* (New York: Harper and Row, 1980), 294.

7. Quoted in Bluestone and Harrison in *Capital and Communities*, 191.

8. Reproduced in *The Apparel Industry Moves South*, (n.3), p.14.

9. Ibid., 13.

10. See n.7, p.50, Emphasis in original.

11. "Profits Without Productivity," Seymour Melman, ed., *The War Economy of the United States, Readings on Military Industry and Economy* (New York: St. Martin's Press, 1971), 126-28.

12. NACLA, *Electronics*, op.cit., 13.

13. *Conglomerate Mergers*, op.cit., (see ch.2,n.3) pp.21-22.

14. Ibid., 24.

X

1. Secy. of Transportation, *The U.S. Auto Industry 1980* (Washington: Dept. of Transportation, 1981), Introduction, p.2 (hereafter cited as *Auto 1980*).

2. Ibid., Letter of transmittal, p.1.

3. *Auto 1980*, p.88.

4. U.S. Dept. of Commerce, *United States Automobile Industry, Status Report*, submitted to the U.S. Senate Comm. on Finance, Subcomm. on International Trade, 1981, p.4, (hereafter cited as *US Auto Status*).

5. *Auto 1980*, 86-7.

6. Alfred P. Sloan, Jr., *My Years with General Motors* (New York: Anchor Books, 1972), 70.

7. Ibid., 76.

8 Ibid., 308

9. Blair, op.cit., (see ch. IV, n.4), p.502.

10 Ibid., 482.

11 Subcommittee on Trade of the Comm. on Ways and Means, U.S. House of Repr. (Washington: Govt. P.O., 1980), p.53.

12. John Z. De Lorean and J. Patrick Wright, *On a Clear Day You Can See General Motors* (New York: Avon Books, 1979), 211.

13. Ibid., 212-13

14. Ibid., 63.

15. *Consumer Reports*, April, 1980, as quoted in *Auto Situation 1980*, p.54.

16. *Auto Situation 1980*, 27-8.

17. *Auto 1980*, 56.

18. *Auto 1980*, p. xii.

19. *New York Times*, 11-9-80.

20. *Auto 1980*, 58.

21. "Detroit Downsizes U.S. Jobs," *The Nation*, 10-11-80, 346-47.

22. *Auto 1980*, 85-6.

23. *New York Times*, 10-14-81.

24. "The Chrysler Crisis," *Dollars and Sense*, Jan., 1980.

25. *Newsweek*, 8-13-79.

26. *New York Times*, 11-4-79.

27. *New York Times*, 9-23-79.

28. *New York Times*, 11-11-79.

29. *New York Times*, 4-21-83.

30. *New York Times*, 4-23-83.

31. *New York Times*, 4-28-83.

32. *US Auto Status*, p.4.

XI

1. American Iron and Steel Institute, *Steel at the Crossroads: The American Iron and Steel Industry in the 1980s* (Washington: January, 1980), p.5. Hereafter cited as *Steel Crossroads*.

2. Ibid., p.10.

3. *New York Times, Wall Street Journal*, Dec. 28, 1983.

4. Council on Wage and Price Stability, *Report to the President on Prices and Costs in the United States Steel Industry* (Washington: Govt. P.O., 1977), p.19.

5. Ibid., p.20.

6. Ibid.

7. Ibid.

8. *Labor Today*, March, 1981.

9. *Steel Crossroads*, pp. 21, 23.

10. Ibid., p. 33.

11. Ibid., p.11.

12. *New York Times*, Nov. 20, 1981.

13. Helen Shapiro and Steven Volk, *Steelyard Blues: New Structures in Steel* (New York: NACLA, Jan-Feb., 1979), pp. 15-17.

14. *New York Times*, Dec. 29, 1983.

15. *Wall Street Journal*, Dec. 20, 1983.

16. *Auto 1980*, p.76

17. *Wall Street Journal*, Sept. 28, 1978.

18. *Steel Crossroads*, pp. 69, 71.

19. See n.4, p.37.

20. *Steel Crossroads*, p.72

21. *New York Times,* Nov. 23, 1981.

22. *New York Times,* Feb. 28, 1983; Dan Swinney, David Bensman, Jack Metzger, eds., "The Crisis in Steel: Jobs, Profits, Communities," in *Labor Research Review,* (East Chicago, IN: Midwest Center for Labor Research, Winter, 1981), p.53.

23. Jane Slaughter, *Concessions and How to Beat Them!* (Detroit: Labor Education Research Project, 1983), p.53.

24. *Steel Crossroads,* p.8.

25. *"The Crisis in Steel",* op.cit., p.29.

26. *"Concessions . . ."* op.cit., pp. 22, 62.

27. *New York Times,* Sept. 29, 1980.

XII

1. Lenin, "Imperialism, the Highest State of Capitalism," *C.W. XXII,* p.277.

2. Ibid., pp. 279-80.

3. Ibid., p.300.

4. A report prepared for the AFL-CIO Maritime Trades Department Executive Board Meeting, February 15-16, 1973. The report appears in Hearings Before the Subcomittee on International Trade, Committee on Finance, U.S. Senate, 93rd Congress (Washington: Govt. P.O., 1973), p.448.

5. *Steel Labor,* March-April, 1983.

6. *New York Times,* June 20, 1982.

7. U.S. Dept. of Labor, Bureau of Labor Statistics, *Employment and Earnings January 1982* (Washington, Govt. P.O.), p.172.

8. "High Tech, Low Hopes," *New York Times* Op Ed page, May 15, 1983.

9. *New York Times, Wall Street Journal,* Feb. 23, 1983.

10. *Daily World,* April 28, 1983.

11. *Business Week,* March 28, 1983, p.87.

12. Ibid., p.96.

13. Calculated from military expenditures given in Stockholm International Peace Research Institute, *World Armaments and Disarmament, SIPRI Yearbook 1981* (London: Taylor and Francis, 1981), pp. 156, 159; and *SA 1981,* pp. 867-68.

14. Joint Economic Committee, U.S. Congress, "The U.S. Economy and Productivity: Where Do We Go from Here?" in *Productivity: The Foundation of Economic Growth,* Special Study on Economic Change, X (Washington: Govt. P. O., 1980), p.22.

15. Op. cit., (VI, n.1); italics in original.

16. "Trends in Technology-Intensive Trade," *Report of the President on U.S. Competitiveness,* p.10; also Statement accompanying report, p.9.

17. *SA,* 1982-83, p.592.

18. Office of Technology Assessment, U.S. Congress, *U.S. Industrial Competitiveness, A Comparison of Steel, Electronics and Automobiles* (Washington: Govt.P.O.,1981),p.52.

19. *SA,* 1982-83, p.835, and *SA,* 1971, pp. 773, 778.

20. Stanley H. Ruttenburg & Assoc., *Needed: A Constructive Foreign Trade Policy,* A Special Study Commissioned and Published by the Industrial Union Dept., AFL-CIO, Washington, 1971, p.124.

XIII

1. Op.cit. (I, n.13), pp. 66-67.

2. Ibid., p.129.

3. Ibid., pp. 126-27.

4. Marx, op. cit., I, p.725.

5. Ibid., p.705.

6. Ibid., p.726

7. Ann B. Schnare, *The Persistence of Racial Segregation in Housing* (Washington: The Urban Institute, 1978), pp. 1-3.

8. *H.Stat. I*, p.107; *SA* 1981, p.88.

9. EPICA Task Force, *Puerto Rico: A People Challenging Colonialism* (Washington: 1976), p.49.

10. Schnare, op.cit., p.16.

11. Joint Economic Committee, U.S. Congress, *New York City's Financial Crisis* (Washington: Govt. P.O., 1975), pp. 12-13.

12. "Trends in Central City Employment," in Herrington J. Bryce, ed., *Revitalizing Cities* (Lexington, MA: D. C. Heath & Co., 1979), p.4.

13. *New York Times*, March 13, 1982.

14. *Housing Abandonment in New York City* (New York: Homefront), pp. 1 and 8-10.

15. *New York Times*, Oct. 25, 1977.

16. Robert A. Caro, *The Power Broker* (New York: Vintage Books, 1975), p.733.

17. Joint Economic Committee, U.S. Congress, *Trends in the Fiscal Condition of Cities: 1979-81* (Washington: Govt.P.O., 1981), pp 3-4.

18. Ibid., pp. 11, 63.

19. J.E.C., U.S. Congress, *Trends in the Fiscal Condition of Cities: 1978-80* (Washington: Govt. P.O., 1980), pp. 6-7.

20. Rona B. Stein, "New York City's Economy—A Perspective on its Problems," *Quarterly Review*, Federal Reserve Bank of N.Y., Summer, 1977, p.50.

21. Ibid., p.57.

22. Congressional Budget Office, *New York City's Fiscal Problem: Its Origins, Potential Repercussions, and some Alternative Policy Responses* (Washington: Govt.P.O., 1975), p.iv.

23. From the text of the memorandum as given in Jack Newfield and Paul Du Brul, *The Abuse of Power, The Permanent Government and the Fall of New York* (New York: Viking Press, 1977), p.42, Italics in original memorandum.

24. Ibid., pp. 187-88.

25. U.S. Dept. of Housing and Urban Development, The President's Urban and Regional Policy Group Report (Washington: 1978).

XIV

1. *Newsweek*, Aug. 2, 1983.

2. Pat Choate and Susan Walter, *America in Ruins, Beyond the Public Works Pork Barrel* (Washington: Council of State Planning Agencies, 1981), pp. 1-2.

3. *New York Times*, June 4, 1982.

4. *New York Times*, April 16, 1978.

5. *New York Times*, April 9, 1978; July 17 and 18, 1982.

6. *Business Week*, Oct. 26, 1981; *Nancy Humphrey, George E. Peterson and Peter Wilson, The Future of Cleveland's Capital Plant* (Washington: The Urban Institute, 1979), pp. 23-26.

7. *Newsweek*, op.cit., n.1.

8. *Deteriorating Infrastructure in Urban and Rural Areas*, Hearing before the Subcommittee on Economic Growth and Stabilization of the J.E.C., U.S. Congress, June 18 and August 30, 1979 (Washington: Govt. P.O.,1979), p.109.

9. Ibid., p.44.

10. Grossman, *The Future of New York City's Capital Plant*, (Washington, The Urban Institute, 1979), pp. 77-79.

11. Deputy Comptroller for the City of New York, "Estimates of Deferred

Maintenance Needs and Fiscal 1982 Maintenance Requirements as Furnished by Certain City Agencies and Covered Organizations," (New York: Office of the State Comptroller, 3-8-82), p.ii.

12. Ibid., p.17; Grossman, op.cit., pp. 64-68, 82-3.

13. Ibid., n.11, pp 4a, 5 and Tables I, II.

14. Urban Inst., *Cleveland*, op.cit., pp.22, 36.

15. Ibid., pp. 16-17

16. Ibid., pp. xv, 24-5, 39.

17. Daniel E. Chall, "The Economic Costs of Subway Deterioration," *Quarterly Review*, Federal Reserve Bank of New York, Spring, 1981.

18. Morgan Guaranty Survey, July, 1982.

XV

1. U.S. Dept. of Health, Education and Welfare, *Income and Resources of the Aged* (Washington: Govt. P.O., January, 1980), pp. 18-19.

2. President's Commission on Pension Policy, *An Interim Report* (Washington: Govt. P.O., Nov. 18, 1980), pp. 18, 19, 22; American Council of Life Insurance, *Pension Facts 1980* (Washington), pp. 47-49.

3. *Consumer Reports*, March 1982, p.126.

4. James Gollin, *The Star-Spangled Retirement Dream* (New York: Scribner's, 1981), p. 105.

5. Obtained from the Bronx office of the Social Security Administration, New York.

6. *New York Times*, Nov. 30, 1980.

7. Stockman, op. cit., p. 45. Italics in original.

8. *U.S. News & World Report*, Feb. 15, 1982.

9. Committee on Finance, U.S. Senate, *Staff Data and Materials Relating to Social Security Financing* (Washington: Govt. P.O., 1977), p.15.

9. Commitee on Finance, U.S. Senate, *Staff Data and Materials Relating to Social Security Financing* (Washington: Govt. P.O., 1977), p.15.

10. Transmitted by the Secy. of HEW to the Committee on Ways and Means, U.S. House of Representatives (Washington: Govt. P.O., 1980), p.47.

11. "The Current State of Social Security Financing," *New England Economic Review*, Federal Reserve Bank of Boston, May/June 1983, p.48.

12. Stockman, op. cit., p.44.

13. "Social Security: America's Best Bet," Statement presented to the President's Commission on Pension Policy, March 13, 1980. Emphasis in original.

14. Quoted in letter by Cong. Matthew J. Rinaldo to the *New York Times*, 3-20-83.

15. Special Committee on Aging, U.S. Senate, *Social Security in Europe: The Impact of an Aging Population* (Washington: Govt.P.O., 1981), p.13.

XVI

1. E. Richard Brown, *Rockefeller Medicine Men, Medicine and Capitalism* (Berkeley: Univ. of California Press, 1979), pp. 98-100.

2. Bernhard Stern, *Society and Medical Progress* (Princeton: Princeton Univ. Press, 1941), p.107.

3. Moscowitz, Katz and Levering, *Everybody's Business*, p.217.

4. Ibid., 216.

5. SA 1981, pp. 103, 529.

6. Robert M. Gibson and Daniel R. Waldo, "National Health Care Expenditures 1981," *National Health Care Financing Review*, Sept., 1982, p.1.

7. Quoted in Richard Harris, *A Sacred Trust* (New York: New American Library, 1966), pp. 215-16.

8. "Family Income, Ill Health, and Medical Care of U.S. Children," *Journal of Public Health Policy,* Sept., 1982), pp. 245-46.

9. Ibid., pp. 247-48.

10. Public Health Service, U.S. Dept. of Health and Human Services, Hyattsville, Md., Sept. 1980, passim.

11. Margaret C. Thompson, ed., *Health Policy, The Legislative Agenda* (Washington: Congressional Quarterly Inc., 1980), p. 51.

12. Berkeley: McCutchan Publishing Corp., 1975, p.422.

13. *Cost and Quality of Health Care: Unnecessary Surgery,* Report of the Subcommittee on Oversight and Investigation of the Committee on Interstate and Foreign Commerce, U.S. House of Representatives (Washington: Govt. P.O., 1976), p.111.

14. Quoted in Martin Gross, *The Doctors* (New York: Dell Publishing Co., 1967), p.582.

15. Quoted in Spencer Klaw, *The Great American Medicine Show* (New York: Viking Press, 1975), p.79.

16. U.S. Dept. of Health and Human Services, "Who Are the Uninsured?", Data Preview, National Health Expenditures Study (Hyattsville: no date), pp. 1-2.

17. Richard Carter, *The Doctor Business* (New York: Pocket Books, 1967), p.156.

18. *U.S. News & World Report,* Aug. 17, 1981.

19. Robert V. Pattison, Ph.D., and Hallie M. Katz, M.B.A., M.S.P.H., "Investor-Owned and Not-for-Profit Hospitals," *New England Journal of Medicine,* 8-11-83.

20. Monograph entitled *Medicare and Medicaid: The Process, Value, and Limits of Health Care Reforms,* (June, 1982), pp. 18-19.

21. Ibid., pp. 22-23.

22. Ibid.

23. Marion Gornick, "Ten Years of Medicare: Impact on the Covered Population," Social Security Bulletin, July, 1976.

24. *SA* 1981, p. 102; *ERP* 1982, p. 291.

25. Gibson and Waldo, op. cit. (see n.6), p.3.

26. *SA* 1981, p.111.

XVII

1. *SA,* 1982-83, p.429.

2. U.S. Dept. of Commerce, Bureau of the Census, *Money Income and Poverty Status of Families and Persons in the United States,* 1982,(Washington, 1983), p.21.

3. Elin Schoen, *New York Times Magazine,* Jan. 2, 1983.

4. *New York Times,* July 19, 1983.

5. *ERP* 1983, pp. 206-7.

6. Ibid., pp. 196-7; *New York Times,* 8-14-83.

7. October 10, 1982.

8. *New York Times,* 11-3-82.

9. *ERP* 1982, p.264; *Money Income and Poverty Status,* op.cit., p.9.

10. *Money Income . . .* op.cit., p.10.

11. U.S. Dept. of Labor, Bureau of Labor Statistics, *Employment and Earnings January 1983* (Washington: Govt. P.O.), pp. 53-54.

12. *Money Income . . .* op.cit. p.21.

13. Cited in Steve Talbot, *Roots of Oppression, The American Indian Question* (New York: International Publishers Co., Inc., 1981), p.180.

14. (New York: The New York Times Company, 1968), pp. 402-3.

15. *Money Income . . .* op.cit., p.10.

16. Richard O. Boyer and Herbert Morais, *Labor's Untold Story* (New York: United Elec. R & M, 1974), p.70.

17. Ibid., p. 66.

18. For a fuller discussion, see Victor Perlo, *Economics of Racism* (New York: International Publishers Co., Inc., 1975), especially Chap.8, "Capitalist Responsibility."

19. *Employment and Earnings, Jan.1982*, pp. 164, 186, plus data on unemployment by job obtained at the N.Y. City office of the Bureau of Labor Statistics.

20. Ibid.

21. *Employment and Earnings, July 1983*, p.62.

22. *New York Times*, 4-21-83.

23. *WSJ*, 8-2-83.

24. *Money Income* . . . op.cit., p.27.

25. SA 1982-83, p.383.

26. *Money Income* . . . op.cit., p. 20.

XVIII

1. Lenin, *C.W.* XXI, p.40.

INDEX